What Readers Are Saying About *Domain-Driven Design Using Naked Objects*

Over the years I have watched Dan strive to find the best ways to develop complex systems, and I'm glad he has taken this opportunity to share with you just some of his insights and experiences. As well as a champion of using the Naked Objects framework, Dan has now become one of its major contributors and committers, and I must say we are lucky to have his energy and enthusiasm directed at this project.

▶ **Robert Matthews**
Creator, the Naked Objects framework

This is a tutorial, a Naked Objects manifest, a software architecture book, and a user reference, all at the same time and combined amazingly well. You'll find this book to be the best way of developing enterprise apps without repeating yourself.

▶ **Sebastián Slutzky**
Software engineer, Department of Family and Social Affairs, Ireland

Domain-driven design comes alive in this book, as it is demonstrated by example on every page. Furthermore, Naked Objects is shown to be the ideal support for the approach, focusing as it does on the core concepts of a system's domain. Dan Haywood's easy style means that the complex ideas in this book come across very clearly. Don't just read this book...mark, learn, and inwardly digest!

▶ **Andy Carmichael**
CEO, OpenXprocess Ltd

This is a great hands-on guide to implementing domain-driven solutions using the innovative Naked Objects open source framework.

▶ **Dylan Hayes**
Solutions architect, Deloitte Consulting

Domain-Driven Design
Using Naked Objects

Domain-Driven Design

Using Naked Objects

Dan Haywood

The Pragmatic Bookshelf

Raleigh, North Carolina   Dallas, Texas

Many of the designations used by manufacturers and sellers to distinguish their products are claimed as trademarks. Where those designations appear in this book, and The Pragmatic Programmers, LLC was aware of a trademark claim, the designations have been printed in initial capital letters or in all capitals. The Pragmatic Starter Kit, The Pragmatic Programmer, Pragmatic Programming, Pragmatic Bookshelf and the linking *g* device are trademarks of The Pragmatic Programmers, LLC.

Every precaution was taken in the preparation of this book. However, the publisher assumes no responsibility for errors or omissions, or for damages that may result from the use of information (including program listings) contained herein.

Our Pragmatic courses, workshops, and other products can help you and your team create better software and have more fun. For more information, as well as the latest Pragmatic titles, please visit us at

http://www.pragprog.com

ISBN-10: 1-934356-44-1
ISBN-13: 978-1-934356-44-9
Printed on acid-free paper.
P1.0 printing, December 2009
Version: 2009-11-30

Contents

Foreword

Synergy—from the Greek for "working together"—occurs when a combination has a greater value than the sum of its parts. It would be hard to find a better example of synergy than between domain-driven design and Naked Objects. The former is an approach to designing application software that advocates capturing the very essence of the business in the form of a domain model; the latter is a technology for developing and deploying object-oriented applications, where the only thing you actually develop are the domain objects.

The Naked Objects pattern arose, at least in part, from my own frustration at the lack of success of the domain-driven approach. (Eric Evans coined the term *domain-driven design* in his 2004 book of that name, but the broad principles of the approach are as old as object modeling itself.) Good examples were hard to find—as they are still.

A common complaint from DDD practitioners was that it was hard to gain enough commitment from business stakeholders, or even to engage them at all. My own experience suggested that it was nearly impossible to engage business managers with UML diagrams. It was much easier to engage them in rapid prototyping—where they could see and interact with the results—but most forms of rapid prototyping concentrate on the presentation layer, often at the expense of the underlying model and certainly at the expense of abstract thinking.

Even if you could engage the business sponsors sufficiently to design a domain model, by the time you'd finished developing the system on top of the domain model, most of its benefits had disappeared. It's all very well creating an agile domain object model, but if any change to that model also dictates the modification of one or more layers underneath it (dealing with persistence) and multiple layers on top (dealing with presentation), then that agility is practically worthless.

The other concern that gave rise to the birth of Naked Objects was how to make user interfaces of mainstream business systems more "expressive"—how to make them feel more like using a drawing program or CAD system. Most business systems are not at all expressive; they treat the user merely as a dumb *process-follower*, rather than as an empowered *problem-solver*. Research had demonstrated that the best way to achieve expressiveness was to create an object-oriented user interface (OOUI). In practice, though, OOUIs were notoriously hard to develop.

Sometime in the late 1990s, it dawned on me that if the domain model really did represent the "ubiquitous language" (Evans' term) of the business and those domain objects were behaviorally rich (that is, business logic is encapsulated as methods on the domain objects rather than in procedural scripts on top of them), then the UI could be nothing more than a reflection of the user interface. This would solve both of my concerns. It would make it easier to do domain-driven design, because one could instantly translate evolving domain modeling ideas into a working prototype. And it would deliver an expressive, object-oriented user interface for free. Thus was born the idea of Naked Objects.

In my opinion, this book performs an immensely valuable service both in explaining the synergy between these two ideas and in providing practical guidance for applying them. I cannot think of a better person to write it than Dan Haywood. Over the years that I have known him, he continues to astound me with the speed at which he acquires, integrates, and deploys new ideas and new technologies: he reminds me of that scene in *The Matrix* where Trinity, with agents in hot pursuit, runs toward an empty helicopter, calling her colleague Tank on her mobile phone and demanding to have the skill for flying a helicopter downloaded immediately! (Dan doesn't like the analogy.)

I have worked extensively with Dan at the Department of Social and Family Affairs in Ireland—one of the largest and purest applications both of Naked Objects and of domain-driven design anywhere in the world. During that time, Dan has not only helped formulate many best practices but has also made significant contributions to the technology itself. Much as I would have liked to see Dan's work published sooner, now that we have the book, I can say that it was definitely worth the wait.

Richard Pawson
Henley-on-Thames, UK, 2009

Acknowledgments

First thanks should go to Richard Pawson and Robert Matthews for, respectively, conceiving the Naked Objects pattern and for implementing it in the Naked Objects framework. I've been working with Richard and Rob since meeting them in 2002, and we are still learning from each other.

I must also thank all those at the Irish government's Department of Social and Family Affairs (DSFA). Back in 2004, the DSFA gave the go-ahead for the development of a major application for the administration of state benefits, running on Naked Objects. Developed jointly by Bearing Point Ireland and Naked Objects Group Limited, the system went fully live in 2006 and is now the strategic platform for all future benefits administration in the department. In the process, we've learned a lot about large-scale domain-driven design and how Naked Objects makes this achievable, but we couldn't have done so without DSFA's original commitment to the project.

My deep thanks to my editor, Susannah Pfalzer, who has worked tirelessly and patiently to help me tighten up and focus this book on the stuff that matters. Thanks also to Dave Thomas and Andy Hunt for publishing me; the Pragmatic Bookshelf is the ideal vehicle for a book such as this.

Thanks too of course to the reviewers of the book: Gojko Adzic, George Ball, Aidan Coughlan, Eelco Hillenius, Kevin Gisi, Dave Klein, Robert Matthews, Richard Pawson, Sebastián Slutzky, Jeremy Sydik, Phil Wills, and Eoin Woods. Your feedback was invaluable!

Finally, my love and thanks to my wonderful wife, Sue, and beautiful daughter, Phoebe. I couldn't have done this without your love and support.

Preface

There's no doubt that writing enterprise applications is hard. To bring the thing together, you must master numerous technologies: frameworks to handle presentation, APIs to deal with persistence, yet more technology for remoting and authentication. . . the list goes on. Yet none of this matters to the business users asking for the system in the first place.

Domain-driven design is an approach to building application software that focuses on the bit that matters in enterprise applications: the core business domain. Rather than putting all your effort into technical concerns, you work to identify the key concepts that you want the application to handle, you try to figure out how they relate, and you experiment with allocating responsibilities (functionality). Those concepts might be easy to see (Customers, Products, Orders, and so on), but often there are more subtle ones (Payable, ShippingRecipient, and RepeatingOrder) that won't get spotted the first time around. So, you can use a team that consists of business domain experts and developers, and you work to make sure that each understands the other by using the common ground of the domain itself.

Even with your domain experts' help, building these domain models isn't always that easy. You need to be precise as to what the domain concepts actually mean, but that's easier said than done, especially if you're automating previously manual business processes. But if you can develop a deep and insightful model, then the benefits can be enormous. Not only will it deliver benefits to the business (reduced operational costs and the like), it will also be easy to extend and maintain (reducing time to market for future requirements).

So, there's your challenge: how do you bring the domain model to life so that it can be checked, verified, and refined? Static UML diagrams don't hack it; they are too technical for business users to understand.

No, what a nontechnical audience needs to see is rapidly developed working prototypes. And Naked Objects, an open source Java framework, gives you this capability. You write the classes that make up the domain model as plain old Java objects (pojos). Naked Objects then automatically renders those domain classes in an object-oriented user interface, running either as a rich client app or (with no extra coding) as a web application. You run the application using whichever user interface the business users find most comfortable.

With Naked Objects taking care of the presentation layer for you, you can focus solely on the domain. If you make a change to a domain class, you'll see the change immediately when you run the application, and that gives you the feedback loop you need for experimentation. You work with the business's domain experts trying out new ideas; if they come to naught, then it will have cost you little in terms of development effort, and your compensation will be a deeper knowledge of the domain.

This book is about using Naked Objects for domain-driven design, but it's not just about building prototypes. You will also see how Naked Objects defines a straightforward architecture for your domain-driven applications, making it easy to get started. You use Naked Objects' integration with the FitNesse acceptance testing framework, allowing you and your domain experts to work together to specify your application's functionality through scenario tests. And you see how to deploy a domain model as a fully working application using either Naked Objects' own object-oriented user interfaces or a custom user interface.

Who This Book Is For

This book is mostly targeted at developers working on enterprise applications, especially those working on line-of-business operational applications. When I say "developer," I use a broad brush. Naked Objects uses Java as its language, so if you have a Java background, then you'll be right at home. However, even if you typically use only the .NET languages or another object-oriented language, you'll find nothing too complex in the code here.[1]

---

1. If you are a .NET developer, you might like to know there is a commercial version of Naked Objects offering broadly equivalent functionality. See http://www.nakedobjects.net for further details.

More specifically, this book is for developers who also do business analysis, or at least work with business analysts; after all, domain-driven design requires an interest in thinking about domains. If your job title is plain business analyst, then you'll get a lot out of this book too—so long as the thought of some code doesn't scare you. And if you are a database specialist, you'll also find something of interest; there's a lot of common ground between logical data modeling and domain modeling.

If you are a project manager, you'll find this book opens up some new approaches for your development process. In particular, you might be interested in the ability to rapidly prototype (which takes in requirements capture), in writing scenario tests, and in the various deployment options that Naked Objects makes available. And if you were originally from a development background, you might also fancy the chance to do a bit of coding again!

How the Book Is Organized

This book is not a theoretical discourse on how to practice domain-driven design; instead, it's a "wade in there and get your hands mucky" sort of book. It breaks down into three parts.

In the first part, *Tools*, you'll learn the building blocks for developing domain-driven applications. You'll use Naked Objects to build up a single domain application, learning the conventions that make up the Naked Objects programming model as you go.

In the second part, *Techniques*, you'll look at ways to develop deeper insight within your domain models and to ensure that your domain applications are maintainable. You will lean on existing "prior art" for building object-oriented applications, but always from our domain-driven design/Naked Objects perspective. You'll also learn about two different ways to test your domain-driven applications.

In the third part, *Practices*, you'll explore the development process and deployment options. At one end of the spectrum, you'll look at using Naked Objects just as a design tool within development; at the other, you'll look in detail at how to integrate and deploy Naked Objects applications into production (taking in custom web interfaces, persistence, and enterprise integration). We finish up by looking at the various ways to deploy your domain-driven application and briefly discuss one of the largest domain-driven applications (600+ users), built with and deployed on Naked Objects.

There are also several reference appendixes, covering the Naked Objects programming model and other resources.

The book has an accompanying website from which you can download (as a single ZIP) the various code snippets scattered throughout the book.[2] The code download also includes the various versions of the example case study (discussed in the next section) as we build it up through the chapters.

By the end of the book your hands should be well and truly dirty! You will have seen the power of the Naked Objects approach for building domain-driven applications firsthand and will be ready to put it into use for your own domain applications.

Case Study and Exercises

Throughout the book you'll be using a single case study called CarServ, a vehicle-servicing application for a garage. CarServ suits a domain-driven approach because it's an enterprise system supporting core operational business requirements. It also suits our purposes as an example to learn from because it's a domain that most can relate to.

As each new idea is introduced, you'll immediately apply it to CarServ; and because Naked Objects generates the user interface for you, you'll also be able to *see* it in use. In the first two parts of the book, all the changes you need are fully described, so you can follow along either at your computer or in your head. As already mentioned, though, multiple versions of CarServ are available for download from the book's website. Each of these are self-contained and runnable without reference to previous versions, so you can pick up the story at any point. In Part III, because we are integrating with some other technologies, the CarServ downloads already have the necessary changes made, so you can download them and try them out; all the relevant code snippets are also in the book if you're not at your computer.

CarServ also acts as a good basis for structuring your own applications. One of the things that domain-driven design requires is a strict layered architecture, but figuring out how to put this together can be a challenge. CarServ demonstrates how Naked Objects provides a standard approach for the domain layer. As mentioned previously, the chapters

---

2. http://www.pragprog.com/titles/dhnako

in Part III explain how to integrate the domain layer with the other layers of the architecture.

At the end of every chapter are a number of exercises. Many of these ask you to enhance CarServ—for example, by adding an additional type of business rule. But the point of the book isn't about developing CarServ; it's so you can learn the skills to develop your own domain applications. Therefore, an ongoing exercise is for you to select an application and build it up alongside the case study; I guarantee it'll be worth your time.

Conventions

You'll see a few conventions throughout this book:

- Short sidebars (with a "DDD" icon) briefly explain domain-driven design terminology. Since this is a practical book rather than theoretical, use these sidebars as jumping-off points to further reading. I've used the same terms for domain-driven design as Eric Evans does in his book, *Domain-Driven Design* [Eva03].
- You'll occasionally see sidebars with a "Joe Asks" icon. Joe is the Pragmatic Bookshelf's mythical developer, and he likes to ask the odd question related to the text.
- ***Bold italics*** indicate when there is a version of the CarServ case study. You'll find these in the code download ZIP under the casestudy directory.
- Each code snippet appears with a little gray lozenge above it, specifying its location in the code download ZIP. This should save you typing if you are following along. And if you have bought the PDF version of the book, clicking the link goes directly to the code.

Before we start, let me just provide you with some further pointers.

Further Resources

This book will give you a great start toward writing fully fledged domain-driven applications. However, it's not the be-all and end-all; you should know about some other places. Since this is a "PragProg" book, there are the usual resources:

- The book's website is at http://www.pragprog.com/titles/dhnako.
- The book's errata is at http://www.pragprog.com/titles/dhnako/errata.
- The discussion group is at http://forums.pragprog.com/forums/106.

In addition, I've put together a blog that aims to supplement and extend the ideas in this book:

- http://danhaywood.com, "the blog of the book"

Finally, there are the websites for Naked Objects and its sister projects:

- Naked Objects is hosted via http://nakedobjects.org.

- Scimpi is hosted at http://scimpi.org.

- The sister projects that we use in some of the later chapters are collectively signposted from http://starobjects.org.

So, that's about it. I'm eager to get started, and I hope you are too. In Chapter 1 we're going to look at some of the key concepts of domain-driven design and see them in action by running our first Naked Objects application. See you there!

Part I

Tools

Getting Started

To stop himself from procrastinating in his work, the Greek orator Demosthenes would shave off half his beard. Too embarrassed to go outside and with nothing else to do, his work got done.

We could learn a lesson or two from old Demosthenes. After all, we forever seem to be taking an old concept and inventing a new technology around it (always remembering to invent a new acronym, of course)—anything, it would seem, instead of getting down to the real work of solving business problems.

Domain-driven design (hereafter DDD) puts the emphasis elsewhere, "tackling complexity in the heart of software." And Naked Objects—an open source Java framework—helps you build your business applications with ease. No beard shaving necessary, indeed.

In this chapter, we're going to briefly describe the key ideas underlying DDD, identify some of the challenges of applying these ideas, and see for ourselves how Naked Objects makes our task that much easier.

1.1 Understanding Domain-Driven Design

There's no doubt that we developers love the challenge of understanding and deploying complex technologies. But understanding the nuances and subtleties of the business domain itself is just as great a challenge, perhaps more so. If we devoted our efforts to understanding and addressing those subtleties, we could build better, cleaner, and more maintainable software that did a better job for our stakeholders. And there's no doubt that our stakeholders would thank us for it.

A couple of years back Eric Evans wrote his book *Domain-Driven Design* [Eva03], which is well on its way to becoming a seminal work. In fact, most if not all of the ideas in Evans' book have been expressed before, but what he did was pull those ideas together to show how predominantly object-oriented techniques can be used to develop rich, deep, insightful, and ultimately useful business applications.

So, let's start off by reviewing the essential ideas of DDD.

1.2 The Essentials of DDD

There are two central ideas at the heart of domain-driven design. The *ubiquitous language* is about getting the whole team (both domain experts and developers) to communicate more transparently using a domain model. Meanwhile, *model-driven design* is about capturing that model in a very straightforward manner in code. Let's look at each in turn.

Creating a Ubiquitous Language

It's no secret that the IT industry is plagued by project failures. Too often systems take longer than intended to implement, and when finally implemented, they don't address the real requirements anyway.

Over the years we in IT have tried various approaches to address this failing. Using waterfall methodologies, we've asked for requirements to be fully and precisely written down before starting on anything else. Or, using agile methodologies, we've realized that requirements are likely to change anyway and have sought to deliver systems incrementally using feedback loops to refine the implementation.

But let's not get distracted talking about methodologies. At the end of the day what really matters is communication between the domain experts (that is, the business) who need the system and the techies actually implementing it. If the two don't have and cannot evolve a shared understanding of what is required, then the chance of delivering a useful system will be next to nothing.

Bridging this gap is traditionally what business analysts are for; they act as interpreters between the domain experts and the developers. However, this still means there are two (or more) languages in use, making it difficult to verify that the system being built is correct. If the analyst mistranslates a requirement, then neither the domain expert

in context...

Ubiquitous Language

Build a common language between the domain experts and developers by using the concepts of the domain model as the primary means of communication. Use the terms in speech, in diagrams, in writing, and when presenting.

If an idea cannot be expressed using this set of concepts, then go back and extend the model. Look for and remove ambiguities and inconsistencies.

nor the application developer will discover this until (at best) the application is first demonstrated or (much worse) an end user sounds the alarm once the application has been deployed into production.

Rather than trying to translate between a business language and a technical language, with DDD we aim to have the business and developers using the same terms for the same concepts in order to create a single *domain model*. This domain model identifies the relevant concepts of the domain, how they relate, and ultimately where the responsibilities are. This single domain model provides the vocabulary for the *ubiquitous language* for our system.[1]

Creating a *ubiquitous language* calls upon everyone involved in the system's development to express what they are doing through the vocabulary provided by the model. If this can't be done, then our model is incomplete. Finding the missing words deepens our understanding of the domain being modeled.

This might sound like nothing more than me insisting that the developers shouldn't use jargon when talking to the business. Well, that's true enough, but it's not a one-way street. A *ubiquitous language* demands that the developers work hard to understand the problem domain, but it also demands that the business works hard in being *precise* in its naming and descriptions of those concepts. After all, ultimately the developers will have to express those concepts in a computer programming language.

---

1. In Extreme Programming, there is a similar idea called a *system of names*. But *ubiquitous language* is much more evocative.

Also, although here I'm talking about the "domain experts" as being a homogeneous group of people, often they may come from different branches of the business. Even if we weren't building a computer system, there's a lot of value in helping the domain experts standardize their own terminology. Is the marketing department's "prospect" the same as sales' "customer," and is that the same as an after-sales "contract"?

The need for precision within the *ubiquitous language* also helps us scope the system. Most business processes evolve piecemeal and are often quite ill-defined. If the domain experts have a very good idea of what the business process should be, then that's a good candidate for automation, that is, including it in the scope of the system. But if the domain experts find it hard to agree, then it's probably best to leave it out. After all, human beings are rather more capable of dealing with fuzzy situations than computers.

So, if the development team (business and developers together) continually searches to build their *ubiquitous language*, then the domain model naturally becomes richer as the nuances of the domain are uncovered. At the same time, the knowledge of the business domain experts also deepens as edge conditions and contradictions that have previously been overlooked are explored.

We use the *ubiquitous language* to build up a domain model. But what do we do *with* that model? The answer to that is the second of our central ideas.

Model-Driven Design

Of the various methodologies that the IT industry has tried, many advocate the production of separate analysis models and implementation models. A recent example is that of the OMG's Model-Driven Architecture (MDA) initiative, with its platform-independent model (the PIM) and a platform-specific model (the PSM).

Bah and humbug! If we use our *ubiquitous language* just to build up a high-level analysis model, then we will re-create the communication divide. The domain experts and business analysts will look only to the analysis model, and the developers will look only to the implementation model. Unless the mapping between the two is completely mechanical, inevitably the two will diverge.

in context...
Model-Driven Design

There must be a straightforward and very literal way to represent the domain model in terms of software. The model should balance these two requirements: form the *ubiquitous language* of the development team and be representable in code.

Changing the code means changing the model; refining the model requires a change to the code.

What do we mean by *model* anyway? For some, the term will bring to mind UML class or sequence diagrams and the like. But this isn't a model; it's a visual *representation* of some aspect of a model. No, a domain model is a group of related concepts, identifying them, naming them, and defining how they relate. What is in the model depends on what our objective is. We're not looking to simply model everything that's out there in the real world. Instead, we want to take a relevant abstraction or simplification of it and then make it do something useful for us. Oft quoted and still true is that a model is neither right nor wrong, just more or less useful.

For our *ubiquitous language* to have value, the domain model that encodes it must have a straightforward, literal representation to the design of the software, specifically to the implementation. Our software's design should be driven by this model; we should have a *model-driven design*.

Here also the word *design* might mislead; some might again be thinking of design documents and design diagrams. But by *design* we mean a way of organizing the domain concepts, which in turn leads to the way in which we organize their representation in code.

Luckily, using *object-oriented* (OO) languages such as Java, this is relatively easy to do; OO is based on a modeling paradigm anyway. We can express domain concepts using classes and interfaces, and we can express the relationships between those concepts using associations.

So far so good. Or maybe, so far so much motherhood and apple pie. Understanding the DDD concepts isn't the same as being able to apply them, and some of the DDD ideas can be difficult to put into practice.

What this book is about is how Naked Objects eases that path by applying these central ideas of DDD in a very concrete way. So, now would be a good time to see how.

1.3 Introducing Naked Objects

Naked Objects is both an architectural pattern and a software framework. The pattern was originally conceived and articulated by Richard Pawson as a means of engaging business stakeholders and experts in developing more expressive domain-driven applications. Richard discusses this in more detail in the foreword.

The framework, then, is an implementation of the pattern to help you rapidly prototype, develop, and deploy domain-driven applications:

- *Rapid prototyping* comes from the fact that you can develop an application without spending any time writing user interface code or persistence code. This creates a very tight feedback loop with your domain experts.

- The *development support* comes from the close integration with developer tools such as *Eclipse* (for coding), *FitNesse* (for testing), *Maven* (for building and packaging), and *Hudson* (for continuous integration).

- The *deployment support* comes from Naked Objects' pluggable architecture allowing different viewers, persistence mechanisms, and security. In fact, the domain model has no runtime dependencies on the framework, so you can deploy your application on any Java-based enterprise architecture with any UI you want.

For more on the original philosophy that drove Naked Objects' development, see Richard Pawson and Robert Matthews' book, *Naked Objects* [PM02], and Richard's later PhD thesis.[2]

I could talk at length in a highly theoretical fashion about Naked Objects and how it relates to DDD for the next thirty pages, but what we're going to do instead is see Naked Objects in action.

---

2. http://www.nakedobjects.org/downloads/Pawson%20thesis.pdf

Joe Asks. . .

How Does Naked Objects Compare to Other Frameworks?

Many other frameworks promise rapid application development and provide automatically generated user interfaces, so how do they compare to Naked Objects?

Some of most significant are *Rails* (for the Ruby programming language), *Grails* (Groovy), and *Spring Roo* (Java with AspectJ).* These frameworks all use the classic *model-view-controller* (MVC) pattern for web applications, with scaffolding, code-generation, and/or metaprogramming tools for the controllers and views, as well as convention over configuration to define how these components interact. The views provided out of the box by these frameworks tend to be simple CRUD-style interfaces. More sophisticated behavior is accomplished by customizing the generated controllers.

For many developers, the most obvious difference of Naked Objects is its deliberate lack of an explicit controller layer; non-CRUD behavior is automatically made available in its generic object-oriented UIs. More sophisticated UIs can be built either by skinning Naked Objects (see Chapter 15, *Integrating with Web Frameworks*, on page 269) or by using a newer viewer that supports easy customization (see Chapter 18, *Deploying the Full Runtime*, on page 333).

Like all of these frameworks, Naked Objects can expose domain objects as a RESTful web service. However, it has some other tricks you may not find in a typical MVC framework: it supports client-server (rich-client) deployments as well as on the Web; it supports non-RDBMS as well as RDBMS object stores, with an in-memory object store for rapid prototyping; it supports domain-driven concepts such as values, repositories, and domain services; it supports agile scenario testing using FitNesse; and it puts the domain metamodel at the center, allowing the programming model to be redefined.

---

*. The frameworks mentioned here are hosted at http://rubyonrails.org/, http://www.grails.org, and http://www.springsource.org/roo.

1.4 Naked Objects in About Five Minutes

Throughout the book we're going to be using Naked Objects 4.0 for Java, an open source framework licensed under Apache License v2.[3] All the other products we're going to use in this book are also open source with similar nonrestrictive licenses. Without further ado, let's get our development environment set up.[4]

Set Up the Development Environment

Naked Objects is a Java framework, so we need Java 5 or higher installed along with an IDE. In this book I'm going to be using Eclipse 3.5: it's extremely capable and freely available. However, there's nothing stopping you from using some other IDE.

In addition, we need to set up Maven, one of the most commonly used tools for building Java software.[5] Naked Objects provides a Maven archetype (a project template) to help get us started, and the case study we'll develop through the book builds on this archetype and so is also a Maven-based project. We won't be using particularly advanced features of Maven, but if you are interested in learning more, then take a look at *Maven, The Definitive Guide* [Com08].

We also need Maven support in our IDE (or at least the ability to import Maven projects). In the case of Eclipse, this means installing a plug-in; if you're using an IDE other than Eclipse, then make sure it has equivalent Maven support. Both NetBeans 6.7 onward and IntelliJ IDEA 7.0 onward have out-of-the-box support, so there's plenty of choice.

And finally, we also need to download the Naked Objects distribution itself. We don't need this for the Naked Objects JARs—we'll get those courtesy of Maven—but the distribution does include a number of resources (such as icons) that we will need, along with an example application that we're going to try in the next section.

So, do the following:

1. Install Java 5 or 6 from http://java.sun.com. Either the JRE or the JDK is fine. I used JDK 1.5_014 for this book. Set the JAVA_HOME environment variable, and update the PATH to include $JAVA_HOME/ bin.

---

3. http://www.apache.org/licenses/LICENSE-2.0.html
4. If you have any problems setting up or running the application, don't forget the book's forum as a place to get help.
5. Maven is hosted at http://maven.apache.org.

2. Download and install Maven 2.0.9 or higher, from http://maven. apache.org/download.html. The Maven website has instructions on installing Maven, but it basically amounts to extracting the ZIP, setting up the M2_HOME environment variable, and updating your PATH to pick up the mvn.bat or mvn.sh batch file.

3. Download and unzip Eclipse 3.5 or higher, http://www.eclipse.org/ downloads. You can use either the standard distribution or the full-blown Java EE enterprise distribution.

4. Install the *m2eclipse* plug-ins into Eclipse, v0.9.7 or higher, http: //m2eclipse.sonatype.org/update. This is an update site from which Eclipse can download and install the software. If you aren't an Eclipse regular, the incantation is: select the Help > Install New Software menu and then press the Add... button to add this site.

5. Download Naked Objects 4.0 from https://sourceforge.net/projects/ nakedobjects/; the file you need is nakedobjects-4.0.0-for-maven.zip (or whichever is the latest release). Unzip this wherever you want; I'll refer to this location as $NO_HOME (though there's no need to set an environment variable).

Included in the Naked Objects download are a number of Eclipse templates that we can use to quickly write short code fragments using Content Assist (that is, `Ctrl`+`Spacebar`). We won't need these until the next chapter, but now is a good time to set them up. So, start up Eclipse in a new workspace, select Window > Preferences > Java > Editor > Templates, and then select Import. Navigate to the $NO_HOME/resources/ide/ eclipse/templates directory, and select the nakedobjects-templates.xml file. Finally, hit OK.

Note, by the way, that these templates are effectively stored in the workspace; if you use File > Switch Workspace, then you'll need to reimport the templates. For easy reference, all the templates are listed in Appendix B, on page 369. When we get to using them, I'll also indicate some of the main ones to use in the text.

OK, let's test our setup by importing and running a very simple claims-processing application written using Naked Objects.

Import and Explore a Naked Objects Application

With Eclipse still running, first make sure you are in the Java perspective (use Window > Open Perspective > Other > Java). Then, use File > Import > General > Maven Projects, and browse to $NO_HOME/examples/ claims. Hit Enter, and a set of Maven projects should be listed.

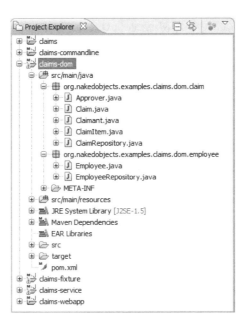

Figure 1.1: The imported dom project

Now hit Finish, and you should be left with a parent project (no suffix) and five further child projects with various suffices. This is the standard way that we tend to organize Naked Objects applications:

- The dom (domain object model) is where most of the action is, containing the domain classes that make up the application.
- The fixture project contains fixtures that provide a working set of objects for demonstration purposes; we cover this in Chapter 4, *Rapid Prototyping*, on page 63.
- The service project provides supporting services to the domain objects; we cover this mostly in Chapter 8, *Isolating Infrastructure Services*, on page 125 and in Chapter 16, *Integrating with the Database*, on page 287.
- The commandline project is where we run the application from during development (throughout the book).
- The webapp project allows us to deploy the application to a web container; we use this at the end of the book, in Chapter 18, *Deploying the Full Runtime*, on page 333.

Open the dom project, as shown in Figure 1.1. There should be three concrete classes: Employee, Claim, and ClaimItem. Employees make

Claims, and Claims are made up of ClaimItems. In addition, there are some interfaces implemented by these domain classes (Approver and Claimant), as well as some repository interfaces (EmployeeRepository and ClaimRepository). These are used to look up Employees and, um, Claims; the implementations are in the services project.

Poke around inside these domain classes. We are of course going to be covering how to write such classes in detail (starting in Chapter 2, *Identifying the Domain Concepts*, on page 23), but for now it should at easy enough to see that an Employee has a Name and an Approver property:

`chapter01/Employee.java`

```
public class Employee extends AbstractDomainObject
                      implements Claimant, Approver {

    // {{ Title
    public String title() {
        return getName();
    }
    // }}

    // {{ Name
    private String name;
    @MemberOrder(sequence="1")
    public String getName() {
        return name;
    }
    public void setName(String lastName) {
        this.name = lastName;
    }
    // }}

    // {{ Approver
    private Approver approver;
    @MemberOrder(sequence="2")
    public Approver getApprover() {
        return approver;
    }
    public void setApprover(Approver approver) {
        this.approver = approver;
    }
    // }}
}
```

Now here's the thing: the domain model we've been looking at is the entire application. Fundamentally, writing a Naked Objects application means writing a domain model, and that's it.

It's time to run the application, methinks.

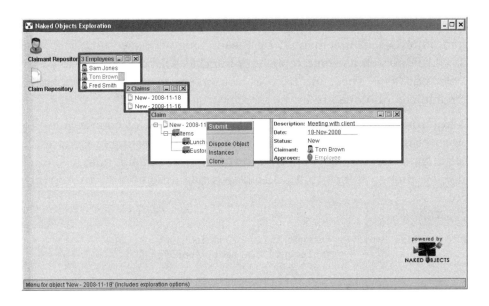

Figure 1.2: THE CLAIMS APP IN THE DND VIEWER

Run the Application

Naked Objects is so called because it automatically displays the domain objects in an *object-oriented user interface* (OOUI). These OOUIs are also generic because they can display *any* domain object in a standardized fashion.

Out of the box, Naked Objects ships with two main OOUI viewers. The *drag-n-drop* (DnD) viewer is a rich client intended for client-side deployment, while the HTML viewer is designed to host your application on the Web. Let's look at the DnD viewer first.

In Eclipse, use Run > Run Configurations to bring up the generated launch configurations. Listed as a Java Application launch configuration should be claims_exploration_dnd.launch (defined in the commandline project). Select this, and then click Run. If using another IDE, all we are doing is running org.nakedobjects.runtime.NakedObjects with a command-line option of --type exploration --viewer dnd.

All being well, the DnD viewer should launch, showing the two repositories as icons. By right-clicking these icons, we can invoke actions on the repositories to retrieve objects. Once we have an object, we can use it to navigate to other referenced objects (click/double-click icons), right-

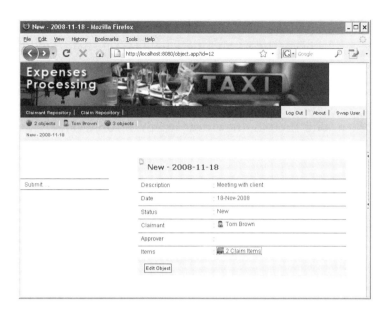

Figure 1.3: THE CLAIMS APP IN THE HTML VIEWER

click to invoke actions, and generally have a good old browse around. We can see the DnD viewer in action in Figure 1.2, on the preceding page.

OK, let's now run the same application using the HTML viewer. Again, using Run > Run Configurations, this time select claims_exploration_html. launch, and click Run. Again, if using another IDE, this is running the same class with flags of --type exploration and --viewer html.

What Naked Objects will do is run the application on an embedded Jetty web server, listening on port 8080. If for some reason you need to use another port number, just edit the *nakedobjects.embedded-web-server.port* property in the config/embedded-web-server.properties file in the commandline project.

Eclipse's console view should indicate that the server is up and running. Now start your favorite web browser, and go to http://localhost:8080/logon.app. You should be logged in automatically and then see links representing the two repositories; these are the HTML equivalents of the icons in the DnD desktop view. Click one of these, and then use the action links to navigate the application as before. We can see the HTML viewer in action in Figure 1.3.

Try running the two viewers side-by-side. Although they look differ-ent, they both provide the same functionality, and that functionality is defined entirely by the domain classes.

We're going to be using both of these viewers extensively throughout the book; they are, after all, the default viewers provided by Naked Objects. I should point out, though, that these aren't the only viewers available. In Chapter 18, *Deploying the Full Runtime*, on page 333, we'll see a number of other viewers either developed or in active development. It's also possible to use a custom interface; see Chapter 15, *Integrating with Web Frameworks*, on page 269.

Before our quick Naked Objects demo, I was asserting that putting DDD ideas into practice isn't necessarily that easy but that Naked Objects eases the path. Now that you've seen Naked Objects "in the flesh" (so to speak!), let's see how.

1.5 How Naked Objects Helps with DDD

The case for DDD might be compelling, but that doesn't necessarily make it easy to do. Let's take a look at some of the challenges that DDD throws up and see how Naked Objects helps address them.

DDD Takes a Conscious Effort

Here's what Evans says about *ubiquitous language*: "With a conscious effort by the [development] team the domain model can provide the backbone for [the] common [ubiquitous] language...connecting team communication to the software implementation."

The word I want to pick up on here is *conscious*. It takes a *conscious* effort by the entire team to develop the *ubiquitous language*. Everyone in the team must challenge the use of new or unfamiliar terms, must clarify concepts when used in a new context, and in general must be on the lookout for sloppy thinking. This takes willingness on the part of all involved, not to mention some practice.

With Naked Objects, though, the *ubiquitous language* evolves with scarcely any effort at all. For the business experts, the Naked Objects viewers show the domain concepts they identify and the relationships between those concepts in a straightforward fashion. Meanwhile, the developers can devote themselves to encoding those domain concepts directly as domain classes. There's no technology to get distracted by; there is literally nothing else for the developers to work on.

DDD Must Be Grounded

Employing a *model-driven design* isn't necessarily straightforward, and the development processes used by some organizations positively hinder it. It's not sufficient for the business analysts or architects to come up with some idealized representation of the business domain and then chuck it over the wall for the programmers to do their best with.

Instead, the concepts in the model must have a very literal representation in code. If we fail to do this, then we open up the communication divide, and our *ubiquitous language* is lost. There is literally no point having a domain model that cannot be represented in code. We cannot invent our *ubiquitous language* in a vacuum, and the developers must ensure that the model remains grounded in the doable.

In Naked Objects, we have a very pure one-to-one correspondence between the domain concepts and its implementation. Domain concepts are represented as classes and interfaces, easily demonstrated back to the business. If the model is clumsy, then the application will be clumsy too, and so the team can work together to find a better implementable model.

Abstract Models Are Difficult to Represent

If we are using code as the primary means of expressing the model, then we need to find a way to make this model understandable to the business.

We could generate UML diagrams and the like from code. That will work for some members of the business community, but not for everyone. Or we could generate a PDF document from Javadoc comments, but comments aren't code and so the document may be inaccurate. Anyway, even if we do create such a document, not everyone will read it.

A better way to represent the model is to show it in action as a working prototype. As we've seen, Naked Objects enables this with ease. Such prototypes bring the domain model to life, engaging the audience in a way that a piece of paper never can.

Moreover, with Naked Objects prototypes, the domain model will come shining through. If there are mistakes or misunderstandings in the domain model, they will be obvious to all.

in context...

Layered Architecture

We partition a complex program into layers, with each layer cohesive and depending only on the layers below.

In particular, we have a layer dedicated to the domain model. The code in this layer is unencumbered with the (mostly technical) responsibilities of the other layers and so can evolve to tackle complex domains as well as simple ones.

Layered Architectures Are Expensive and Easily Compromised

DDD rightly requires that the domain model lives in its own layer within the architecture. The other layers of the application (usually presentation, application, and persistence) have their own responsibilities, and are completely separate.

However, there are two immediate issues. The first is rather obvious: custom coding each of those other layers is an expensive proposition. Picking up on the previous point, this in itself can put the kibosh on using prototyping to represent the model, even if we wanted to do so.

The second issue is more subtle. It takes real skill to ensure the correct separation of concerns between these layers, if indeed you can get an agreement as to what those concerns actually are. Even with the best intentions, it's all too easy for custom-written layers to blur the boundaries and put (for example) validation in the user interface layer when it should belong to the domain layer. At the other extreme, it's quite possible for custom layers to distort or completely subvert the underlying domain model.

Because of Naked Objects' generic OOUIs, there's no need to write the other layers of the architecture. And as we've seen, this makes prototyping cheap. But more than that, there will be no leakage of concerns outside the domain model. All the validation logic *must* be in the domain model because there is nowhere else to put it.

Moreover, although Naked Objects does provide a complete runtime framework, there is no direct coupling of your domain model to the framework. That means it is very possible to take your domain model prototyped in Naked Objects and then deploy it on some other J(2)EE architecture, with a custom UI if you want. Naked Objects guarantees that your domain model is complete.

Naked Objects Extends the Reach of DDD

Domain-driven design is often positioned as being applicable only to complex domains; indeed, the subtitle of Evans book is *Tackling Complexity in the Heart of Software*. The corollary is that DDD is overkill for simpler domains. The trouble is that we immediately have to make a choice: is the domain complex enough to warrant a domain-driven approach?

This goes back to the previous point, building and maintaining a *layered architecture*. It doesn't seem cost effective to go to all the effort of a DDD approach if the underlying domain is simple.

However, with Naked Objects, we don't write these other layers, so we don't have to make a call on how complex our domain is. We can start working solely on our domain, even if we suspect it will be simple. If it is indeed a simple domain, then there's no hardship, but if unexpected subtleties arise, then we're in a good position to handle them.

If you're just starting out writing domain-driven applications, then Naked Objects should significantly ease your journey into applying DDD. On the other hand, if you've used DDD for a while, then you should find Naked Objects a very useful new tool in your arsenal.

In this chapter we've discussed DDD in the context of a layered architecture. We're going to finish off this chapter with a refinement of that idea, which moreover will act as a road map to the rest of the book.

1.6 The Big Picture

A few years ago Alistair Cockburn reworked the traditional layered architecture diagram and came up with the *hexagonal architecture*, as shown in Figure 1.4, on the next page.[6]

What Cockburn is emphasizing is that there's usually more than one way *into* an application (what he called the *user-side' ports*) and more than one way *out of* an application too (the *data-side ports*). This is very similar to the concept of primary and secondary actors in use cases: a

---

6. http://alistair.cockburn.us/Hexagonal+architecture. Another similar (same?) pattern is the onion architecture; see http://jeffreypalermo.com/blog/the-onion-architecture-part-3/.

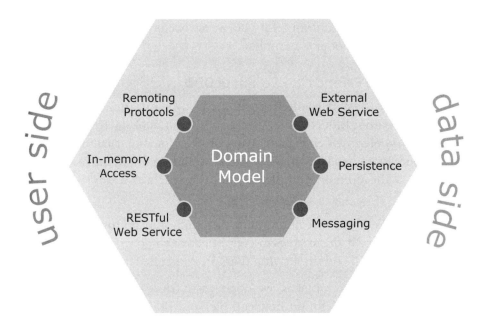

Figure 1.4: The *hexagonal architecture* emphasizes multiple implementations of the different layers.

primary actor (often a human user but not always) is active and initi-
ates an interaction, while a secondary actor (almost always an external
system) is passive and waits to be interacted with.

Associated with each port can be an *adapter* (in fact, Cockburn's alternative name for this architecture is *ports and adapters*). An adapter is
a device (piece of software) that talks in the protocol (or API) of the port.
Each port could have several adapters.

Naked Objects maps very nicely onto the *hexagonal architecture*. As
shown in Figure 1.5, on the facing page, most of the user-side adapters
(that is, viewers) run in the same memory space as the domain layer
and so (using Cockburn's terminology) access the domain layer through
an in-memory port. However, rich client/desktop-based viewers such
as the DnD viewer can also access the domain layer using a remoting protocol port. Naked Objects also supports RESTful web services,
which I've drawn as an adapter, but one could also think of it as an
implementation of a third port providing access to other non-Java on

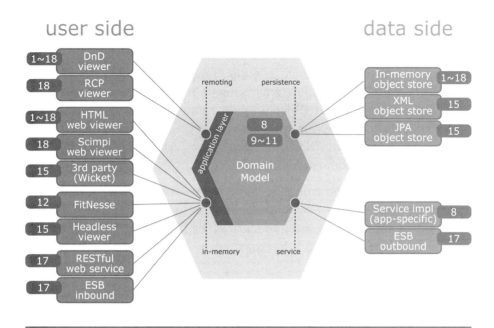

Figure 1.5: THE *hexagonal architecture* FOR NAKED OBJECTS

the user side. An inbound adapter from an *enterprise service bus* (ESB) could also consume events from any other system in the enterprise.

For the data side, we are mostly concerned with persisting domain objects to some sort of object store; this is the persistence port. We might also invoke services; the implementation of these services is specific to the application. These could, for example, call out to an external web service. Alternatively, the service could be a generic mechanism to publish events asynchronously onto an ESB, removing any runtime dependency between our application and the external system.

Doing double duty, Figure 1.5 is a road map for the book; as you might have guessed, the overlaid numbers correspond to the chapters where that component is discussed. As you would expect, much of the book (most of the chapters in Parts I and II) is focused on the domain model. The chapters in Part III focus more on the adapters (viewers and object stores) that interact with the domain model.

Coming Up Next

In this chapter, we talked about the two central ideas of domain-driven design, that of the *ubiquitous language* and of a *model-driven design*. We also got our development environment up and running and used it to run our first Naked Objects application. We then looked at how Naked Objects addresses several issues that you might otherwise struggle with when applying DDD and recast the traditional *layered architecture* instead as the *hexagonal architecture*.

This is very much a learning-by-doing book. Throughout, we're going to be developing our own domain application as a single case study, so in the next chapter we're going to start at the beginning, identifying the main concepts of its domain. See you there.

Exercises

In each chapter of the book there is an "Exercises" section like this, where I'll be asking you to implement the techniques covered in the chapter text.

In addition to the case study in the main text, you might want to develop your own application alongside, something that's close to your heart. So, get your thinking hat on and decide what you'd like to implement as your first Naked Objects (and perhaps domain-driven design) application. In the next chapter's exercises, you'll be in a position to start implementing it.

Identifying the Domain Concepts

The domain model is at the heart of all domain-driven applications, capturing the key domain concepts as classes or as responsibilities of those classes. Our goal is to make the domain model into the *ubiquitous language* that the business domain experts and the IT development team can use to communicate with each other.

But we need a domain to work on. So, allow me to introduce...

2.1   Introducing CarServ

CarServ is an application to allow the service manager to manage car servicing for a garage. Even if you don't own a car, it's a domain that we can all relate to pretty easily. It's a good idea to have some sort of domain vision statement, so here's one to start off with:

CarServ should enable the service manager to record Customers and their Cars and to track the Services performed on the Cars. This information will be used for billing, service reminders, and reordering parts.

---

 in context...

Domain Vision Statement

A *domain vision statement* describes how the domain model serves its stakeholders interests, in other words, its "value proposition." It provides a focus for development at project initiation.

<u>**Working with the Case Study**</u>

This is a hands-on book, so download the case study from the book's website, and follow along on your computer if possible.*

There are at least two versions of the case study per chapter (as at the beginning of the chapter and as at the end), sometimes more. Whenever there's a version to download, you'll see it in parentheses. For example, (*chapter03-02*) refers to the casestudy/chapter03-02 directory in the extracted ZIP.

In Parts I and II, you should be able to start with a version and then follow the guidance in the text to reach the objective. In Part III—when we look in detail at some complex integration and deployment issues—I take a slightly different approach: the case study versions tend to have the changes already made, and the text picks up on the salient points. That's because for these chapters I expect you'll almost certainly want to look at some working code to see how to do likewise for your own domain applications.

To pick up the story at any point, import it into Eclipse using File > Import and then General > Maven Projects. Specify the chapterXX-XX directory as the root directory, refresh, and then click Finish.

---

*. http://www.pragprog.com/titles/dhnako

We're going to be using CarServ throughout the book to develop a domain-driven application using the Naked Objects framework. During Part I of this book, we're mostly going to be learning about Naked Objects' capabilities, so the number of classes in our domain will be very modest. Initially, it might also seem a little naive. However, developing domain applications is an exploration process, with the domain experts our coexplorers. There's nothing wrong with building up the domain model piecemeal.

In Part II we'll be deepening the domain, so things will get a little richer. Here we'll introduce a number of techniques and patterns, as well as learn how to test applications using scenario tests. In Part III, we'll discuss development processes and reflect on how the tools and techniques can be brought to play within real-world development. And then

> ⌣ **Joe Asks...**
>
> **What's a Maven Archetype?**
>
> Maven archetypes are effectively templates for creating Maven projects. They typically generate some example code, and they always generate the Maven-specific pom.xml file that (among other things) defines the classpath and specifies how the code should be compiled, tested, and packaged.

we'll see how to integrate and deploy our CarServ domain model with a number of technologies.

That said, CarServ is always going to be a toy application. We're not actually going to be consulting real domain experts as we build CarServ, and in any case I doubt you bought this book to learn about the vehicle servicing domain. We do discuss the development process and the importance of involvement with domain experts in Chapter 13, *Developing Domain Applications*, on page 241, and by that stage in the book you'll be seeing how Naked Objects lets us genuinely work with domain experts. Meanwhile, CarServ gives us a familiar context to explore new ideas and learn new skills; you can then try out your skills in the book's exercises as you develop your own domain applications.

For this chapter, our objectives are to get to grips with the domain, identify and name our key domain classes, and capture a number of their properties. But before we do that, we need somewhere to put our model.

2.2 Getting Ready

First off, if you haven't yet set up your development environment in the previous chapter, then you'll need to do so. See Section 1.4, *Set Up the Development Environment*, on page 10 for instructions.

As already mentioned, Naked Objects provides a Maven archetype to create an initial project structure. We can use this either at the command line or within Eclipse; let's look at Eclipse first.

Figure 2.1: ECLIPSE LETS US CREATE A NAKED OBJECTS PROJECT USING MAVEN.

Generating the CarServ Projects Within Eclipse

In Eclipse, use File > New > Maven Project to bring up a wizard. Skip to the second page, and make sure that the Nexus Indexer catalog is selected. This catalog automatically indexes and searches for archetypes in the central Maven repository. (It can take several minutes to download the first time around—see the Updating Indexes task in Eclipse's Progress view—so if you are impatient, you can always generate from the command line, described in the next section.)

When Nexus is ready, choose the latest version of the org.nakedobjects: application-archetype archetype, as shown in Figure 2.1. Hit Next, and on the next page, enter the following:

- A group ID of com.pragprog.dhnako (or anything else, but I'll use this domain name throughout)

- An artifact ID of carserv

- A version of 0.0.1-SNAPSHOT (the default)

  The "SNAPSHOT" suffix is a Maven convention, indicating that the code is not yet released.

- A package of com.pragprog.dhnako.carserv

Hit Finish, and the projects should be created and structured the same as the claims project from the previous chapter.

Generating the CarServ Projects from the Command Line

As mentioned earlier, we can alternatively generate the projects from the command line:

chapter02/mvn-archetype-generate.session

```
$ mvn archetype:generate                          \
  -D archetypeGroupId=org.nakedobjects            \
  -D archetypeArtifactId=application-archetype \
  -D archetypeVersion=4.0.0                        \
  -D groupId=com.pragprog.dhnako               \
  -D artifactId=carserv
```

I've shown this over multiple lines, but you should type it in as a single line. We then import the generated projects into Eclipse using File > Import > General > Maven Projects.

Tidying Up

Whichever way you prefer to create the project, you'll find that the archetype automatically generates a single class, DomainObject, in the carserv-dom project and another, DomainObjectRepository, in the carserv-service project. Delete these to get us to a nice clean sheet.

The previous steps have also been done in the code download, so if you prefer, you can just import the relevant version (*chapter02-01*).

OK, after that preamble, let's start thinking about CarServ's domain.

2.3 Creating the Domain Classes

At the heart of our model are the domain classes themselves, so you will need to spend a little up-front time learning something about the domain before you start. Meeting with the domain experts and just talking about their business area is a good starting point, looking out for jargon, concepts, and terms. Even an hour's meeting will give you plenty to go on.

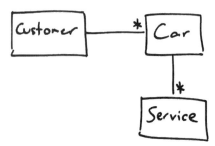

Figure 2.2: INITIAL SKETCH OF THE CARSERV DOMAIN MODEL

You might also be working in a domain where there is formal literature (the finance industry is an obvious example). So, do some prereading if you can; it shows some respect to the domain expert and builds some trust if you are not a complete greenhorn about their domain.

That said, I don't recommend spending too long on analysis. We're going to be getting a domain application up and running very quickly, so the sooner we start putting prototypes in front of our domain experts, the sooner they'll be able to tell us what's missing or wrong. We should also start with very concrete classes rather than try to second-guess inheritance hierarchies and interfaces. We'll have plenty of opportunity to generalize as we develop.

With CarServ, I've purposefully chosen a simple domain to understand and for which the concrete classes are pretty easy to spot. So, let's just wade right in.

Sketch the Domain

In Figure 2.2, we can see an initial sketch of what I reckon are the key classes in the CarServ domain: Customer, Car, and Service. Every Car is owned by a Customer (who can own several Cars), and Cars have Services. The identity of each of these matters—we can't just swap one red Car with another—so they are all *entities*.

We have the beginnings of a domain model; now is the time to start converting it into code.

in context...

Entity

An *entity*, also called a *reference object*, is an object whose identity must be preserved, principally because its state can change over time. Classic examples are Customer or Order.

When entities are persisted (for example into an RDBMS), they are often given a unique ID to preserve their identity across multiple instantiations.

Name the Classes

For our nascent CarServ application, we have three classes to create: Customer, Car, and Service. Select the carserv-dom project; then create a new class in Eclipse (File > New > Class), and specify the following:

- The source folder: carserv-dom/src/main/java (should be the default)

- The package: com.pragprog.dhnako.carserv.dom.customer

- The class: Customer

- The superclass: org.nakedobjects.applib.AbstractDomainObject (more on this in a moment)

Hit Finish. We should end up with this:

`chapter02/Customer.java`

```
package com.pragprog.dhnako.carserv.dom.customer;
import org.nakedobjects.applib.AbstractDomainObject;

public class Customer extends AbstractDomainObject {
    ...
}
```

Repeat for the other two classes, but put Car in the dom.vehicle subpackage and Service in a dom.service subpackage.

So, what's with the AbstractDomainObject superclass? Well, this is part of the Naked Objects application library (or *applib*), and using it will simplify our code a little. The applib also provides a set of annotations that can be used to extend the semantics of the domain model. We'll see some of these in just a moment.

I hasten to add, though, that it *isn't* necessary to subclass from Abstract-DomainObject, and you don't necessarily need to use any annotations either. We will be doing so within our case study, but that said, your domain classes can truly be *plain old Java object*s (pojos) if you want. Chapter 14, *Naked Objects as a Design Tool*, on page 259 covers this topic in more detail.

It's always important to choose a good name for classes, and in Naked Objects it will be apparent if we haven't because that name is going to appear directly in the UI. If the name we want to use isn't acceptable as a Java class name (for example, is a keyword or a name containing symbols or punctuation), then we can override the inferred name using the @Named annotation from the applib. Don't use it otherwise, though; it erodes the *ubiquitous language*.

Another annotation you might also want to apply is @DescribedAs. This allows a longer description of the class to be provided, for example, so that the viewer can display it as a tooltip or equivalent.

Annotations play a big part in Naked Objects. We'll be using many of them as we go through the book, but for the full set, take a look at the *Annotations Reference* on page 366.

OK, we've defined some classes, so let's flesh them out a little.

Add Basic Properties

A couple of basic properties will make our entities seem a little more real. Using the nop (p=property) template (as we imported when we set up the development environment), add a FirstName property for Customer, of type String. You should end up with something like this:

chapter02/Customer-FirstName.java

```
// {{ FirstName
private String firstName;
@MemberOrder(sequence = "1")
public String getFirstName() {
    return firstName;
}
public void setFirstName(final String firstName) {
    this.firstName = firstName;
}
// }}
```

You'll see that a *getter* and a *setter* method are both generated for the property, as well as an instance variable. This is just the standard JavaBean convention. You might also have noticed the @MemberOrder

> ### Use Regions for a Bird's-Eye View
>
> You'll notice when you use the Eclipse templates that they use comments to group together class members that represent each property (or more generally responsibility) of the object.
>
> This convention allows code folding in the editor of the IDE. The *Coffee-Bytes* plug-in for Eclipse can be configured so that each of these regions will fold into a single line.*
>
> Not everyone is a fan of code folding, but I find it invaluable to help navigate a large domain class and get a sense of its responsibilities. If you don't like it, you're free of course to adapt the templates to your preferred coding style.
>
> ───────────
> *. Coffee Bytes is hosted at http://www.realjenius.com/platform_support.

annotation. This is another of the applib annotations, this time being a hint to the viewer as to the order to display the fields in the UI.

Go ahead and add some further properties:

- For the Customer class, add a LastName property (String).

- For the Car class, add a RegistrationNumber property (again, String).

- For the Service class, add a BookedIn property and also an EstimatedReady property (both of type java.sql.Date).

Now that we've defined some classes, let's think about how the end user might want to use the application.

2.4 Using Repositories to Locate Objects

The OOUIs provided by Naked Objects purposefully don't provide wizards and such; instead, the end user goes straight to the domain object that has the functionality they need for, well, whatever it is they are doing.

So, how might our end user want to use the CarServ application; where would they likely start? Well:

- A customer might call on the phone; the service manager would want to look them up on the system.

in context...

Factory and Repository

A *factory* provides a mechanism that encapsulates the creation of objects (or possibly graphs of objects). It also decouples the rest of the model from the concrete classes.

A *repository* provides a mechanism to acquire references to existing objects. It decouples the rest of the model from the persistence mechanism of such objects.

- A mechanic working on a car might want to look at its previous services.

So, most likely the Customer and Car objects are our start points. There probably isn't any valid reason to start with a Service, though, because every Service object belongs to a Car object.

For each of the likely start points—Car and Customer—we create a combined *factory* and *repository* class, with which the end user can either create new objects or locate existing objects. Let's do this now.

Create and Register the Repository Class

Naked Objects allows us to define classes to act as our factory and repository. Normally we combine these responsibilities into a single class; as a consequence, we usually just use the term *repository* even if it can also act as a factory.

So, select File > New > Class, and specify the following:

- The source folder: carserv-dom/src/main/java (should be the default)

- The package: com.pragprog.dhnako.carserv.dom.customer

- The class: CustomerRepository

- The superclass: org.nakedobjects.applib.AbstractFactoryAndRepository

Then repeat for CarRepository, but placing it in the vehicle subpackage. The AbstractFactoryAndRepository is another of our convenience superclasses from the applib.

Next, we need to register these classes with the framework. We do that by editing the *nakedobjects.services* property key in the naked-objects.properties file (in the commandline project). This will already have some entries from the archetype, so replace them with the following:

`chapter02/nakedobjects.properties`

```
nakedobjects.services.prefix = com.pragprog.dhnako.carserv.dom
nakedobjects.services = customer.CustomerRepository,\
                        vehicle.CarRepository
```

This property tells Naked Objects to do a couple of things. First, it will instantiate each of these classes as managed singletons. Second, it will display the repositories as icons on the GUI.[1]

While we're here, let's also comment out the *fixtures* property key:

`chapter02/nakedobjects.properties`

```
#nakedobjects.fixtures.prefix= com.pragprog.dhnako.carserv.fixture
#nakedobjects.fixtures=
```

We'll be looking at fixtures in Chapter 4, *Rapid Prototyping*, on page 63.

Adding Behavior to Create and List Objects

Now let's have both the repositories be able to create a new instance of their corresponding domain object. For CustomerRepository, then, use the noft (ft=factory-transient) template (as installed in Section 1.4, *Set Up the Development Environment*, on page 10) to add the following:

`chapter02/CustomerRepository-newCustomer.java`

```
// {{ Create new (still transient) Customer
public Customer newCustomer() {
    Customer customer = newTransientInstance(Customer.class);
    return customer;
}
// }}
```

The newTransientInstance() method is inherited from the convenience superclass and will return a nonpersisted Customer instance (that is, one that still needs to be inserted into the database). Add a similar method for the CarRepository to return a Car.

---

1. Strictly speaking, the repositories are displayed as icons only provided that they haven't been annotated as @Hidden and the user has permission to use them. You can find more about authorization in Chapter 18, *Deploying the Full Runtime*, on page 333.

At this early stage of development, it'd also be useful to list all the objects (or rather, those that have been persisted). So, let's add another method to CustomerRepository, using the nosa (sa = "search for all") template:

```java
// {{ all Customers
@Exploration
public List<Customer> allCustomers() {
    return allInstances(Customer.class);
}
// }}
```

The inherited allInstances() method just returns all known instances of the specified type, while the @Exploration annotation indicates that this action should be made available only while in exploration mode (more on modes in Chapter 4, *Rapid Prototyping*, on page 63). Write a similar method for CarRepository to return all Cars.

I think we ought to give the application a go. Use Run > Run Configurations..., and then under the Java Application node, select NakedObjects (DnD) or NakedObjects (HTML). With this launch configuration selected, choose Run. All being well, you should see the application running, with our two repositories showing as icons, as shown in Figure 2.3, on the facing page. In the DnD viewer, for example, you should now be able to right-click either of the repositories to create a new, nonpersisted Customer or Car. Because it is still transient, it is automatically rendered with a Save button; clicking this will cause the object to be persisted. Create and persist a couple more instances of Customer, say; close their windows; and then retrieve them using allCustomers() (on CustomerRepository).

Before we move on, let's just do a little tidying up. It's a bit strange in the GUI to see the icons called CustomerRepository and CarRepository. Better names would probably be Customers and Cars. We can do this using the @Named annotation, mentioned earlier:

```java
import org.nakedobjects.applib.annotation.Named;

@Named("Customers")
public class CustomerRepository extends AbstractFactoryAndRepository {
    // code omitted
}
```

Make this change, and try the application again.

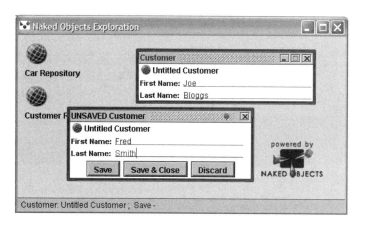

Figure 2.3: CREATING A CUSTOMER

You'll have noticed that I haven't talked at all about setting up any sort of back-end database. Well, Naked Objects is component-based, and one of those components is the object store (also called a *persistor*). By altering the runtime configuration, we can choose to persist the objects in an RDBMS, as XML, or indeed just stored in-memory.

The default configuration is to use the in-memory object store. Since this requires no configuration, it is ideal for rapid development. More-over, because the objects are stored only in memory, it is also great for unit testing our domain objects because there is no need to reset the database to a known state.

Of course, the downside to using the in-memory object store is that the objects aren't persisted between runs of your application. We'll live with the inconvenience for now, but (just so you know where we're heading) we'll address it in Chapter 4, *Rapid Prototyping*, on page 63.

OK, so the application works, but it's hard to distinguish objects or even the types of objects. It's time to fix that.

2.5 Identifying Objects to the User

Everything that the end user sees in the OOUI is a representation of an object or of a collection of objects. To help the user, we emphasize that objects of the same type do the same thing by associating an icon with the class's type. We also help the user distinguish between different

<u>**An Icon?! Now?!**</u>

I remember clearly my own reaction when I first learned about Naked Objects; I honestly couldn't believe it when, having written just a tiny bit of code, we were asked to select icons for the domain objects we had created.

But icons are important—they connect the image-oriented right side of your brain to the domain object as well as the logical left side. You start to have a fuller grasp of the concept.*

They can also be fun. If I don't have an icon that fits, then I'll temporarily choose another one based on a pun or joke. It's a good way to start working together with the domain experts.

---
*. See Andy Hunt's *Pragmatic Thinking & Learning* (Hun08) for similar ideas.

instances of the same type by giving each object a title (a label). Let's look at both of these.

Choose Icons

Though not dependent on them, the Naked Objects viewers use icons to allow us to rapidly distinguish the different types of domain objects.

Some viewers also use icons for the repositories. Usually the icon of a repository should be the same as the icon of the objects that it creates or retrieves.

You can use any icons you want, but Naked Objects provides a set that you are free to use in your own applications. You'll find these in $NO_HOME/resources/icon-library. So, let's copy and rename the following icons into the carserv-dom project:

From	To
hal-icons/32/regular/customer.gif	Customer.gif
hal-icons/32/regular/Car.png	Car.png
tango-icons/32x32/categories/preferences-system.png	Service.png

Naked Objects will automatically match the names of the files with the class names. We also need icons for the two repositories. Although we could copy over an icon with the same name as the repository, an alternative is to write an iconName() method that returns a string indicating the image to use.

chapter02/CustomerRepository-iconName.java

```
// {{ Identification
public String iconName() {
    return "Customer";
}
// }}
```

Go ahead and make these changes; you can use the noid and noidicon templates to speed you. Then we'll move onto the title.

Add a Title

Although an icon is primarily used to distinguish between different types of objects, we also need to distinguish between different instances of the same type. Here we use a *title*—a label for each object. This is just a method called title() that returns a String, typically built up using key properties of the object.

Since we already have some suitable properties for each of our domain classes, we can write our title() methods with no further ado. Using the noid and noidtitle templates if you want, write a title() method for each of Customer, Car, and Service. For example:

chapter02/Customer-Title.java

```
// {{ Identification
public String title() {
    TitleBuffer buf = new TitleBuffer();
    buf.append(getFirstName()).append(getLastName());
    return buf.toString();
}
// }}
```

The TitleBuffer class is just a helper utility provided by the applib that takes care of adding spaces and similar annoyances. OK, we're ready for another try. Run your application, and have a go at creating a Customer. Then, fill in the properties, and check that the title is updated, as per Figure 2.4, on the following page. Also, make sure you can create a customer via the HTML interface.

The icon and the title aren't the only things we can do that influence the presentation of our domain objects in the user interface. Let's look at some other techniques.

Add Rendering Hints

Earlier, in Section 2.3, *Name the Classes*, on page 29, we saw that the @Named annotation can be used to rename classes, and that the

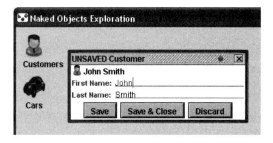

Figure 2.4: CREATING A (TITLED) CUSTOMER

@DescribedAs annotations can be used to provide a tooltip-like description of the class. These annotations can also be applied to the properties:

`chapter02/Customer-Members-Named-Annotation.java`

```
@DescribedAs(
    "The name given to this customer, or by which he/she is known")
public String getFirstName() { ... }
```

Another annotation we can apply is @MemberOrder, mentioned earlier. For those classes where there are multiple properties, update the sequence attribute to specify the relative order that the properties should appear in the user interface. For example:

`chapter02/Customer-Members-MemberOrder-Annotation.java`

```
public class Customer ... {

    @MemberOrder(sequence="1.2")
    public String getFirstName() { ... }
    ...

    @MemberOrder(sequence="1.1")
    public String getLastName() { ... }
    ...
}
```

This will render the LastName property before the FirstName property. For the sequence attribute, you can just use numbers, but it also supports the Dewey decimal format (as used for cataloging in libraries). This cunning plan is so that subclasses can specify where their properties reside relative to the superclass's.

Joe Asks...
Does the Title Need to Be Unique?

There's no need for the title to be unique, at least not so far as Naked Objects is concerned. However, it should be unique *enough* that the end user can distinguish between different objects viewed at the same time.

This isn't something to agonize over, though; your end users will soon tell you whether they need additional information in the title.

Another annotation that we can apply to string properties is @Typical-Length. This is used by the viewer to determine the length of a text field widget. One further annotation I'll just mention, again for string properties, is @MultiLine. Using this, we can specify whether the widget used should be a text box rather than a text field. For example, suppose we add a Notes property to Customer:

`chapter02/Customer-Notes-MultiLine-Annotation.java`

```java
import org.nakedobjects.applib.annotation.MultiLine;

public class Customer ... {
    ...
    @MultiLine(numberOfLines = 10, preventWrapping = false)
    @MemberOrder(sequence = "1.3")
    public String getNotes() { ... }
}
```

In Figure 2.5, on the following page, we see the effect of the @MultiLine annotation under the DnD viewer.

It makes sense to add these annotations early on. Although you might argue they are merely just improving the cosmetics of the user interface, for a nontechnical domain expert's viewpoint this is often impressive stuff. It does no harm to build a little credibility early on!

Now we have some of the basics out of the way, let's turn to slightly more weighty matters and implement some simple business rules.

Figure 2.5: EFFECT OF THE @MULTILINE ANNOTATION

Joe Asks...

Should Annotations Capture UI-Specific Details?

Annotations such as @MemberOrder and @MultiLine influence the UI but do not otherwise have domain semantics, so it's reasonable to ask whether this is right.

Then again, we could equally ask whether it is right for a domain object to be annotated with JPA annotations such as @ManyToOne that capture semantics relating to the persistence layer, such as whether to lazy load.

Ultimately this is a trade-off: we could separate the presentation semantics into separate metadata (just as *Hibernate* does for persistence with its hibernate.cfg.xml file), and indeed Naked Objects' internal architecture does support this. However, it would give the developer two separate sets of artifacts to keep in sync. Naked Objects prefers annotations to keep the information together.

2.6 Capturing Simple Business Rules

Because we are focusing in this chapter on domain objects' properties, we should also think about any business rules associated with those properties.

In fact, we've already started doing this; the very act of deciding on a datatype for a property (such as Integer or String) constrains the values of that property. But over and above the datatype, we might have further business rules, such as only positive numbers, for example, or a date might be allowed only prior to "today."

Naked Objects allows us to capture such business rules in two different ways. Let's look at each.

Capture Declarative Rules

Our first means of capturing business rules is using annotations. These are called *declarative semantics* because they are, well, a declaration of something that should always be true.

A good example is @MaxLength, indicating the maximum number of characters for a String property. Every layer of the application will reflect this characteristic of the property: the viewer's text field will prevent more characters than this from being entered, and similarly the object store will only ever persist this many characters. So, let's revisit our string properties and specify @MaxLength for each:

- A maximum length of 30 for Customer's FirstName.

- Likewise, a maximum of 30 for Customer's LastName.

- 255 for the Customer's Notes.

- An appropriate maximum length for the Car's RegistrationNumber property. In the United Kingdom where I live, the maximum number of characters is 7, as it is in the United States, for example.

Another useful declarative annotation that applies to any type of property is @Optional. If specified, it means that the object can be persisted without any value set for that property. If we look at our Customer and Car objects, then we can see that most properties are mandatory. However, the Customer's Notes property should probably be marked as optional. Go ahead and make this change.

When done, our Notes property, for example, should look like this:

chapter02/Customer-Notes-MaxLength-Optional-Annotation.java

```
@MultiLine(numberOfLines = 10, preventWrapping = false)
@Optional
@MaxLength(255)
@MemberOrder(sequence = "1.3")
public String getNotes() { ... }
```

Although annotations are simple to apply, if there isn't an annotation for the rule you want to specify, then too bad. Naked Objects therefore also provides a more powerful mechanism.

Capture Imperative Rules

How's your Latin? *Imperator* is Latin, broadly meaning "commander," and is the root of the French word *Empereur* and the English word *Emperor*.[2]

And in Naked Objects, an *imperative semantic* represents a rule that is implemented programmatically rather than declaratively.

Previously we added the @MaxLength annotation to specify the maximum number of characters for a Car's RegistrationNumber. However, the number of characters might vary by country. If we wanted to deploy our application to run in different countries, we couldn't use a declarative semantic; we need to program the rule instead.

We do this by writing a method for the property with a *validate* prefix. This returns a String that—if not **null**—is taken to be the reason that the proposed value is wrong. For example, we could validate the registration number as follows:

chapter02/Car-RegistrationNumber-validate.java

```
public String validateRegistrationNumber(String registrationNumber) {
    if (registrationNumber == null) return null;
    String country = Locale.getDefault().getCountry();
    int length = registrationNumber.length();
    if ( ("US".equals(country) && length > 7) ||
        ("GB".equals(country) && length > 7 ) ||
        length > 12) { // everywhere else
        return "Registration number is too long";
    }
    return null;
}
```

---

2. I double-checked this on the Internet, so it must be right!

Figure 2.6: VALIDATING REGISTRATION NUMBERS

In this particular example, the business logic itself isn't too tricky to follow, but much more complex rules could be implemented.

Go ahead and add in this rule; use the nopval template if you want. In Figure 2.6, we can see the rule in action: the save buttons are disabled, there is a warning icon against the field, and (inlaid in the figure) there is a message in the status bar.

Before we wrap up this chapter, there's just one more thing we could do to make our application a bit easier to use. Let's look at this now.

2.7 Providing Choices for Properties

As we saw in the preceding section, sometimes the values that are valid for a property are restricted. When the set of valid values is relatively small, then (rather than the end user having to guess what the valid values might be), we can ask the domain object to return a list of such values. The Naked Objects viewer uses this information to present the list of values in a drop-down.

For example, we might want to capture the formal title of a Customer as a Title property (not to be confused with Naked Objects' own reserved title() method) where the range of available values is Mr, Mrs, Ms, and Miss.

Let's try this by adding a new Title property in the usual way. Then, add a new method called choicesTitle() (using the nopcho template), and complete its implementation like so:

chapter02/Customer-TitleProperty-choices.java

```java
public List<String> choicesTitle() {
    return Arrays.asList("Mr", "Mrs", "Ms", "Miss");
}
```

Figure 2.7: THE CHOICES ARE DISPLAYED AS A DROP-DOWN LIST BOX.

We could also update our Customer's title() implementation to incorporate this new Title property:

chapter02/Customer-Title-updatedWithTitleProperty.java

```java
public String title() {
    TitleBuffer buf = new TitleBuffer();
    buf.append(getTitle());
    buf.append(getFirstName()).append(getLastName());
    return buf.toString();
}
```

If you run the application, you should see a drop-down list box. In Figure 2.7, we can see what this looks like in the DnD viewer.

Note that providing a selection of choices does not actually prevent the user from typing in some other value. So, we should also add a validateTitle() method. I'll leave that as an exercise for now.

Coming Up Next

In this chapter, we used Maven to create a project and started populating it with the domain classes that make up our little CarServ application. We have some objects that we can demonstrate to our domain expert that are identifiable and relevant, look OK in the UI, and even implement some simple business rules.

Right now, though these domain objects are stand-alone, they don't have any relationship to each other. So, in the next chapter, we'll start relating those domain concepts together.

Exercises

If you have just been reading rather than actually coding, now would be a good time to load the final CarServ application (***chapter02-02***), inspect the code, and run the application. Note, by the way, that I updated the banner and some of the CSS for the HTML viewer (in the command-dline project under src/main/webapp). I've also renamed the launch configurations to exploration#viewer_dnd.launch and exploration#viewer_html. launch. . . as the case study develops, we'll be running our application in other ways, so it'll help to distinguish them from the outset.

Try adding a validateTitle() method to ensure that only those titles listed in choicesTitle() may be selected. You could also explore iconName(). We saw this for repositories, but it works for domain objects too, and moreover it is dynamic. So, you could change the icon based on the selected Title if you wanted.

In the previous chapter's exercise, I suggested you think about an application of your own you might want to write. So, why not start it now and develop it side-by-side with my CarServ one? If you're not feeling inspired, try one of these: a to-do list manager, a recipe organizer, a dinner party planner, an album organizer, or (a perennial favorite) a library management system.

Chapter 3

Relating Objects Together

In the previous chapter, we made a start on our *ubiquitous language* for the CarServ domain. We have three domain classes—Car, Customer, and Service—with properties, icons, and titles for each. In short, we understand that these are indeed meaningful classes within our domain.

However, in order for our *ubiquitous language* to be useful for the team, we need to start linking these concepts together, explaining how they relate. For example, we want to be able to say that Cars are owned by Customers and that Cars have Service histories. In terms of code, that means associating the domain objects that correspond to these domain concepts.

In this chapter (**chapter03-01**[1]), we're going to associate our objects using both uni- and bidirectional relationships. We'll also be extending our *ubiquitous language* by adding some describing concepts. But let's start with relationships.

3.1 Associating Objects

Much of the richness of object-oriented designs comes from the way in which the objects interact. This is as true for domain objects as it is for any other type of object.

Some of the key insights that (we hope) we'll uncover about our domain objects will revolve around these interactions and associations. For now, though, we'll start with very concrete relationships, just as we did with domain entities.

---

1. Includes solutions to Chapter 2's exercises

Looking back to the initial sketch of the domain model in Figure 2.2, on page 28, we can see that the relationships we need are between Car and its owning Customer, as well as between Service and Car.

Adding Scalar Associations

To add scalar associations between classes, we just use properties, meaning we can use the same nop template as we used in the preceding chapter. However, rather than the property's type being a String or a java.sql.Date, instead it will be the type of the referenced object. For instance, the reference from Car to its owning Customer is as follows:

chapter03/Car-OwningCustomer.java

```java
private Customer owningCustomer;
@Optional
@MemberOrder(sequence = "1.2")
public Customer getOwningCustomer() {
    return owningCustomer;
}
public void setOwningCustomer(final Customer owningCustomer) {
    this.owningCustomer = owningCustomer;
}
```

Add this property now. Note that I've made it @Optional so that we can create Cars without necessarily having to specify who owns them.

When you run your application in the DnD viewer, you should be able to drag and drop one of your Customers into the slot representing the Car's OwningCustomer property. For the HTML viewer, there is no drag and drop. Instead, first retrieve the object that you want to associate, so that is "known" to the viewer. When you go to do the association, the object should appear in the drop-down list.

OK, this works and will do for now, but it is also rather manual and open to user error. Don't worry, it'll get more sophisticated in Chapter 5, *Creating Behaviorally Complete Objects*, on page 79.

Now you've created a reference from Car to Customer, repeat for Service and Car. Then, update the title of the Service to include the Car's registration number:

chapter03/Service-TitleAndCarProperty.java

```java
public class Service extends AbstractDomainObject {
    public String title() {
        TitleBuffer buf = new TitleBuffer();
        buf.append(getCar().getRegistrationNumber())
            .append(":", getBookedIn());
        return buf.toString();
    }
}
```

```
    private Car car;
    public Car getCar() { ... }
    public void setCar(final Car car) { ... }
    ...
}
```

Right, we're halfway there. We can associate one object with another *single* object, but we also need to be able to associate an object with a whole *collection* of objects.

Adding Vector Associations

Our Car knows its owning Customer (and Service knows its owning Car). However, a Customer could own multiple Cars, and Cars undoubtedly require more than one Service throughout their lifetimes. We need to manage collections of objects.

Like a property, a collection has a *get*ter and a *set*ter along with some supporting methods. However, the type of the collection is either a java.util.List (order preserved, duplicates optionally allowed) or a java.util.Set (order may or may not be preserved, duplicates not allowed).

To quickly add a collection, we can use either the nocl (collection-list) or nocs (collection-set) template. Let's add a list for the Customer-to-Car relationship:

chapter03/Customer-Cars.java

```
private List<Car> cars = new ArrayList<Car>();
@MemberOrder(sequence = "1.4")
public List<Car> getCars() {
    return cars;
}
public void setCars(final List<Car> cars) {
    this.cars = cars;
}
```

When we run the application, we should see that the Customer has a collection of Cars. In the DnD viewer, you should be able to drag and drop objects into this collection, and likewise, in the HTML viewer, you should (once you've initially retrieved the object to add) be able to add new objects from the drop-down. Compare your application against that shown in Figure 3.1, on the next page.

That's a big step forward... but we're not done quite yet. For a start, we need to manually associate the Customer with the Car and then (once the Car is saved) associate the Car with the Customer. As a consequence, it is possible to have a Car reference a Customer but not vice versa. Equally, a Customer can reference a Car, but that Car could refer to

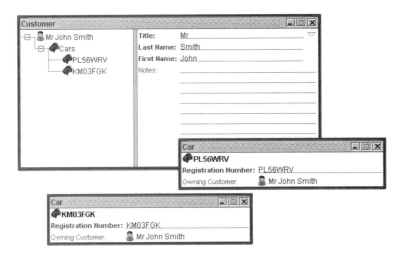

Figure 3.1: CUSTOMER'S CARS COLLECTION IN THE DND VIEWER

some *other* Customer. In other words, there is no referential integrity here.

What we really need to do is ensure that these associations keep in sync. The most straightforward approach is the *mutual registration* pattern, whereby the object on one side of the relationship (say Customer) is responsible for wiring up both associations, and the other (say Car) just delegates up.[2]

To accomplish this, we need to add some supporting methods. If a collection has an addToXxx() or a removeFromXxx() method, then the framework will call these rather than simply calling add() and remove() on the collection returned from the *get*ter. Similarly, if a property has a modifyXxx() or a clearXxx() method, then these will be called rather than the *set*ter. This allows us to implement the *mutual registration* in these supporting methods.

Let's make the changes we need. For the Customer's Cars collection, use the nocmod template to add new addToCars() and removeFromCars() methods.

---

2. For more on the *mutual registration* pattern, see http://www.two-sdg.demon.co.uk/curbralan/papers/MutualRegistration.pdf.

chapter03/Customer-Cars-nocmod.java

```java
public void addToCars(final Car car) {
    // check for no-op
    if (car == null || getCars().contains(car)) {
        return;
    }
    // associate new
    getCars().add(car);
    // additional business logic
    onAddToCars(car);
}
public void removeFromCars(
        final Car car) {
    // check for no-op
    if (car == null || !getCars().contains(car)) {
        return;
    }
    // dissociate existing
    getCars().remove(car);
    // additional business logic
    onRemoveFromCars(car);
}
protected void onAddToCars(final Car car) {
}
protected void onRemoveFromCars(final Car car) {
}
```

The implementation generated by this template does the exact same thing that the framework would otherwise have done. Likewise, for the Car's Customer property, use the nopmod template to add supporting modifyOwningCustomer() and clearOwningCustomer() methods:

chapter03/Car-OwningCustomer-nopmod.java

```java
public void modifyOwningCustomer( final Customer owningCustomer) {
    Customer currentOwningCustomer = getOwningCustomer();
    // check for no-op
    if (owningCustomer == null ||
        owningCustomer.equals(currentOwningCustomer)) {
        return;
    }
    // associate new
    setOwningCustomer(owningCustomer);
    // additional business logic
    onModifyOwningCustomer(currentOwningCustomer, owningCustomer);
}
public void clearOwningCustomer() {
    Customer currentOwningCustomer = getOwningCustomer();
    // check for no-op
    if (currentOwningCustomer == null) {
        return;
    }
```

```
    // dissociate existing
    setOwningCustomer(null);
    // additional business logic
    onClearOwningCustomer(currentOwningCustomer);
}
protected void onModifyOwningCustomer(
        final Customer oldOwningCustomer,
        final Customer newOwningCustomer) {
}
protected void onClearOwningCustomer(
        final Customer oldOwningCustomer) {
}
```

Again, this generated implementation doesn't change what the framework would have done.

Now we can implement the *mutual registration* pattern. First, in the Customer's addToCars(), we update both the Customer's own Cars collection and also the Car's reference to the Customer. We replace this:

```
chapter03/Customer-Cars-replaced.java
```

```
// associate new
getCars().add(car);
```

with the following:

```
chapter03/Customer-Cars-Bidir.java
```

```
// dissociate arg from its current parent (if any).
car.clearOwningCustomer();
// associate arg
car.setOwningCustomer(this);
getCars().add(car);
```

In the removeFromCars() method, we have similar functionality to clear the relationship from both sides, replacing this:

```
chapter03/Customer-Cars-replaced.java
```

```
// dissociate existing
getCars().remove(car);
```

with the following:

```
chapter03/Customer-Cars-Bidir.java
```

```
// dissociate arg
car.setOwningCustomer(null);
getCars().remove(car);
```

Meanwhile, in the Car's modifyOwningCustomer() method, we simply delegate up to the provided Customer (because, as we've seen, the Customer will set up the relationship on both sides).

We replace this:

`chapter03/Car-OwningCustomer-replaced.java`

```
// associate new
setOwningCustomer(owningCustomer);
```

with the following:

`chapter03/Car-OwningCustomer-Bidir.java`

```
// delegate to parent to associate
owningCustomer.addToCars(this);
```

And similarly, in the clearOwningCustomer() method, we delegate to the current owning Customer to clear the relationship on both sides, replacing this:

`chapter03/Car-OwningCustomer-replaced.java`

```
// dissociate existing
setOwningCustomer(null);
```

with the following:

`chapter03/Car-OwningCustomer-Bidir.java`

```
// delegate to parent to dissociate
getOwningCustomer().removeFromCars(this);
```

OK, with those edits done, run the application again. This time the associations stay in sync.

In the generated implementations, note some additional methods: onAddToCars(), onRemoveFromCars(), onModifyOwningCustomer(), and onClearOwningCustomer(). These are the places to put any additional business logic you might need to perform over and above maintaining a bidirectional relationship. If we need to convert a unidirectional relationship into bidirectional, we can then apply other templates rather than manually edit the code.

For example, the noc-1m template sets up a bidirectional one-to-many relationship for a collection, and the nop-m1 template sets up a corresponding bidirectional many-to-one relationship for a property. We can find variants, such as bidirectional one-to-one relationships, in Appendix B, on page 369. All of these templates replace the supporting methods but leave untouched any hook methods with business logic you might have added.

In our CarServ domain model, there is another relationship, namely, Car-to-Service. We already have one direction (from Service back up to Car). Add a list of Services for a Car, and then (using the *mutual registration* pattern) convert it into a bidirectional relationship in the same way.

We've now associated our three main domain objects together. Let's see how relationships can further enrich our model.

3.2 Adding Describing Concepts

Our objective is to develop a rich model to act as the *ubiquitous language* for the domain. If this is to succeed, then we should look to extend that domain model as and when we need to.

There's very often a reluctance to do this, because by using "traditional" frameworks, the impact of adding a new domain class to the model can be quite substantial. For example, using a web framework such as Struts, you would need to write new web forms, write new controllers, and develop *data transfer objects* (DTOs)—all this as well as the domain model and its back-end database schema. A similar degree of work would be required if writing a rich client.

When developing in Naked Objects, many of these artifacts just don't exist. The (small) cost of having to develop a new domain object is more than outweighed by the expansion of our *ubiquitous language*. The common language with our business means we don't have to waste time translating between the actual domain concepts and an incomplete domain model that doesn't adequately capture them.

We can enrich our language by introducing additional domain classes that describe or are related to the existing classes. Very often properties start off being defined using simple Strings or **int**s but then later become references to full-blown domain classes. And once we have these classes, we can start to push responsibilities onto them. The classes introduced are very often read-only—what in RDBMS terms might be called *reference data* or standing data. (And by the by, the term I use for nonreference classes is *transactional classes*.)

So, let's introduce some describing objects in our CarServ domain.

Introducing the Title Concept

In Section 2.7, *Providing Choices for Properties*, on page 43, we added a Title property to Customer. Our code currently looks something like this:[3]

```
private static List<String> TITLES =
    Arrays.asList("Mr", "Mrs", "Ms", "Miss");
public List<String> choicesTitle() {
    return TITLES;
}
public String validateTitle(final String title) {
    if (title == null) return null;
    if (!TITLES.contains(title)) {
        return "Invalid title";
    }
    return null;
}
```

The list of titles that we want to allow is quite restricted: Mr, Mrs, Ms, and Ms. In other words, it is a well-defined, bounded set. We could instead create a new domain class (an *entity* in DDD terms) to represent this concept. Let's do so and call it Title (in the customer package):

`chapter03/Title.java`

```
import org.nakedobjects.applib.annotation.Bounded;

@Bounded
public class Title extends AbstractDomainObject {

}
```

Note the @Bounded annotation of Title. This tells Naked Objects that there is only a static, well-defined set of instances and therefore (as for an **enum**) likely to be small in number. The viewers use this information by displaying all instances of the class as a drop-down list.

Update the Title class by adding a Name property (of type String), and write a title() method using this Name property. Also select an icon from the icon library.

Then, let's update the Customer's Title property to simply be of this type:

```
private Title title;
public Title getTitle() { ... }
public void setTitle(final Title title) { ... }
```

---

3. This assumes you've done the exercises at the end of Chapter 2. Download **chapter03-01** if not.

Also remove the earlier choicesTitle() and validateTitle() methods; they are about to become defunct.

Now that we have Title as a domain concept, we can give it some responsibilities. One of the exercises for Chapter 2 (implemented in the **chapter03-01** version of the case study) suggested using the icon-Name() method to dynamically change the icon based on the Title property. The best implementation I could come up with was nevertheless rather clunky:

chapter03/Customer-iconName.java

```java
public String iconName() {
    if ("Mr".equals(getTitle()))
        return "Man";
    if ("Mrs".equals(getTitle()))
        return "Woman";
    if ("Ms".equals(getTitle()))
        return "Woman";
    if ("Miss".equals(getTitle()))
        return "Woman";
    return null; // default
}
```

So, let's add an IconName property (of type String, with a *get*ter and *set*ter as usual) to the Title domain class and then refactor Customer:

chapter03/Customer-iconName-refactored.java

```java
public String iconName() {
    return getTitle() != null? getTitle().getIconName(): null;
}
```

That's all very nice, but where does this bounded set of valid Titles come from? Let's look at this now.

Setting Up Titles

We've said that there are a bounded set of Titles, but it'd be nonsensical to require the user to have to create them; they should exist already. When we get to production, they will have been seeded into the database. However, for the moment, we're using the in-memory object store, meaning objects are not persisted between runs of the application. We therefore need to create a TitlesFixture to populate the object store and instruct the framework to install the fixture for us as part of its initialization.

Because fixtures are not part of the domain model, we put them instead into the fixture project. So, select the carserv-fixture project and then, using File > New > Class, specify the following:

- The package name: com.pragprog.dhnako.carserv.fixture.customer

- The name: TitlesFixture

- The superclass: org.nakedobjects.applib.fixtures.AbstractFixture

AbstractFixture is another of the convenience superclasses in the applib. Modify the class to read as follows:

chapter03/TitlesFixture.java

```
public class TitlesFixture extends AbstractFixture {
    public void install() {
        createTitle("Mr", "Man");
        createTitle("Mrs", "Woman");
        createTitle("Ms", "Woman");
        createTitle("Miss", "Woman");
    }
    private void createTitle(final String name, final String iconName) {
        Title title = newTransientInstance(Title.class);
        title.setName(name);
        title.setIconName(iconName);
        persist(title);
    }
}
```

The persist() method, inherited from AbstractFixture, saves the object to the (in-memory) object store.

Then, register in nakedobjects.properties (in the commandline project's config directory):

chapter03/nakedobjects-fixture-Titles.properties

```
nakedobjects.fixtures.prefix=com.pragprog.dhnako.carserv.fixture
nakedobjects.fixtures=customer.TitlesFixture
```

With all that done, run your application again. This time there should be some Titles to select from automatically.

Now we have that working, but I doubt it seems like a particularly compelling addition to our *ubiquitous language*. Let's add some more concepts with a little more meat on them.

Introducing the Concepts of Make and Model

Since this is a car-servicing application, one of the concepts that seems relevant is the make and model of the car. For example, a Ford Focus is serviced every 12,500 miles, whereas a Toyota Corolla is serviced every 10,000 miles. These are properties of the Car's Model rather than the Car itself.

So, have a go at adding the following:

1. Add a Make class (in dom.vehicle package).

   Give the Make class a Name property, implement its title() method, and choose an icon.

   Annotate as being @Bounded so that the Make instances appear as a drop-down. But we should also annotate them as @Immutable. This makes them noneditable in the viewer and triggers an exception if there is any attempt to modify them programmatically. Very often reference data classes are annotated with both @Bounded and @Immutable.

2. Add a Model class (also in the dom.vehicle package).

   Give the Model class a Name property, and, like for Make, implement its title() method, choose an icon, and add the @DescribedAs annotation. Also annotate as being @Bounded and @Immutable.

3. Add a bidirectional relationship between Make and Model.

   A Make has a collection of Models, and a Model has a reference to its associated Make.

Because Make and Model are reference data, we will need fixtures for them. Since the two classes have a bidirectional relationship, the easiest approach is to set up both in the same fixture.

Therefore, create a new MakesAndModelsFixture (in the fixture.vehicle package) to set up Model instances (for example Ford or Toyota), and also set up Make instances (for example, Ford Focus, Ford Mustang, Toyota Corolla, Toyota Yaris). The following code will do the job:

chapter03/MakesAndModelsFixture.java

```java
public class MakesAndModelsFixture extends AbstractFixture {
    public void install() {
        Make fordMake = createMake("Ford");
        Make toyotaMake = createMake("Toyota");
        createModel(fordMake, "Focus");
        createModel(fordMake, "Mustang");
        createModel(toyotaMake, "Corolla");
        createModel(toyotaMake, "Yaris");
    }
```

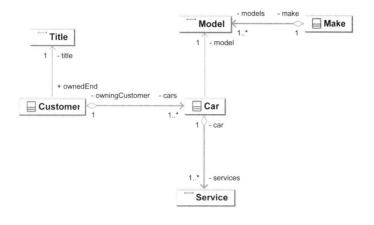

Figure 3.2: CARSERV WITH DESCRIBING CONCEPTS

```
    private Make createMake(String name) {
        Make make = newTransientInstance(Make.class);
        make.setName(name);
        persist(make);
        return make;
    }
    private Model createModel(Make make, String name) {
        Model model = newTransientInstance(Model.class);
        model.setName(name);
        make.addToModels(model);
        persist(model);
        return model;
    }
}
```

Finally, we need to register our new fixture with Naked Objects so that
it is installed when we run the application:

chapter03/nakedobjects-fixture-Titles-MakesAndModels.properties

```
nakedobjects.fixtures.prefix=com.pragprog.dhnako.carserv.fixture
nakedobjects.fixtures=customer.TitlesFixture,\
                      vehicle.MakesAndModelsFixture
```

We're done adding the Make and Model classes, so let's now add a simple
unidirectional association from Car to Model. In Figure 3.2, we can see
(as a UML class diagram) the new classes in our model. We'll be able to
exploit this relationship in subsequent chapters. Run the application
again to make sure all is in order.

As already discussed, adding classes that act as describing concepts extends the vocabulary of our *ubiquitous language*. As we saw with the Title's IconName property, it also enables more natural implementations: we were able to replace a horrid set of **if** statements in the original icon-Name() method with polymorphism. You'll find much more on patterns such as this in Part II of the book, by the way.

In the previous chapter, we saw how to validate proposed values for properties. One thing missing from our toolbox is to perform similar validation when modifying collections. Let's look at that now.

3.3 Capturing Business Rules for Collections

You'll recall that we can specify simple business rules on properties to restrict the set of values that they can take. In the previous chapter, we did this for simple value types (such as String); the same approach also works for properties representing associations between classes.

We can similarly restrict the objects that can be placed in a collection:

- To prevent a new object from being added to a collection, we use a validateAddToXxx() method (where Xxx is the name of the collection).

- To prevent an existing object from being removed from a collection, we use a validateRemoveFromXxx() method.

For example, suppose we want to prevent a Customer from owning more than three Cars. We can do this as follows (using the nocval template):

chapter03/Customer-Cars-validate.java

```
public String validateAddToCars(final Car car) {
    return getCars().size() >= 3 ?
            "No more than 3 cars per customer":null;
}
public String validateRemoveFromCars(final Car car) {
    return null;
}
```

To try this, create a Customer and then create three Cars, associating each with the customer. Now add a fourth Car, but *don't associate* with the Customer; just save instead. Now try to add the Car to the Customer's collection by dragging and dropping; the viewer should prevent this. In Figure 3.3, on the next page, we can see what this looks like in the DnD viewer (I've inlaid the validation message that appears in the viewer's status bar).

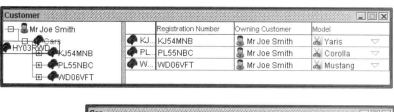

Figure 3.3: VALIDATION PREVENTS OBJECTS FROM BEING ADDED OR REMOVED.

However, there's a bug in this code. Instead of adding the Car to the Customer, drop the Customer into the Car's OwningCustomer property slot. There is no validation for this property, so the modifyOwningCustomer() method is called, setting up the bidirectional relationship and breaking our rule. The fix is to add a validateOwningCustomer() method and make it delegate up to Customer (just as the modifyOwningCustomer() method does):

chapter03/Car-OwningCustomer-validate.java

```java
public String validateOwningCustomer(final Customer owningCustomer) {
    if (owningCustomer != null) {
        return owningCustomer.validateAddToCars(this);
    } else {
        // clearing association
        if (getOwningCustomer() == null) {
            return null;
        }
        return getOwningCustomer().validateRemoveFromCars(this);
    }
}
```

Now it shouldn't be possible to associate too many Cars with the Customer, no matter which way we approach it.

Coming Up Next

In this chapter, we've come a long way in developing a *ubiquitous language* for our little CarServ application. Our domain classes are now associated together using references and collections, and we've seen how introducing additional relatively simple describing concepts (such as Title, Make, and Model) extends the language further.

With the ability to add properties and collections to our objects, we should be able to start validating our domain model with our customer. To do that, we're going to need to be able to demonstrate the application in use with some realistic business data. So, in the next chapter, that's what we'll be focusing on.

Exercises

If you weren't coding along, load this chapter's version of CarServ from the book's website (***chapter03-02***), and make sure you understand how associations and their respective validation are implemented. Also review the use of fixtures in the nakedobjects.properties file.

As an additional exercise, add a new property to allow a Customer to specify their favorite Car. Add validation to ensure that they can reference only one of their own Cars, not some other Customers.

And then, I suspect you're itching to get back to developing your own application. Have a go at adding the following:

- A reference property and a collection in a *bidirectional* relationship.

- A new describing class (like our Title) to represent a concept in the domain. Create and register a fixture for this describing class, and annotate it as @Immutable and (possibly) as @Bounded.

- A property from one of the transactional classes to this describing class.

- Validation of at least one of your reference properties and your collections.

Then, run your application and admire your work!

Chapter 4

Rapid Prototyping

As we've seen over the past few chapters, Naked Objects allows us to develop and demonstrate our domain model very quickly, because we only having to worry about one layer: the domain layer. The framework takes care of the presentation layer for us, and because we are only storing objects in-memory, there is no coding needed for the persistence layer either.

However, we want our prototypes to do more than just demonstrate some classes; they should tell a story. In the previous chapter, we learned how fixtures can be used to create an initial set of reference objects. . . but they can also be used to create transactional objects too. We can therefore use different fixtures sets for each scenario that we want to explore, demonstrating the application to our domain experts in the context of that scenario.

More generally, a fixture in Naked Objects is anything that sets up the runtime environment in some way. There are a number of other types of fixtures in addition to those that simply create instances of objects. In this chapter (**chapter04-01**), we'll be looking at all the different fixture types, and we'll also see how to organize fixtures. We'll end up with a single fixture, CustomerCarsMaintenanceFixture, that we'll use for much of the rest of the book; as I say, you'll normally have one fixture per scenario being prototyped.

We'll start off with fixtures that set up the object store.

4.1 Fixtures for Setting Up Domain Objects

From the framework's viewpoint, there are only object fixtures, but from our viewpoint, it's worth splitting them into two:

- First we have reference object fixtures creating instances of read-only domain classes. Such domain classes can reference each other but must not (since they are immutable) reference transactional domain classes that get created and deleted. Examples of such classes in CarServ are Title, Make, and Model.

  The reference domain objects are often the same between prototyping and ultimate deployment into production, so developing such fixtures is a good way of developing the seed scripts to give to the DBA. Such reference fixtures are typically shared between scenarios.

- We also have transactional object fixtures that create sets of objects for a particular scenario. Examples of such classes in CarServ are Customer, Car, and Service.

  Unlike reference objects, the transactional objects created are merely representative for the scenario. We probably would want to have a few Customers, one with a single Car, one with a few Cars, and one with maybe no Cars. And for each of those Cars, there should be differing numbers of Services. However, they ought to be as realistic as possible: we want to demo an application to our domain experts that looks credible.

We've already had a first look at reference object fixtures in Section 3.2, *Introducing the Title Concept*, on page 55. The process for creating sample transactional objects is exactly the same: we write the fixture class and then configure the framework to install this fixture for us.

However, the fixtures we've written so far have been self-contained. In contrast, fixtures for transactional objects often need to get hold of an already persisted object in order to create further objects. For example, in CarServ, we will need to get hold of a Title before we can create a Customer, and we will need to get hold of a Customer and a Model in order to create a Car. If we use AbstractFixture as the fixture superclass (as we did previously), then we can use one of its helper methods to locate these dependent objects.

Let's see this by creating a JoeBloggsCustomerFixture and then a JoeBloggsCarFixture, starting with the Customer first. Since we will most likely want to create lots of Customers, create a new AbstractCustomerFixture class (in the fixture.customer subpackage) as follows:

```
chapter04/AbstractCustomerFixture.java

public abstract class AbstractCustomerFixture extends AbstractFixture {
    public abstract void install();
    protected Customer createCustomer(
            final String titleName,
            final String lastName, final String firstName) {
        Customer customer = newTransientInstance(Customer.class);
        customer.setTitle(findTitle(titleName));
        customer.setLastName(lastName);
        customer.setFirstName(firstName);
        persist(customer);
        return customer;
    }
    protected Title findTitle(final String titleName) {
        return firstMatch(Title.class, new Filter<Title>() {
            public boolean accept(Title title) {
                return title.getName().equals(titleName);
            }
        });
    }
}
```

The interesting bit here is the call to the inherited firstMatch() method. Naked Objects will iterate through all known instances and return the first instance matching the supplied Filter (from the applib). There are other methods such as allMatches() and uniqueMatch() that work in a similar way.

Now we can write the JoeBloggsCustomerFixture fixture (again in fixture. customer):

```
chapter04/JoeBloggsCustomerFixture.java

public class JoeBloggsCustomerFixture extends AbstractCustomerFixture {
    public void install() {
        createCustomer("Mr", "Bloggs", "Joe");
    }
}
```

Add this to the end of the (comma-separated value for the) *naked-objects.fixtures* property key in the nakedobjects.properties configuration file, and then run your application. You should automatically have a *Joe Bloggs* Customer created. (If you don't, try putting a breakpoint on the install() method to ensure that the fixture gets called, or look at the logging messages from the framework itself.)

We can write an AbstractCarFixture and JoeBloggsCarsFixture similarly. Let us do AbstractCarFixture first:

chapter04/AbstractCarFixture.java

```java
public abstract class AbstractCarFixture extends AbstractFixture {
    public abstract void install();
    protected Car createCar(
            final Customer customer, final Model model,
            final String registrationNumber) {
        Car car = newTransientInstance(Car.class);
        car.modifyOwningCustomer(customer);
        car.setModel(model);
        car.setRegistrationNumber(registrationNumber);
        persist(car);
        return car;
    }
    protected Make findMake(final String name) {
        return firstMatch(Make.class, new Filter<Make>() {
            public boolean accept(Make make) {
                return make.getName().equals(name);
            }
        });
    }
    protected Model findModel(final Make make, final String name) {
        return firstMatch(Model.class, new Filter<Model>() {
            public boolean accept(Model model) {
                return model.getMake() == make &&
                        model.getName().equals(name);
            }
        });
    }
    protected Customer findCustomer(
            final String lastName, final String firstName) {
        return firstMatch(Customer.class, new Filter<Customer>() {
            public boolean accept(Customer customer) {
                return customer.getLastName().equals(lastName) &&
                        customer.getFirstName().equals(firstName);
            }
        });
    }
}
```

And now JoeBloggsCarsFixture:

chapter04/JoeBloggsCarsFixture.java

```java
public class JoeBloggsCarsFixture extends AbstractCarFixture {
    public void install() {
        Customer joeBloggs = findCustomer("Bloggs", "Joe");
        createCar(joeBloggs,
            findModel(findMake("Ford"), "Focus"), "M321RNP");
        createCar(joeBloggs,
            findModel(findMake("Toyota"), "Yaris"), "KL56WGF");
    }
}
```

Again, update the *nakedobjects.fixtures* property key in the nakedobjects.properties configuration file, and run your application. *Joe* should have some Cars.

I should point out that it is up to the object store implementation whether the fixtures that are defined in nakedobjects.properties are actually used. The in-memory object store that we use for prototyping *does* of course load up all fixtures every time; that's the whole point of us creating them. However, object store implementations that persist objects between runs (such as the ones we'll see in Chapter 16, *Integrating with the Database*, on page 287) generally use fixtures only for the initial population of the persistence store but otherwise ignore the fixtures at runtime.

Most of the time the fixtures we create are to set up objects. There are other fixture types too, though, so let's look at them now.

4.2 Fixtures for Setting Up the Clock

We use date fixtures to "mock the clock," allowing us to create representative object sets that look like they were created at some previous point in history; this is great for demos. We can also use date fixtures to set the effective date/time that the application itself is running; any time an object asks for the current time, the time set up in the fixture will be provided. This way, the domain experts will be able to validate any time-specific behavior being demoed.

Instead of using java.util.Calendar to obtain the time, our domain objects should use the applib's Clock class. Clock is a singleton that allows different implementations to be installed, but by default will lazily instantiate an implementation that just returns the time according to the computer's system clock.

Specifying any fixtures at all will automatically install a different implementation; FixtureClock.FixtureClock behaves the same as SystemClock unless we call the setDate() and/or setTime() methods on it, typically using helper methods in AbstractFixture. Subsequent calls will then return the date/time that's been set. Calling resetClock() will get us back to using the system's time.

Let's see how to do this.

Changing the Clock While Installing Fixtures

Suppose we wanted to know who our long-standing customers are, perhaps so we can send them a Christmas greeting each year. Go ahead and model this by adding a new Since property (as in "customer since 1988") to the Customer class. Make it of type java.sql.Date.

Now we want this property to be defaulted to the current date when the Customer is first created, something we can do with a defaultXxx() supporting method. Therefore, go ahead and add a defaultSince() (using the nopdef template if you want):

chapter04/Customer-Since.java

```
public Date defaultSince() {
    return new java.sql.Date(Clock.getTime());
}
```

Back in the JoeBloggsCustomerFixture, set the date to 23 Sep 1988 (to choose a date at random):

chapter04/JoeBloggsCustomerFixture-SetDate.java

```
public class JoeBloggsCustomerFixture extends AbstractCustomerFixture {
    public void install() {
        setDate(1988,9,23);
        createCustomer("Mr", "Bloggs", "Joe");
    }
}
```

When we run the application, we should see the property's time set correctly, as shown in Figure 4.1, on the facing page.

As things stand, this set of fixtures will leave the clock set to some historical value, which is probably not what we want. Instead, we should leave the application running with a (well-defined) date to represent "now." We can solve this by refactoring the previous example.

Setting the Clock for the Running Application

Rather than setting up the clock on an ad hoc basis, an alternative is to have a fixture whose only job is to set the date, and to support this, the Naked Objects applib has a DateFixture. When browsing through the fixtures, this makes it easier to see what the effective date is, which is useful when there are lots of objects being set up for some scenario. This approach also solves the problem already highlighted; we can also use a DateFixture to set the clock at the end, once all the other fixtures have been installed.

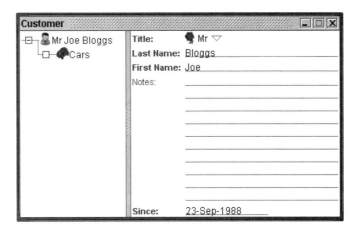

Figure 4.1: PROPERTY DEFAULTED FROM FIXTURECLOCK

So, let's refactor to use this approach instead:

1. Remove the setDate() call in JoeBloggsCustomerFixture.

2. Subclass DateFixture (in the root fixture package). First let's have a historical date fixture:

`chapter04/DateIs23Sep1988Fixture.java`
```java
public class DateIs23Sep1988Fixture extends DateFixture {
    public DateIs23Sep1988Fixture() {
        super(1988,9,23);
    }
}
```

and then let's have another more recent date fixture to represent "now":

`chapter04/DateIs09Jul2008Fixture.java`
```java
public class DateIs09Jul2008Fixture extends DateFixture {
    public DateIs09Jul2008Fixture() {
        super(2008,7,9);
    }
}
```

3. Finally, update nakedobjects.properties, putting the historical date fixture first and the "now" fixture last:

```
chapter04/nakedobjects-fixture-Date.properties
```

```
nakedobjects.fixtures.prefix=com.pragprog.dhnako.carserv.fixture
nakedobjects.fixtures=DateIs23Sep1988Fixture,\
                customer.TitlesFixture,\
                vehicle.MakesAndModelsFixture,\
                customer.JoeBloggsCustomerFixture,\
                vehicle.JoeBloggsCarsFixture,\
                DateIs09Jul2008Fixture,\
```

Run the application, and check it still works as required.

Setting up the clock is one way in which we can take control of the runtime environment. Another thing we can do is use fixtures to control who has actually logged on.

4.3 Fixtures for Setting Up User Sessions

A session encapsulates the identity of the user who has logged onto the application, as well as their roles. Whereas a date fixture changes the "when," a session fixture changes the "who." So, we can use a session fixture to influence who the effective user is for subsequent objects set up by our object fixtures, and (a great time-saver when prototyping) we can also use a session fixture to simulate logging onto the application as such-and-such a user.

Note that we're not talking here about authorization. Naked Objects does support authorization, but we don't enable it during initial proto-typing; we can worry about restricting permissions later. Also, gener-ally our domain objects don't care who is using them, and it's arguably bad practice to hard-code information about specific user roles (such as "supervisor") within them. There's further coverage of authorization in Section 18.2, *Securing the Application*, on page 342. Let's start by changing the effective user.

Changing the User While Installing Fixtures

To change the effective user running a fixture, we use the AbstractFix-ture's switchUser() method (analogous to the setDate() method used ear-lier to change the date and time).

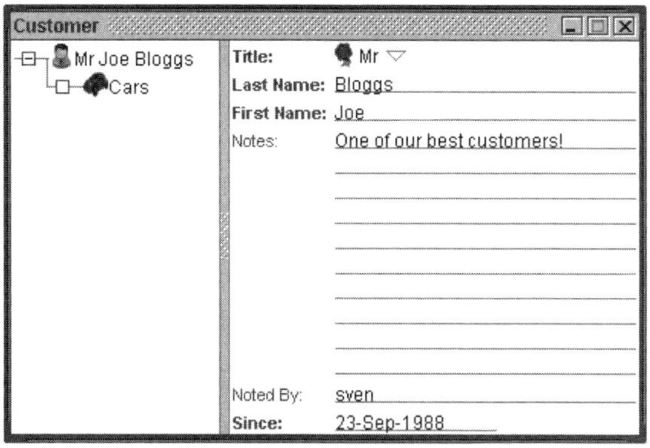

Figure 4.2: EFFECTIVE USER WHEN FIXTURE INSTALLED

To see this, let's add a new (optional) *NotedBy* property, of type String, in our Customer. The idea is that if someone adds a Note, we can also capture who made that note:

chapter04/Customer-NotedBy.java

```
@MemberOrder(sequence = "1.5.5")
@Optional
@MaxLength(16)
public String getNotedBy() { ... }
```

Since we want to perform some additional processing when we add a note, use the nopmod template to also add hook methods for the Customer's Notes property:

chapter04/Customer-Notes-nopmod.java

```
public void modifyNotes(String notes) {...}
public void clearNotes() {...}
public void onModifyNotes(String oldNotes, String newNotes) {...}
public void onClearNotes(String oldNotes) {...}
```

Then we change our onModifyNotes() hook method:

chapter04/Customer-Notes-onModify.java

```
protected void onModifyNotes(String oldNotes, String newNotes) {
    setNotedBy(getUser().getName());
}
```

Note the use of the inherited getUser() method from AbstractDomainObject; we'll look at this in Chapter 8, *Isolating Infrastructure Services*, on page 125.

Let's now update JoeBloggsCustomerFixture and create a note:

chapter04/JoeBloggsCustomerFixture-withNotes.java

```java
public class JoeBloggsCustomerFixture extends AbstractCustomerFixture {
    public void install() {
        Customer customer = createCustomer("Mr", "Bloggs", "Joe");
        switchUser("sven");
        customer.modifyNotes("One of our best customers!");
    }
}
```

In Figure 4.2, on the previous page, we can see the NotedBy property picking up the effective user when the fixture was installed.

As an alternative to the switchUser() method, we can subclass from SwitchUserFixture, analogous to DateFixture. Switching users in this way lets us control who fixtures are installed as but doesn't tackle the problem of automatically logging in as a known user. For this we use a different fixture class. But first, a quick digression.

Setting the User for the Running Application

So far, we've been running our application in exploration mode (using the exploration#viewer_dnd or exploration#viewer_html launch configurations). This means that there's no need to log on explicitly. Nevertheless, there is a current user set up for us: the "exploration" user.

We can get hold of a representation of this user through any object, including repositories, using the getUser() method. For example, add the following to the CustomerRepository:

chapter04/CustomerRepository-currentUser.java

```java
@Debug
public UserMemento currentUser() {
    return getUser();
}
```

If we run the application using the DnD viewer, we'll see a representation of this exploration user, as shown in Figure 4.3, on the facing page.

The useful @Debug annotation, by the way, indicates that the action is for diagnostics or debugging and so can be invoked only through an accompanying "gesture." For the DnD viewer, this means that by pressing the ⟨Shift⟩ key at the same time for the HTML viewer, it calls http://localhost:8080/debugon.app first to enable debug mode.

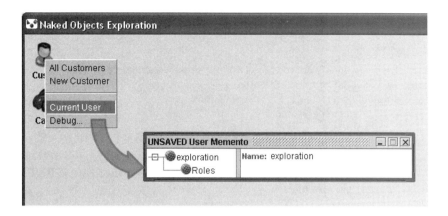

Figure 4.3: THE "EXPLORATION" USER

If we want to demonstrate a "real" user, then we have a choice. One option is to add a new *nakedobjects.exploration.users* property key into nakedobjects.properties, for example:

chapter04/nakedobjects-exploration-users.properties

```
nakedobjects.exploration.users=sven:role1, dick:role2, bob:role1|role2
```

This defines three users (*sven*, *dick*, and *bob*) in different roles. When we run the application, the user will be *sven*, but the viewers let us easily switch to another user. For example, in the DnD viewer, just right-click the background workspace; for the HTML viewer, there's a Swap User link at the top right by the Log Out link.

Alternatively, we can run the application in prototype mode (using the --type prototype command-line flag); doing so will require us to log in. The default authentication manager is a simple file-based implementation that reads the config/passwords file in the commandline project, so you can see for example that there is a user called *sven* with a password of *pass*. Run the application in prototype mode, and you'll be presented with a logon dialog. You should be able to log in using *sven* or any of the other defined users.

OK, digression over; let's get back to the fixtures. By subclassing Logon-Fixture (in the applib as ever), we can provide an autologon as a specified user.

Add the following in the root fixture package:

chapter04/LogonAsFredSmithFixture.java

```
public class LogonAsFredSmithFixture extends LogonFixture {
    public LogonAsFredSmithFixture() {
        super("fsmith",
                "service_manager", "user");
    }
}
```

The first parameter in the constructor is the username; the remainder is the (varargs) set of roles.

Update the nakedobjects.properties configuration file with this fixture class, and then run your application. If you now run in either exploration or prototype mode, you should be automatically logged in as the user *fsmith*.

We've now seen how to create domain objects, controlling when they were created and who they were created by. We've also seen ways to ensure that the clock and also the current user are set up as well. Let's now see how we might organize them.

4.4 Organizing Fixtures into Hierarchies

Currently, all the fixtures we've created are listed in the *nakedobjects. fixtures* property key in the nakedobjects.properties file. This is a somewhat error-prone approach, though. It's better to organize our fixtures according to the different scenarios that they represent.

If we assemble fixtures into a hierarchy, then the root is a single fixture that effectively names the scenario that we're setting up. This top-level fixture recursively delegates to more finely grained fixtures, which in turn can potentially be reused across scenarios at any level of the hierarchy that makes sense.

In Figure 4.4, on the next page, we can see a design to assemble our existing fixtures into a hierarchy. The top-level CustomerCarsMaintenanceFixture fixture represents the scenario. It references a FredSmithSessionFixture, which sets up the session for user *Fred Smith*. It also includes ReferenceDataFixture, which references the fixtures we have for our reference domain objects. And finally, it has CustomerCarsMaintenanceTransactionalFixture, the actual representative transactional objects for the scenario. Using the same base name for the top-level fixture and

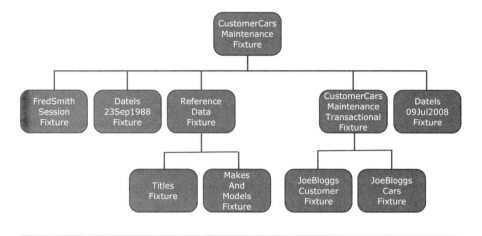

Figure 4.4: FIXTURES CAN BE ARRANGED INTO A HIERARCHY.

the underlying transactional object fixture makes it easy to see these go together.

The AbstractFixture superclass (that we've used so far) has built-in support for creating composite fixtures, through its addFixture() method. Let's create the top-level CustomerCarsMaintenanceFixture as follows:

`chapter04/CustomerCarsMaintenanceFixture.java`

```java
public class CustomerCarsMaintenanceFixture extends AbstractFixture {
    public CustomerCarsMaintenanceFixture() {
        addFixture(new FredSmithSessionFixture());
        addFixture(new DateIs23Sep1988Fixture());
        addFixture(new ReferenceDataFixture());
        addFixture(new CustomerCarsMaintenanceTransactionalFixture());
        addFixture(new DateIs09Jul2008Fixture());
    }
}
```

Similarly, create the other two composite fixtures:

1. ReferenceDataFixture should compose TitlesFixture and MakesAndModelsFixture.

2. CustomerCarsMaintenanceTransactionalFixture should compose JoeBloggsCustomerFixture and JoeBloggsCarsFixture.

With this fixture hierarchy defined, we then register *just* the top-level fixture within nakedobjects.properties:

chapter04/nakedobjects-fixture-CustomerCarsMaintenance.properties

```
nakedobjects.fixtures.prefix=com.pragprog.dhnako.carserv.fixture
nakedobjects.fixtures=CustomerCarsMaintenanceFixture
```

Run the application, and check that *Joe* and his Cars, plus all the reference domain objects, are still being created automatically. Alternatively, we can run the application with a command-line option:

```
-D nakedobjects.fixtures=CustomerCarsMaintenanceFixture
```

In fact, any of the properties in nakedobjects.properties can be overridden in this way, very much following the approach for overriding Java system properties.

Coming Up Next

Putting fixtures together takes a little time, but it is time worth spending. When you are doing your demos to the domain expert, you'll appreciate having a consistent set of objects to work with, and you'll soon get to know those objects (like Joe and his Cars). In Chapter 12, *Scenario Testing*, on page 217, we'll learn about an alternative way to manage our fixtures, at which time they become an even more valuable asset as an integral part of our testing.

It's time to move on. Right now our domain objects are still not particularly behaviorally rich; they don't *do* very much yet. For example, in our fixtures when we created *Joe* and his Cars, we had to create each separately and then manually wire them together. So, it's time to start making our objects work harder for us, which is the topic of Chapter 5, *Creating Behaviorally Complete Objects*, on page 79.

Exercises

If you weren't coding along, then load up this chapter's version of CarServ (**chapter04-02**), and inspect the fixture hierarchy. In particular, note the use of date fixtures and session fixtures and of composite fixtures. Note that I've also created two additional launch configurations, prototype#viewer_dnd.launch and prototype#viewer_html.launch, so that we can easily run the application in prototype mode.

Then, if you've been developing your own application, have a go at sorting out your fixtures:

- Create a logon fixture to specify the current username and the set of roles.

- Create a set of fixtures for your reference domain objects, organized into a composite using the addFixture() method.

- Create fixtures for the transactional domain objects. Use the inherited firstMatch() or uniqueMatch() to look up other objects. Use a composite fixture that represents the scenario you are developing and have a separate fixture per instance of your core transactional classes.

Once you've done all this, you should be in a good position to demonstrate more in-depth functionality of your application.

Creating Behaviorally Complete Objects

Naked Objects is sometimes dismissed as merely being a way to build simple CRUD-style applications—in other words, those of limited applicability. Sure, you can use Naked Objects to create simple CRUD-style applications; then again, you could just use Microsoft Access.

Now, some architectures do use CRUD-style domain models and use an application layer to expose richer functionality, coordinating interactions between the underlying domain objects. However, such architectures can lead to a procedural rather than OO programming style: behavior (in the application layer) is separated from data (in the domain layer).

In contrast, Naked Objects deliberately has *no* explicitly coded application layer. Instead, its ability to expose actions in the user interface means that we go beyond simple CRUD applications while reinforcing an OO approach. Actions elegantly allow us to create *behaviorally complete* objects, each with their own distinct responsibilities. And it's these actions that deliver much of the business benefit of the system, automating previously manual business processes.

This then is the focus of this chapter (**chapter05-01**): adding actions to our domain objects and repositories. We'll also look at how the programming model supports validation and other usability features.

5.1 Adding Behavior to Domain Objects

In Naked Objects an action is basically just a **public** method, exposed automatically in the user interface. Both domain objects and repositories/factories can have actions, though their representation in the UI will depend on which is being viewed.

Actions can accept parameters, with each of the parameters being either a domain object or a scalar value.[1] If the action returns a non-null value (of any type), then this is rendered automatically by the viewer.

Actions are one of the defining characteristics of Naked Objects. Whereas other architectures require custom code to marshal between the gestures in the presentation layer (menu item clicks and button presses) through to the objects in the domain layer, in Naked Objects there is a direct equivalence between the two. Being able to directly see the responsibilities of the underlying domain objects helps us to decide with our domain experts whether they are correctly assigned.

Looking at CarServ, in fact we've already created a couple of simple actions on our repositories: the allCustomers()/allCars() and the new-Customer()/newCar() methods. But let's now add some actions to our domain objects; we'll beef up our repositories later in the chapter.

Create a Car Through the Customer

Right now our application is a little fiddly to use because one must separately create the Customer and the Car and only separately associate the two together. A cleaner design would be to have the Customer create the Car object: the Customer could then automatically associate itself with the Car.

In the CarRepository, we still have a newCar() action. Since Cars should now only ever be created by Customers, let's start by removing this action from CarRepository. Then, let's add a newCar() action to Customer (using the noa template or by just typing it in):

```
chapter05/Customer-newCar.java

@MemberOrder(sequence = "1.1")
public Car newCar(
        final Model model,
        @Named("Registration Number")
```

---

1. Neither collections nor arrays can be a parameter to an action. This restriction might be lifted in a future version of the Naked Objects framework.

```
       final String registrationNumber) {
    Car car = newTransientInstance(Car.class);
    car.setModel(model);
    car.setRegistrationNumber(registrationNumber);
    car.modifyOwningCustomer(this);
    persist(car);
    return car;
}
```

The persist() method we can see here is inherited from the AbstractDomainObject convenience superclass (similar to the method in the AbstractFixture we used in the previous chapter). As you might imagine, it saves the domain object to the object store.

This is a common idiom for "owning" relationships: the owner (in our case Customer) has an action that prompts for all the mandatory properties of the child object (in our case, Car) and then creates the child object and sets up the relationships in one go.

Run the application using either viewer. In the DnD viewer, actions can be invoked by right-clicking the object's icon (similar to repositories), while for the HTML viewer, actions are shown as links. Verify that it all works as expected.

Delete Car

So much for creating the Car. If a Customer sells their Car, then we presumably no longer care about it; we should delete it along with its service history.

One design would be to simply have a delete() action on the Car itself:

chapter05/Car-delete.java

```
@MemberOrder(sequence="1.1")
public void delete() {
    clearOwningCustomer();
    remove(this);
}
```

The remove() method is also inherited from the convenience superclass.

Go ahead and make this change to the CarServ application, and then run the application and verify that it all works as expected.

An alternative design for deleting the Car would be to have a deleteCar() action on Customer. However, it would only make sense to try to delete a Car that the Customer owned. We know from previous chapters that we can validate changes to properties (Section 2.6, *Capturing Simple Business Rules*, on page 41) and collections (Section 3.3, *Capturing Business Rules for Collections*, on page 60), so it'll come as no surprise to learn that action arguments can be validated too.

5.2 Validating Action Arguments

As we've learned already, if we want to modify the value of a property or the contents of a collection, then we can validate the change first. These are preconditions to the modification.

Many actions will also change the state of an object (indeed, possibly of several objects), so we can likewise specify an action's preconditions by validating its arguments. When identifying actions, we should also think about these preconditions. Although it might seem like more work to do, they simplify the implementation of the action itself because the action does not need to deal with invalid arguments.

We can validate arguments either imperatively or declaratively.

Adding Imperative Validation

We validate action arguments imperatively using a validateXxx() method, where xxx() is the name of the action. As for property and collection validation, this returns a String value where any non-**null** value is taken to be the reason why the (in this case) arguments are invalid. The parameters to the validateXxx() method must be identical to that of the action method itself.

So, let's add that deleteCar() action on the Customer, along with its validation (use the noa and noaval templates):

chapter05/Customer-deleteCar.java

```
@MemberOrder(sequence = "1.2")
public void deleteCar(final Car car) {
    car.delete();
}
public String validateDeleteCar(final Car car) {
    return getCars().contains(car) ?
        null :"Customer does not own this car";
}
```

To test this, you'll need to create a couple more Customers and Cars. Go ahead and do this by writing a few fixtures and adding them to the transactional objects fixture.

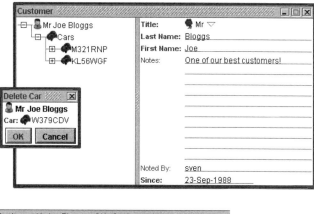

Figure 5.1: ACTIONS WITH INVALID ARGUMENTS CANNOT BE INVOKED.

Now, if we attempt to remove a Car that isn't owned by the Customer, we should see a warning message and be unable to invoke the action. In Figure 5.1, we can see how this appears in the DnD viewer. Try this for yourself, and make sure it works as expected.

Just as we can use annotations to validate properties, we can use declarative validation for action parameters too. Let's see how.

Adding Declarative Validation

The newCar() action we added a few pages back for Customer takes a Model and a (string) registration number. Suppose we now realize that there are rules for the format of a registration number—that it should contain only alphanumeric characters. We can express this using a regular expression:

`chapter05/Customer-newCar-regex.java`

```java
public Car newCar(
    final Model model,
    @RegEx(validation="[A-Z0-9]+")
    @Named("Registration Number")
    final String registrationNumber ) {
    // omitted
}
```

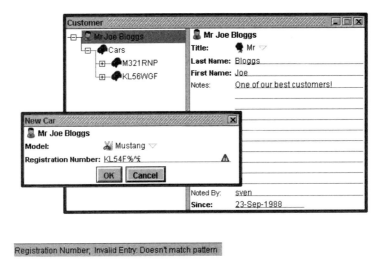

Figure 5.2: ACTION ARGUMENTS CAN BE VALIDATED DECLARATIVELY.

The @RegEx annotation ensures that the registration number complies with the specified regular expression. In Figure 5.2, we see that Naked Objects won't allow the action to be invoked until we fix the argument value.

However, we're only halfway there in terms of implementing this rule because our errant user could still change the registration number property of the Car to an invalid format. Therefore, we should also update the property definition itself in the Car class:

chapter05/Car-RegistrationNumber-regex.java

```
private String registrationNumber;
@RegEx(validation="[A-Z0-9]+")
public String getRegistrationNumber() { ... }
```

If you haven't already done so, apply these changes, and test for yourself that registration numbers must follow the pattern for both the action and the property.

Note by the way that we've violated the *don't repeat yourself* (DRY) principle (from Andy Hunt and Dave Thomas' *Pragmatic Programmer* [HT00] book): we've needed to specify the @RegEx annotation in two places. If the State of California were to suddenly allow exclamation marks in registration numbers, then we would have to update our code

> \// Joe Asks. . .
> ₂£
> ~   __Shouldn't @RegEx Be on the Setter?__
>
> Since @RegEx (and some other annotations) validates the input,
> you might think it should go on the *setter* rather than the *getter*.
>
> For simplicity, though, the Naked Objects framework always
> looks for these annotations on the *getter*. These conventions
> aren't cast in stone, though; if you wanted to, you could modify
> the framework to search for such annotations on the *setter* too;
> see Chapter 14, *Naked Objects as a Design Tool*, on page 259
> for some further discussion.

in at least two places. Not nice—in this way bugs are born. Fear not;
we'll be addressing this in Chapter 7, *Using Value Types*, on page 109.

You'll remember with the Customer's Title property that we were able
to provide a drop-down list of choices. Let's see how to do something
similar for action parameters.

5.3   Making Actions Friendlier to Use

In the same way that we use supporting methods to validate, we can
provide choices and indeed defaults using similarly named methods.

As we saw in Section 2.7, *Providing Choices for Properties*, on page 43, if
the set of valid values for a property is well-defined, then we can implement our domain object to provide this set of valid values. It therefore
makes sense for us to do this for action parameters at the same time as
thinking about validation. In addition, we can also indicate the default
value of the parameter.

The Naked Objects viewer shows this as a drop-down list, with the
default indicating the initially selected item. For example, if a Customer
owns two Cars, then only these Cars should be offered as valid arguments to the deleteCar() action. And if a Customer has only a single Car,
then we should provide this as a default argument to the action. In
Figure 5.3, on the next page, we see how this would look in the DnD
viewer.

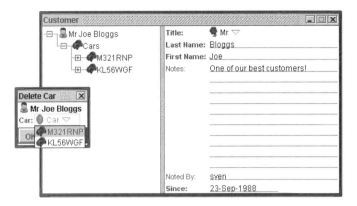

Figure 5.3: PARAMETER CHOICES HELP THE USER SUPPLY THE CORRECT ARGUMENTS.

Let's add the supporting method to offer up parameter choices first (use the noacho template):

chapter05/Customer-choices0DeleteCar.java

```
public List<Car> choices0DeleteCar() {
    return getCars();
}
```

Similarly, we can provide a default, such as if the Customer owns only a single Car (use the noadef template):

chapter05/Customer-default0DeleteCar.java

```
public Car default0DeleteCar() {
    return getCars().size() == 1? getCars().get(0): null;
}
```

There can be multiple *choices* and *default* methods per action, one per parameter. The digit in the method name indicates the parameter to which the method corresponds.

Implementing choices and defaults is a really nice way to give your application that professional touch, and I'd certainly expect the majority of your actions to provide choices and defaults, as well as validation.

As you can see, writing actions is really pretty straightforward. But they are also at the very heart of the Naked Objects approach to domain-driven design.

Let's finish off the chapter by beefing up our repositories with some additional actions of their own.

5.4 Adding Finders to Repositories

Currently in CarServ our repositories let us create new objects and list all objects. In a real-world application, we're likely to want to search for a specific domain object using some sort of identifier (such as a customer ID). We might also want to provide a more generic search capability based on other properties (such as the customer's name).

Applying this to CarServ, what we probably need is the means to search for Customer(s) and Car(s). Let's add an action to look up a Car first, using its RegistrationNumber. Clearly this should live on the CarRepository:

chapter05/CarRepository-findByRegistrationNumber.java

```java
public Car findByRegistrationNumber(
        @RegEx(validation="[A-Z0-9]+")
        @Named("Registration Number")
        final String regNumber) {
    return firstMatch(Car.class, new Filter<Car>() {
        public boolean accept(final Car car) {
            return car.getRegistrationNumber().equals(regNumber);
        }});
}
```

If you're getting a sense of deja-vu, that's because we used the same firstMatch() method when writing object fixtures in Chapter 4, *Rapid Prototyping*, on page 63. Note also the @RegEx annotation again on the registration number parameter.

For Customers, let's write a similar finder that uses the Customer's First-Name and LastName properties. Since there might be more than one matching Customer, we should return a List:

chapter05/CustomerRepository-findByName.java

```java
public List<Customer> findByName(
        @Optional
        @Named("Last Name")
        final String lastName,
        @Optional
        @Named("First Name")
        final String firstName) {
    return allMatches(Customer.class, new Filter<Customer>() {
        public boolean accept(final Customer customer) {
            return matches(customer, firstName, lastName);
        }});
}
```

Repositories vs. Start Points

Because the repositories are the first things an end user sees, they are in a sense a facade to the entire application. In this book, we use repositories for this purpose, but an alternative approach is to think of them as "start points" and provide actions around a number of common use cases.

The implementation of start points is actually the same as repositories, so in a sense this just comes down to the naming of the classes. You could, though, have start points delegate to underlying (and hidden) repositories; we'll be revisiting the broader topic of services in Chapter 8, *Isolating Infrastructure Services*, on page 125.

```
public String validateFindByName(
        final String lastName, final String firstName) {
    if (lastName == null && firstName == null) {
        return "Must specify at least one name";
    }
    return null;
}
private static boolean matches(
        final Customer customer,
        final String firstName, final String lastName) {
    return nullSafeEquals(customer.getFirstName(), firstName) &&
            nullSafeEquals(customer.getLastName(), lastName);
}
private static <T> boolean nullSafeEquals(final T s1, final T s2) {
    return s1 == null || s2 == null ||
            s1 != null && s2 != null && s1.equals(s2);
}
```

This action uses the allMatches() method to return a List of Customers.

If you weren't already doing so, add these new finders into the repositories (use the noa template), and run the application. You might want to tweak your fixtures to demonstrate the various possibilities (for example, two Customers with the same last name).

And that just about wraps up this chapter. Quite short, very sweet!

Coming Up Next

In this chapter, we saw how to implement actions on domain objects and on repositories. Ultimately, actions are little more than **public** methods, with supporting methods to validate parameters and to provide choices and a default for parameters.

Looking back over the past few chapters, we've learned how to write domain classes, properties, collections, and now actions: the real core of writing Naked Objects applications. We've also seen how to write supporting methods to validate values, provide choices, and provide defaults, all types of business rules.

The Naked Objects programming model supports additional types of business rules too, though. In the next chapter, we're going to see how.

Exercises

Load up this chapter's version of CarServ, and make sure you understand how actions appear as menus and can be invoked (*chapter05-02*).

If you've been developing your own application, then try the following:

- Add actions in existing objects to create new objects. Use the inherited newTransientInstance() method to create objects, and use getContainer().persist(obj) to persist them once initialized.

- Add some new repository actions; mark them as @Exploration if they are only for demo purposes or @Debug if they provide debugging/diagnostics.

- Add validation of parameters to one of your new actions, either declarative or imperative.

- Provide a default and/or also choices for one of your actions' parameters.

Then show your application to your granny. She might not understand it, but she'll probably say something nice.

Implementing Business Rules

Picture the scene. There you are demonstrating your prototype application to the domain expert, and he or she asks to have a go. You agree (of course!), but in the back of your mind you're waiting for the application to crash when they do something that they "shouldn't."

As developers, when we use our own application, we tend to do so in a way that we know will work. However, the application isn't for us or even (often) our domain experts; it's for a broader end-user community. When we eventually roll out our application into production, it needs to be usable by everyone.[1]

What we're focusing on in this chapter is how to safeguard the application so that the domain objects can be interacted with correctly so that the application doesn't crash. And we do this by writing business rules that enforce preconditions for object interactions.

In fact, we've already met one type of precondition: the various declarative and imperative validation mechanisms. For example, new values for an object's property must be valid, and its actions should not invoked with nonsense arguments. But validation is just one of three types of business rule supported by Naked Objects, with the other two being disabling and hiding. Or more pithily: Can you see it? Can you use it? Can you do it?

---

1. Douglas Adams: "A common mistake people make when trying to design something completely foolproof is to underestimate the ingenuity of complete fools." Of course, I'm sure your application won't be used by fools, but you can never be sure.

In this chapter (***chapter06-01***), we'll look at each of these in turn. But since we have encountered validation already, let's kick off with a quick recap.

6.1 Validation Recap

We can add validation for properties, for collections, and for actions:

- We can validate a property to check a new candidate value before it is accepted.

  One way to do this is declaratively, using annotations. We can use an @MaxLength annotation to specify the maximum length of a string property. Or the lack of the @Optional annotation can indicate that a property is mandatory.

  Alternatively and more flexibly, we can perform validation imperatively using the supporting validateXxx() method. If this returns a non-null value, then this is used as the error message, and the proposed new value is rejected.
- We can also validate collections to check new objects being added or verify that objects may be removed.

  We do this imperatively using a supporting validateAddToXxx() or validateRemoveFromXxx() method.
- We can validate action parameters before invoking the action.

  Again, we can use the imperative approach, using a validateXxx() method. Or, we can perform some declarative validation on action arguments using any of the annotations we saw for properties.

Whenever we can (if there's an annotation available), we prefer the declarative approach to the imperative; another developer reading our code can take the declaration at face value (for example, @MaxLength) rather than wading through lines of code and wondering whether there is a bug in it.

Of course, there's a big "if" at the beginning of that sentence: *if* there's a suitable annotation. Although it is possible to extend the set of annotations that Naked Objects understands (discussed in Chapter 14, *Naked Objects as a Design Tool*, on page 259), Naked Objects also has a declarative annotation that is a sort of halfway house, allowing us to write declarative-style validations with the full power of the imperative approach underneath. Let's explore this now.

in context. . .
Specification

A *specification* captures a business rule that does not obviously fit the responsibility of an *entity* or *value*. It is a predicate that indicates whether the domain object (or a member) does or does not satisfy some criteria.

Validating Using Specifications

A *specification* is used to say something about how an object, or object's property or parameter, should be. We use the @MustSatisfy annotation to indicate that such-and-such a *specification* applies. The implementation of the *specification* is imperative, but the name of the *specification* can at least indicate the intent in a declarative style.

Let's convert one of our existing imperative validations into a *specification*. Currently we have logic on a Car's RegistrationNumber property that says that the maximum length is 7 in the United Kingdom and the United States and 12 everywhere else:

`chapter06/Car-RegistrationNumber-validate.java`

```java
public String validateRegistrationNumber(final String registrationNumber) {
    if (registrationNumber == null) return null;
    String country = Locale.getDefault().getCountry();
    int length = registrationNumber.length();
    if ( ("US".equals(country) && length > 7) ||
        ("GB".equals(country) && length > 7) ||
        length > 12) { // everywhere else
        return "Registration number is too long";
    }
    return null;
}
```

We write a *specification* by implementing Specification in the applib, but the easiest way is to subclass AbstractSpecification:

`chapter06/RegistrationNumberSpecification.java`

```java
public class RegistrationNumberSpecification
            extends AbstractSpecification<String> {
    @Override
    public String satisfiesSafely(final String registrationNumber) {
        if (registrationNumber == null) return null;
        String country = Locale.getDefault().getCountry();
```

> **Health Warning**
>
> One downside to *specifications* is that they can lead to slightly unbalanced domain objects. *Specifications* place the pre-condition business rules into a separate object, but the post-conditions (for example, the body of the action) are still implemented in the domain model. There's a lack of symmetry here.
>
> But we could argue in their favor too, because *specifications* are very easy to test and separate out the "unhappy" cases (where the validation fails for such-and-such a reason) from the "happy" case (where the validation succeeds and the action is performed). Experiment with them to see what you think.

```java
        int length = registrationNumber.length();
        if ( ("US".equals(country) && length > 7) ||
             ("GB".equals(country) && length > 7) ||
             length > 12) { // everywhere else
            return "Registration number is too long";
        }
        return null;
    }
}
```

Then for the Car's RegistrationNumber property, add the annotation, and remove the validateRegistrationNumber() method:

chapter06/Car-RegistrationNumber-MustSatisfy.java

```java
@MemberOrder(sequence = "1.1")
@RegEx(validation="[A-Z0-9]+")
@MustSatisfy(RegistrationNumberSpecification.class)
public String getRegistrationNumber() { ... }
```

We ought also to apply the annotation to the Customer's newCar() action:

chapter06/Customer-newCar-MustSatisfy.java

```java
@MemberOrder(sequence = "1.1")
public Car newCar(
        final Model model,
        @RegEx(validation="[A-Z0-9]+")
        @Named("Registration Number")
        @MustSatisfy(RegistrationNumberSpecification.class)
        final String registrationNumber) {
    // ...
}
```

Run your application to make sure it all works as expected.

So much for validation. However, implementing such rules still allows our user to *attempt* to modify the property or collection or to *attempt* invoke the action. What if we said that once it's set, you shouldn't be able to modify the Car's RegistrationNumber *at all*? For this, we need to make the property read-only. In Naked Objects parlance, we *disable* it.

6.2 Disabling Class Members

Disabling a class member is a stronger constraint than validation; it prevents the property or collection from being modified or an action from being invoked. . . period. Typically this is because using the class member doesn't make sense given the current state of the domain object. For example, if one action is called "go" and the other "stop," then presumably only one is active at a time.

In terms of the user interface, you can think of a disabled class member as being grayed out, and you might want to describe it in these terms when demonstrating and discussing the domain model with your domain experts. Indeed, in non–Naked Objects applications you have built, you've almost certainly implemented this responsibility within the presentation layer. But this is an area where Naked Objects has strong opinions: such responsibilities should reside in the domain layer, not the presentation layer. In any case, the discussion is moot; we implement the rule on the domain object because in Naked Objects there is literally nowhere else to put it!

As for all the business rules, we can disable class members either declaratively or imperatively. Let's use CarServ to look at each.

Disabling Declaratively

Preventing our user from changing the Car's RegistrationNumber property declaratively really couldn't be much simpler:

`chapter06/Car-RegistrationNumber-disabled.java`

```
@Disabled
public String getRegistrationNumber() { ... }
```

Make this change, and then run the application. As shown in Figure 6.1, on the next page, you shouldn't be able to modify the property.

The @Disabled annotation can also be applied to collections and to actions. Indeed, it is one of the most commonly used annotations, and

Figure 6.1: DISABLED PROPERTIES CANNOT BE EDITED.

there a couple of places in CarServ where we ought to use it. Cars are now created only by Customers (as opposed to using the CarRepository). However:

- Currently we *can* remove a Car from a Customer's Cars() collection, leaving an orphaned Car with no owner. We can fix this by annotating the collection as @Disabled.

- For the other side of this relationship, Car's OwningCustomer property, we should also annotate this property as @Disabled (and remove the redundant @Optional annotation).

Similarly, we should make the Car-Service bidirectional relationship read-only, by annotating both Car's Services collection and Service's Car property as @Disabled.

In a similar vein, it doesn't really make sense to change the Model of a Car once it has been created. So, also add the annotation to the Car's Model property.

Go ahead and apply all these changes and check that this works. Then we'll move onto the imperative approach.

Disabling Imperatively

To disable imperatively, we write a disableXxx() supporting method, analogous to the validateXxx() methods we saw for validation. The framework looks for the presence of this method and, if it exists, will call it first to determine whether to make the property or collection modifiable/action invokable.

To demonstrate this, let's consider the Customer's deleteCar() action. It doesn't make much sense to try to invoke this for a Customer that has no Cars, so we should disable it in these cases.

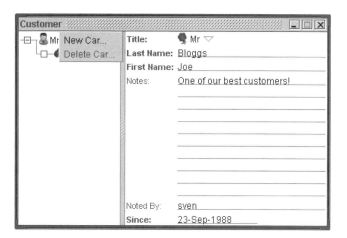

Figure 6.2: THE OBJECT'S STATE MAY DISABLE MEMBERS.

That's easily done:

`chapter06/Customer-deleteCar-disable.java`

```java
public String disableDeleteCar() {
    return getCars().size() == 0? "No cars to delete": null;
}
```

Add this code, and try your revised application (use the nopdis template). As shown in Figure 6.2, the action should be disabled.

As I already mentioned, we can also use a disableXxx() method for properties and collections. To see this in action, let's add a rule to prevent the Customer's Notes property from being updated unless the Customer has at least one Car. It's a bit contrived as an example but easy enough to implement:

`chapter06/Customer-Notes-disable.java`

```java
public String disableNotes() {
    return getCars().size() == 0?
        "Can only add notes for customers with cars":null;
}
```

Disabling is stricter than validation because although validation *might* let a change through (so long as the value you provide is valid), disabling will *never* do so. Our final category of business rule is even stricter—not being able to see the class member in the first place.

Factor Out Ruthlessly

Both our deleteCar() action and our Notes property now have a rule that has to do with there being no Cars in the Cars collection. To better express intent, factor this out:

chapter06/Customer-Notes-disable-refactored.java

```java
public String disableDeleteCar() {
    return doesntOwnAnyCars()?  "No cars to delete": null;
}
...
public String disableNotes() {
    return doesntOwnAnyCars()?
        "Can only add notes for customers with cars":null;
}
private boolean doesntOwnAnyCars() {
    return getCars().size() == 0;
}
```

It's a simple change but a great improvement!

6.3 Hiding Class Members

The strongest of our three rules is the first one that the framework checks: should the class member even be visible?

For disabling class members, I made the observation that you may be more accustomed to implementing that type of rule in the presentation layer. If that's the case, then you almost definitely will have implemented this rule in the presentation layer too. Even so, it too is fundamentally a domain responsibility. For example, when an object transitions between two states, some of its members might be relevant in only one of those states. If the user selects to pay by credit card, then the properties for capturing the credit card details are relevant (and so should be shown); if they pay by cash, then these same properties are irrelevant (and so should be hidden).

Having said that, the most common reason for hiding a class member is because it is really part of the "inner workings" of the object, not to be exposed in a Naked Objects viewer. This occurs with methods that are intended to be called programmatically but that—for whatever implementation reason—happen to have **public** visibility.

As for the other two rule types, we can hide the class member either declaratively or imperatively. Let's look at the declarative case first.

Hiding Declaratively

In Section 5.4, *Adding Finders to Repositories*, on page 87, we implemented a version of the findByName() action on the CustomerRepository. Let's take a look at this code again:

chapter06/CustomerRepository-findByName.java
```java
public List<Customer> findByName(
        @Optional
        @Named("Last Name")
        final String lastName,
        @Optional
        @Named("First Name")
        final String firstName) {
    return allMatches(Customer.class, new Filter<Customer>() {
        public boolean accept(final Customer customer) {
            return matches(customer, firstName, lastName);
        }});
}
// ...
private static boolean matches(
        final Customer customer,
        final String firstName, final String lastName) {
    return nullSafeEquals(customer.getFirstName(), firstName) ||
            nullSafeEquals(customer.getLastName(), lastName);
}
private static <T> boolean nullSafeEquals(final T s1, final T s2) {
    return s1 == null && s2 == null ||
            s1 != null && s2 != null && s1.equals(s2);
}
```

That matches() method doesn't look right on CustomerRepository. Far nicer would be for Customer to do the matching itself. Let's change CustomerRepository first:

chapter06/CustomerRepository-findByName-refactored.java
```java
public List<Customer> findByName(
        @Optional
        @Named("Last Name")
        final String lastName,
        @Optional
        @Named("First Name")
        final String firstName) {
    return allMatches(Customer.class, new Filter<Customer>() {
        public boolean accept(final Customer customer) {
            return customer.matches(firstName, lastName);
        }});
}
```

Subtractive Programming

One of the main responsibilities of a business analyst is to identify business rules, documenting them in specifications documents or in UML, or even semiformally using the Object Constraint Language (OCL). Meanwhile, the developer's responsibility is to implement the functionality up to the point where the constraints are... but no further!

If there's a gap between what the application *can* do and what the spec says it *mustn't* do, then we're left wondering: is this an omission in the application or an omission in the spec?

With Naked Objects this problem doesn't arise. We start off with an application that has all degrees of freedom, just like a UML diagram with no constraints. Then, as we analyze and explore our domain and identify the constraints, we can write code just as we might have once added an OCL constraint.

I call this *subtractive programming*: adding constraints subtracts functionality. Putting aside the fact that Naked Objects is a highly productive development environment, this is also a much more *honest* way of developing software.

And now let's move the matches() method to Customer:

chapter06/Customer-matches.java

```java
@Hidden
public boolean matches(final String firstName, final String lastName) {
    return nullSafeEquals(this.getFirstName(), firstName) ||
            nullSafeEquals(this.getLastName(), lastName);
}
private static <T> boolean nullSafeEquals(final T s1, final T s2) {
    return s1 == null && s2 == null ||
            s1 != null && s2 != null && s1.equals(s2);
}
```

To ensure that this new **public** method of Customer doesn't appear as an action in the user interface, we annotate it as @Hidden. Run your application to make sure. To double-check, temporarily comment out the @Hidden annotation and see the action appear.

Let's now look at the imperative method of hiding members.

Hiding Imperatively

Suppose we'd like to capture feedback from our most valuable Customers, which we'll (slightly naively) define as those that own two or more Cars. To do this, let's define a new (multiline, optional) Feedback property on Customer, using the nop template. You should end up with the following methods:

```
chapter06/Customer-Feedback.java
```

```java
private String feedback;
@MultiLine(numberOfLines = 5, preventWrapping = false)
public String getFeedback() { ...  }
public void setFeedback(final String feedback) { ... }
```

Now let's implement the business rule. Since there's no point in displaying the Feedback property for Customers that don't qualify as being valuable, we'll just hide it (use the nophid template):

```
chapter06/Customer-Feedback-hide.java
```

```java
public boolean hideFeedback() {
    return !isValuableCustomer();
}
private boolean isValuableCustomer() {
    return getCars().size() >= 2;
}
```

Note that hideFeedback() must be **public** for the framework to call; on the other hand, because isValuableCustomer() is **private**, it won't appear in the UI. If we wanted to (and there's probably a good argument for this because it does sound like it is part of the *ubiquitous language*), we could make the latter **public** too; it would then appear as a derived read-only property.

Try adding this code and then adding and removing Cars to your Customers. You should find that when they have two or more Cars, then the Feedback property magically appears; otherwise, it will be hidden, as illustrated in Figure 6.3, on the following page.

Note that whereas the disableXxx() and validateXxx() supporting methods return the reason as a String, the hideXxx() method simply returns a boolean. All that the framework needs to know is, should the class member be displayed or not?

That takes us through the three main categories of business rules that Naked Objects supports. However, the declarative forms of disabling and hiding (@Disabled and @Hidden) are a little more powerful than I let on. Let's look at that now.

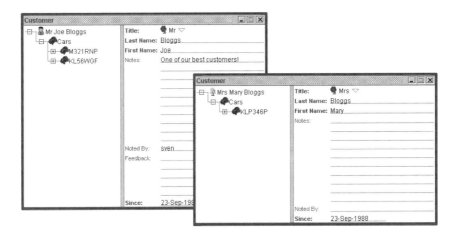

Figure 6.3: THE OBJECT'S STATE MAY HIDE MEMBERS.

6.4 Declarative Rules and the Object Life Cycle

Very often class members can be used or are visible dependent on the object's state only, in particular whether the object is persistent. A property may be disabled if the object is still unsaved; conversely, an action might be visible only when the object has been saved.

Because this is a common requirement, the @Disabled and @Hidden annotations both provide support for this. Each optionally takes an attribute—an instance of the When enumerated type (also in the applib). The default value is When.ALWAYS, so if omitted, we are stating that the class member should be disabled or hidden at all times. The other values of the When enum, though, allow us to qualify when these annotations apply, based on whether the object is persistent or not.

For example, imagine we were building a security management system where we capture Users as domain objects. When first created, the administrator might select the username and enter an initial password; to do that, they will obviously need a field in the UI to fill in. However, once the new User object has been persisted, we almost certainly don't want the password visible, not even to the administrator. To capture this rule, we would use an @Hidden(When.ONCE_PERSISTED). Conversely, an action to *change* the password would be annotated as @Hidden(When.UNTIL_PERSISTED).

> ## Joe Asks...
> ### Shouldn't Domain Objects Be Persistence Agnostic?
>
> In Naked Objects, domain objects don't know how persistence is done. However, that's not the same thing as saying that they don't know *that* persistence is done.
>
> For example, if I have a CreditCard object, then I might want to display it in full while it is being initially entered, but thereafter (that is, once persisted), I might only ever want the title to show the last four digits.

To see this in action, let's revisit the newCar() action for Customer that we looked at earlier:

`chapter06/Customer-newCar-MustSatisfy.java`

```java
@MemberOrder(sequence = "1.1")
public Car newCar(
        final Model model,
        @RegEx(validation="[A-Z0-9]+")
        @Named("Registration Number")
        @MustSatisfy(RegistrationNumberSpecification.class)
        final String registrationNumber) {
    // ...
}
```

There's a subtle violation of the DRY principle going on here. Right now the only mandatory properties of Car are Model and RegistrationNumber. But if we were to add another mandatory property, we'd most likely need to update this action to either prompt for its initial value or at least default it somehow.

The problem really arises from the fact that the action needs to persist the Car before it returns it. Let's mark the original version of newCar() as @Hidden and then write a new version like so:

`chapter06/Customer-newCar-transient.java`

```java
public Car newCar() {
    Car car = newTransientInstance(Car.class);
    car.setOwningCustomer(this);
    return car;
}
```

Rather than prompt for all the parameters, we just instantiate the Car, wire it up to its OwningCustomer, and then return it still transient. Notice, though, that we now call setOwningCustomer() rather than modifyOwningCustomer(). The Car needs to know who its owning Customer will be, but the Customer shouldn't be associated with the Car until we persist the latter:

`chapter06/Car-persisting.java`

```java
public void persisting() {
    getOwningCustomer().addToCars(this);
}
```

This persisting() method is called automatically by the framework when we save the Car; its job is to complete the wiring up between the owning Customer and the Car. This persisting() method is just one of a bunch of so-called life-cycle-aware methods. You'll find them all listed in Section A, *Reserved Methods*, on page 367. There are also a number of templates to use (called nol*).

With our new design for creating Cars, we now need to loosen up those constraints on its Model and RegistrationNumber properties a little. Rather than a simple @Disabled annotation, replace each with @Disabled(When.ONCE_PERSISTED), and for RegistrationNumber add back in the @RegEx and @MustSatisfy constraints:

`chapter06/Car-disabled-oncePersisted.java`

```java
@MemberOrder(sequence = "1.1")
@Disabled(When.ONCE_PERSISTED)
@RegEx(validation="[A-Z0-9 ]+")
@MustSatisfy(RegistrationNumberSpecification.class)
public String getRegistrationNumber() { ... }
...
@MemberOrder(sequence = "1.3")
@Disabled(When.ONCE_PERSISTED)
public Model getModel() { ... }
```

Try this, and you'll notice a couple of things. First, the transient Car is automatically displayed with a Save button, as shown in Figure 6.4, on the facing page. Second, the Model and RegistrationNumber properties remain editable up until we save the Car, at which point they become disabled just as we require.

The previous little refactoring focused on the @Disabled annotation, but exactly the same usage applies for the @Hidden annotation.

In this section, we've seen how @Disabled and @Hidden can be extended to interact with the object's life cycle. But we've still only ever been

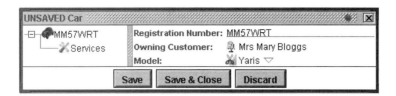

Figure 6.4: TRANSIENT OBJECTS DISPLAY WITH A SAVE BUTTON.

validating a single property or collection at a time. Often we also need to check that an object's properties and collections are consistent with *each other*. Let's see how.

6.5 Validating the Entire Object

Using the persisting() life-cycle method, we've seen that we can perform additional processing when an object is saved. But it is also possible to perform additional validation *before* allowing the save to proceed. This allows us to ensure that the object's state (its properties and collections) is internally consistent.

To illustrate this, we'll flesh out CarServ a bit. As of now we don't actually have the capability to book Cars in for servicing. Let's fix this by adding a new bookService() action on Car:

chapter06/Car-bookService.java

```java
@MemberOrder(sequence="1.1")
public Service bookService( ) {
    Service service = newTransientInstance(Service.class);
    service.setCar(this);
    return service;
}
```

As you can see, we're using the same general design as for the Customer-Car relationship. That means we also need to have a persisting() method to fix up the bidirectional relationship as we persist the Service:

chapter06/Service-persisting.java

```java
public void persisting() {
    getCar().addToServices(this);
}
```

Figure 6.5: BOOKING IN A CAR FOR SERVICE

As you might recall, a Service has two dates, one being the date the Car is booked in and the other the date that the Car is expected to be ready. To make our application a little easier to use, let's default both to tomorrow:

```
chapter06/Service-BookedIn-EstimatedReady-default.java
public Date defaultBookedIn() {
    return todayPlus(1);
}
// ...
public Date defaultEstimatedReady() {
    return todayPlus(1);
}
// ...
private static final long MILLIS_PER_DAY = 24 * 60 * 60 * 1000;
private static Date todayPlus(final int days) {
    Date midnight = new Date(Clock.getTime());
    return new Date(midnight.getTime() + MILLIS_PER_DAY * days);
}
```

Run your updated application to make sure this functionality all works as expected, as shown in Figure 6.5.

Now it's time for a bit of validation. Most of the time a Car will be ready for pickup the same day as it is booked in. On occasion, the EstimatedReady might be a day or two after the BookedIn date. The trouble is, at the moment there's nothing to prevent the user from entering an EstimatedReady date that is *before* the BookedIn date.

To fix this, we use the validate() method, which allows us to validate an object's entire state. If this method exists, then Naked Objects will call it prior to persisting a new object or indeed when updating an existing object.

Figure 6.6: USE THE VALIDATE() METHOD TO CHECK THE ENTIRE OBJECT.

So, make the following changes (use the noval template):

chapter06/Service-validate.java

```java
public String validate() {
    return getEstimatedReady() != null &&
           getBookedIn()        != null &&
           getEstimatedReady().getTime() < getBookedIn().getTime() ?
           "The 'estimated ready' date cannot be before "+
           "the 'booked in' date"
           :null;
}
```

Run your application, and check first that the object cannot be saved if the EstimatedReady date is before the BookedIn date, and check second that once saved, it also isn't possible to update either of the EstimatedReady or BookedIn dates to violate this rule. In Figure 6.6, we can see this in action.

While we are on the subject, the AbstractDomainObject convenience superclass also defines isValid() and validate() methods, both accepting an Object as an argument. These allow your code to discover whether a given object is valid—that is, that all its properties and collections are valid and that the object is valid with respect to its validate() (no-args) method.

Coming Up Next

In this chapter, we saw how Naked Objects allows us to implement both declarative and imperative business rules for properties, collections, and actions, and along the way we learned something about the object life cycle and how to validate entire objects rather than just single class members. Using these tools, we should be able to write applications that can be safely used by anyone.

Thus far, the properties in our objects have ultimately consisted of simple numbers, dates, and strings. If we wanted to manipulate or validate these values, then that logic would have to live in our domain objects. However, Naked Objects allows us to shift these responsibilities on the value objects themselves. This powerful idea is the topic of the next chapter.

Exercises

As ever, if you weren't coding along, then load up this chapter's version of CarServ (**chapter06-02**), and test the different business rules that are implemented there.

As a couple of additional exercises, go through the application, and make sure that all actions are disabled when necessary. Also, have a go at rewriting Service's validate() method as an object-level *specification* (BookedInBeforeEstReadySpec or something similar). Finally, we could simplify the AbstractCustomerFixture's newCar() method to use Customer's newCar() action instead.

If you've been developing your own application, then try one of each of the following:

- Use the @Disabled and/or @Hidden annotations to ensure that class members that are maintained through actions cannot be edited directly.

- Use the disableXxx() and hideXxx() supporting methods to add more complex imperative-style business rules.

- Modify existing actions to return still-transient objects, and then use the validate() and persisting() methods to ensure the object is valid before it is persisted.

- Experiment with using created() and the other life-cycle methods; set a breakpoint in them to see when they are called.

Your application should be progressing nicely. Don't give up the day job just yet, though.

Chapter 7

Using Value Types

When we start developing domain applications, it's usually pretty easy to find some likely looking *entities* (in CarServ, Customer, Car, and Service); we identify and implement their properties and start giving them behavior. However, if we just charge on headlong, we can end up with a less maintainable and more complex system than we bargained for.

Here's why. Our *entities* are made up of more basic objects—such as Strings and Dates—or of primitives. These building blocks are called *value object*s or *value type*s because, well, all they represent are values. Generic value types get us going quickly, but because they are generic, they cannot implement any business rules themselves. So, if we used an Integer to store a number and had a rule that said only positive numbers could be stored, we end up putting that rule in the only place we're able: the *entity object*. If the same rule is repeated in every entity, that's where we get unmaintainability. Good OO design is all about assigning responsibilities correctly. Rather than use generic value types, we can write our own types and implement those rules once and only once.

We can go further than this, though. Value types often define a closed or semiclosed set of operations. Think of numbers (add(), multiply(), . . .) or dates and intervals (overlap(), between(), . . .). Making the manipulation of values a responsibility of the *value type* itself will also substantially simplify the *entity object*s whose state they represent.

The Naked Objects framework has a number of its own value types, but we can also define our own value types or, indeed, use third-party types. Learning how is the topic of this chapter (***chapter07-01***[1]).

---

1. Includes solutions to Chapter 6's exercises

> **DDD in Context: Value Objects**
>
> *Value objects* capture the state of other (*entity*) objects. What is interesting about them is not their identity but the value that they represent. Classic examples are numbers, strings, and dates (think: number 5, "Bloggs," or 1-May-2009).
>
> Value objects should be immutable and often have a closed set of operations that define an "algebra" for the type.

7.1 Identifying Value Types

Whether writing domain-driven applications or otherwise, my experience is that value types tend to be underused. It's worth contrasting them with entity types.

Characteristic	*Value Types*	*Entity Types*
Mutability	Should be immutable	Usually mutable
Equality	Compare by value, as in a.equals(b)	Compare by identity, as in a==b
Scale	Typically small in scale	Of any size
Serializability	Should be serializable; may be parseable	Need not be serializable
Comparability	Often have a natural order: 1, 2, 3. . .	Typically no natural sort order
Defaults	Often have a natural default: the number 0, or "today"	No natural default
Closure (or Algebra)	Often have a closed set of operations: 2 + 2 = 4	Unlikely to have any closed set of operations
Identity	May represent an identifier, such as an SSN	Something that is identified, such as a Person
User Interface	Have dedicated widgets: checkbox, calendar. . .	Coded by hand (unless using Naked Objects!)

Some immutable, small-scale value types are also *internable*, meaning that they are taken from an internal pool of constants. java.lang.String is internable, for example, as are some java.lang.Integer values. This is not quite an implementation detail because it means more than one object could reference a value object. Value objects are therefore *not* aggregated (or wholly owned) by the object that references them.

With these insights, let's see what value types look like in practice.

7.2 Pushing Business Rules onto a Value Type

Back in Section 5.2, *Validating Action Arguments*, on page 82, we noticed a violation of the DRY principle; we had to annotate with @RegEx both the Car's RegistrationNumber property and an action parameter in Customer representing this registration number. Since then, we have worked around that by removing the problematic action, but there is still at least one other place where registration number crops up, which is in the CarRepository finders.

Our problem is that the regular expression and the maximum length are characteristics of the *concept* of "registration numberness," rather than a characteristic of the fact that a Car has a registration number. In object-oriented languages, each concept is a class, so what we need to do is introduce a RegistrationNumber class.

However, it doesn't make sense to make RegistrationNumber an entity object; all we really need is a wrapper for a String. Crucially, though, it will also include the additional business rules that will then automatically apply wherever we use our new value type.

Writing the Value Type

Create the RegistrationNumber type (in the vehicle subpackage):

chapter07/RegistrationNumber.java

```java
@RegEx(validation="[A-Z0-9]+")
@MustSatisfy(RegistrationNumberSpecification.class)
public final class RegistrationNumber implements Serializable {
    private static final long serialVersionUID = 1L;
    public RegistrationNumber(String value) {
        this.value = value;
    }
    private final String value;
    public String getValue() {
        return value;
    }
    @Override
    public boolean equals(final Object other) {
        return other != null &&
                RegistrationNumber.class == other.getClass() &&
                equals((RegistrationNumber)other);
    }
    public boolean equals(final RegistrationNumber other) {
        return other != null &&
                getValue().equals(other.getValue());
    }
```

```
    @Override
    public int hashCode() {
        return getValue().hashCode();
    }
    @Override
    public String toString() {
        return getValue();
    }
}
```

Note this class is immutable (it has no methods to modify its state) and has equal-by-content semantics (overridden equals() and hashCode() methods). Now we have our value type, let's use it in the domain model.

Refactor Our Domain Objects

Let's update the Car's RegistrationNumber property so that it is a reference to a RegistrationNumber value type rather than a String.

chapter07/Car-RegistrationNumber.java

```
@MemberOrder(sequence = "1.1")
@Disabled(When.ONCE_PERSISTED)
public RegistrationNumber getRegistrationNumber() { ... }
```

We also need to change a finder in CarRepository:

chapter07/CarRepository-findByRegistrationNumber.java

```
public Car findByRegistrationNumber(
        final RegistrationNumber registrationNumber) { ... }
```

Remember to remove the @RegEx and @MustSatisfy annotations in both of these. We can also remove the @Named annotation from the parameter, because Naked Objects can infer the parameter's name from the type.

Finally, we also need to modify the AbstractCarFixture:

chapter07/AbstractCarFixture-createCar.java

```
protected Car createCar(
        final Customer customer, final Model model,
    final String registrationNumber) {
    Car car = newTransientInstance(Car.class);
    car.modifyOwningCustomer(customer);
    car.setModel(model);
    car.setRegistrationNumber(
            new RegistrationNumber(registrationNumber));
    persist(car);
    return car;
}
```

That's pretty straightforward. However, the missing bit of the puzzle is to tell Naked Objects to treat RegistrationNumber as a value rather than as an entity. Let's see how.

Write a Provider and Configure Naked Objects

Although we have our value type, Naked Objects doesn't yet *know* it is a value type. We tell it using the @Value annotation. So, add the following to your RegistrationNumber:

chapter07/RegistrationNumber-ValueAnnotation.java

```
@Value(semanticsProviderClass=
            RegistrationNumberValueSemanticsProvider.class)
@RegEx(validation="[A-Z0-9]+")
@MustSatisfy(RegistrationNumberSpecification.class)
public final class RegistrationNumber {
    ...
}
```

What we're doing here is providing the framework with a class by which it can obtain the information it requires to treat RegistrationNumber as a value type. The class provided (RegistrationNumberValueSemanticsProvider) has to implement the ValueSemanticsProvider interface in the applib.

To make life easier, we can just subclass from the convenience Abstract-ValueSemanticsProvider adapter (put the class in the vehicle subpackage):

chapter07/RegistrationNumberValueSemanticsProvider.java

```
public class RegistrationNumberValueSemanticsProvider extends
        AbstractValueSemanticsProvider<RegistrationNumber> {
    @Override
    public Parser<RegistrationNumber> getParser() {
        return new Parser<RegistrationNumber>() {
            public RegistrationNumber parseTextEntry(
                    RegistrationNumber context, String entry) {
                return new RegistrationNumber(entry);
            }
            public String displayTitleOf(RegistrationNumber object) {
                return object.getValue();
            }
            public String displayTitleOf(RegistrationNumber object,
                                        String usingMask) {
                return displayTitleOf(object);
            }
            public String parseableTitleOf(
                            RegistrationNumber existing) {
                return displayTitleOf(existing);
            }
```

```
            public int typicalLength() {
                return 8;
            }
        };
    }
}
```

The bit of magic is the getParser() method, which returns an instance of Parser (again, in the applib). As you can see, we are also required to provide the title of the value, both for display once entered and in a potentially simpler parseable form. For RegistrationNumber, there is no difference between these two, but the second example in this chapter will make a distinction.

It's time to try your application. You should still be able to create a new Car for a Customer, and the regular expression validation should carry on working. Behind the scenes, the framework is delegating to the parser to convert the string into a RegistrationNumber and is setting that as the property on the Car.

Now that you know how to add value types, do use them in your domain. Although simple, they can make a significant contribution to your *ubiquitous language*. You may also find that these value types— basic building blocks as they are—end up being reusable across different applications. Identifiers, especially those that reside in a hierarchy, are good ones to start with, such as a file path or an XPath expression. Or (slightly more domain specific) how about a URN to a piece of hardware within a network? Indeed, you might want to consider creating your own in-house library of such value types.

But why write your own library if there's already one out there? An increasing number of open source projects are dedicated to developing value types, so let's look at integrating one now.

7.3 Adding a Third-Party Value Type

Value types are arguably easier to write than entities, but it's still possible to get them wrong. A good example is Java's own java.util.Date class. As a value type, there are multiple things awry: it's misnamed (it represents both a date and a time), it's mutable (all the mutating methods were deprecated in Java 1.1 but have never been removed), and it doesn't define much of an algebra (there are before() and after() methods, but not between(), for example).

\\\//
  Joe Asks...
 ~∑
  __Are There Any Downsides to Value Types?__

As you've seen, using value types requires some Naked Objects–specific configuration. It's possible that the persistent object store may also require equivalent configuration.

If you are using Naked Object's own in-memory object store, then there's nothing to be done. However, the object stores we use in Chapter 16, *Integrating with the Database*, on page 287 do require some configuration.

The java.util.Date class is also not **final**, which means that it can be subclassed. As Joshua Bloch explains in his excellent book, *Effective Java* [Blo08], allowing subclasses breaks the contract for equality, the most fundamental of the rules for value types. And sure enough, we have java.sql.Date and java.sql.Time, both of which subclass java.util.Date but do not even honor the *substitutability* ("is-a-kind-of") principle. It's all a bit of a mess to be honest.

There's a good lesson here: if even the designers of Java—a lot of very smart people—can get it wrong, we should tread carefully when writing our own value types, following the guidelines in Section 7.1, *Identifying Value Types*, on page 110 carefully.

Better still then would be to reuse a (good!) third-party library. After all, our domain application probably has no specific requirements for dates; they are something that we should be able to take for granted. We shouldn't be devoting effort building a replacement for java.util.Date.

Some of the more significant third-party libraries are *JScience* (which deals primarily with scientific measures) and *JodaTime* (which reworks Java's date and time classes).[2] As I write this, *JScience* is the basis for JSR-275 and JodaTime is the basis for JSR-310, so something like them may appear in a future version of Java.

Another good example of a third-party library is Eric Evan's own *time-andmoney* library, which provides value types relating to, well, time

---

2. The JScience library is at http://jscience.org/. The JodaTime library is at http://joda-time. sourceforge.net/.

and money.[3] Focusing on the "time" bit of it, the library goes further than just dates and times; by supporting a more complete algebra of operations, it also brings in concepts such as intervals.

We can put this to good use in CarServ. The Service class has two properties, BookedIn and EstimatedReady, both of which are java.sql.Dates. We also have a business rule that says that the EstimatedReady date comes after the BookedIn date. Although the implementation of that business rule (using a validate() method or a Specification) is not that complex, its presence at all is a hint that we're missing the concept of an interval of time.

Let's see how we can use timeandmoney's interval concept to simplify the Service class. To start with, we'd better grab hold of the library.

Add the Library to the Classpath

Before we get going, we're going to need to add the library to our classpath. Since this hasn't been published to any Maven repository, we'll have to do a bit of the grunt work ourselves.

First, download both the library (timeandmoney-v0_5_1.jar) and its source (timeandmoney-src-v0_5_1.zip) from the project website.

Next, install the library into your local Maven repository:

```
chapter07/mvn-install.session
$ mvn install:install-file              \
    -D file=timeandmoney-v0_5_1.jar \
    -D groupId=com.domainlanguage   \
    -D artifactId=timeandmoney      \
    -D version=0.5.1                \
    -D packaging=jar                \
    -D generatePom=true
```

Enter this all on one line; I've just broken it up to fit onto the page.

If you want to browse to the source in the IDE, then you'll need to unzip timeandmoney-src-v0_5_1.zip and then rezip just the source code:

```
chapter07/jar-sources.session
$ jar xvf timeandmoney-src-v0_5_1.zip
$ cd TimeAndMoney/src
$ jar cvf timeandmoney-src.jar com
```

---

3. The timeandmoney library is at http://timeandmoney.sourceforge.net/.

Then, we can install the library's source code similarly:

`chapter07/mvn-install-sources.session`

```
$ mvn install:install-file        \
    -D file=timeandmoney-src.jar  \
    -D groupId=com.domainlanguage \
    -D artifactId=timeandmoney    \
    -D version=0.5.1              \
    -D packaging=jar              \
    -D classifier=sources         \
    -D generatePom=true
```

The file property is different, and there is also a classifier property.

Now we need to declare which version of timeandmoney we are using. In the parent pom.xml (in the carserv directory), add the following under project/dependencyManagement/dependencies:

`chapter07/pom.xml`

```
<dependency>
    <groupId>com.domainlanguage</groupId>
    <artifactId>timeandmoney</artifactId>
    <version>0.5.1</version>
</dependency>
```

Finally, we must add the dependency itself. In the carserv-dom project's pom.xml, add the following under project/dependencies:

`chapter07/pom-dom.xml`

```
<dependency>
    <groupId>com.domainlanguage</groupId>
    <artifactId>timeandmoney</artifactId>
</dependency>
```

OK, with the housekeeping done, let's get on with our implementation.

Refactor Our Domain Objects

Since we're reusing a third-party library, there's no value type to write, but we still need to find the appropriate class to use. Casting about in the timeandmoney library, we can see that there is a CalendarInterval class (in the com.domainlanguage.time package). A quick check up the class hierarchy shows it is immutable and has equal-by-content semantics, while the documentation confirms it is intended to be used as a value type.

Let's change our Service class first so that we know where we're headed. Delete the BookedIn and EstimatedReady properties in Service, and add instead a new BookedInAndReady property.

chapter07/Service-BookedInAndReady.java

```
@MemberOrder(sequence = "1.1")
public CalendarInterval getBookedInAndReady() { ... }
```

Doing that is going to introduce some compile errors, so let's fix 'em. First up, the Service's own title() method:

chapter07/Service-title.java

```
public String title() {
    TitleBuffer buf = new TitleBuffer();
    if (getCar() != null) {
        buf.append(getCar().getRegistrationNumber());
    }
    buf.append(":",
        getBookedInAndReady().start().toString("MMM dd, yyyy"));
    return buf.toString();
}
```

The original properties used to have a default, so likewise let's provide a default for our new BookedInAndReady property:

chapter07/Service-BookedInAndReady-default.java

```
public CalendarInterval defaultBookedInAndReady() {
    CalendarDate start =
        CalendarDate.from(todayPlus(1).toString(), "yyyy-MM-dd");
    return CalendarInterval.startingFrom(start, Duration.days(1));
}
```

The BookedInAndEstReadySpecification class can simply be deleted: it will not be possible to create a CalendarInterval that violates the rule of its start before its end. Remove the @MustSatisfy annotation from Service as well.

The next step—just as for our custom value types—is to tell Naked Objects about this type.

Write a Provider

As for RegistrationNumber, we need to write an implementation of Value-SemanticsProvider. Since there's a bit more to this implementation, we'll look at it in sections:

chapter07/CalendarIntervalValueSemanticsProvider.java

```
public class CalendarIntervalValueSemanticsProvider extends
        AbstractValueSemanticsProvider<CalendarInterval> {

    private static final String PARSEABLE_PATTERN = "yyyyMMdd";
    private static final String TITLE_PATTERN = "MMM dd, yyyy";
```

```
    @Override
    public Parser<CalendarInterval> getParser() {
        return new Parser<CalendarInterval>() {
            // more to follow
        };
    }
}
```

We've defined two PATTERN constants that we're going to use for formatting the date in two different ways. The first is used in the business end of our Parser implementation, the parseTextEntry() method:

chapter07/CalendarIntervalValueSemanticsProvider-parseTextEntry.java

```
@Override
public Parser<CalendarInterval> getParser() {
    return new Parser<CalendarInterval>() {
        public CalendarInterval parseTextEntry(
                final CalendarInterval context, final String entry) {
            String[] split = entry.split(":");
            String dateEntry = split[0];
            String durationEntry = split.length > 1?split[1]:null;
            CalendarDate start = parseDate(dateEntry, PARSEABLE_PATTERN);
            int howMany = parseDays(durationEntry);
            return start != null?
                CalendarInterval.startingFrom(
                    start, Duration.days(howMany+1)):
                null;
        }
        private CalendarDate parseDate(
                final String dateEntry, final String candidatePattern) {
            try {
                return CalendarDate.from(dateEntry, candidatePattern);
            } catch(NullPointerException ex) {
                return null;
            } catch(IllegalArgumentException ex) {
                return null;
            }
        }
        private int parseDays(final String daysEntry) {
            if (daysEntry == null) { return 0; }
            try {
                return Integer.parseInt(daysEntry);
            } catch(NumberFormatException ex) {
                return 0;
            }
        }
        // more to follow...
    };
}
```

This parses a string in the form yyyyMMdd:NNN, where the first component (up to the : separator) is a start date and the second component is a number of days duration. If the string is invalid and doesn't match this format, we just return null.

The other PATTERN constant is used in the last bit of our implementation, which has methods for the title and typical length:

```
chapter07/CalendarIntervalValueSemanticsProvider-title.java
public String displayTitleOf(CalendarInterval object) {
    return String.format("%s ~ %s",
        object.start().toString(TITLE_PATTERN),
        object.end().toString(TITLE_PATTERN));
}
public String displayTitleOf(CalendarInterval object,
                                    String usingMask) {
    return displayTitleOf(object);
}
public String parseableTitleOf(CalendarInterval object) {
    return String.format("%s:%d",
        object.start().toString(PARSEABLE_PATTERN),
        object.lengthInDaysInt());
}
public int typicalLength() {
    return 30;
}
```

Unlike the RegistrationNumber example earlier, here we distinguish the parseable title from the displayable title. This allows viewers to potentially display an easily edited and parseable representation of the object that we give focus in the UI, as well as a more user-friendly representation as we leave the field.[4]

One more thing to do: tell Naked Objects that CalendarInterval is a *value type*, not an *entity*.

Configure Naked Objects

With RegistrationNumber, we used the @Value annotation on the value type itself, but because CalendarInterval is third-party code, that isn't an option here. Instead, we register the value type using the naked-objects.properties file.

---

4. Note that the DnD viewer and HTML viewers don't yet support this and only ever show the display title. To enter a new value, it is therefore necessary to delete the displayed title and enter in its parseable form.

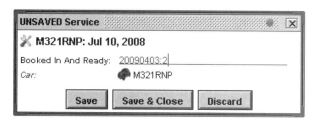

Figure 7.1: ENTER THE VALUE IN ITS PARSEABLE FORM.

chapter07/nakedobjects-VSP.properties

```
nakedobjects.reflector.java.facets.value.XXX.semanticsProviderName=YYY
```

where:

- *XXX* is the fully qualified class name of the value type that we are registering:

  com.domainlanguage.time.CalendarInterval.

- *YYY* is the fully qualified name of the value semantics provider implementation:

  com.pragprog.dhnako.carserv.dom.service.CalendarIntervalValueSe-manticsProvider

Incidentally, this approach can be used for our own custom value types as well; there's no need to include the @Value annotation. I prefer to use @Value annotation where possible.

Anyway, make the changes shown earlier, and give your application a whirl. Create a new Service for a Car, and enter a valid value such as 20090403:2 (two days starting on the April 3, 2009), as in Figure 7.1.

When you hit Enter, Naked Objects will parse the string by delegating to our parser and will then rerender the value using the displayTitleOf() method, as shown in Figure 7.2, on the next page.

So far we've been focusing on parsing, and this is where you'll need to put in the most effort. However, it's also possible to tell Naked Objects about other characteristics of our value types. For example, we are currently defaulting the CalendarInterval to tomorrow, using the default-BookedInAndReady() supporting method. However, we could argue that

Figure 7.2: ONCE ENTERED, THE DISPLAY TITLE IS USED.

this is a reasonable default for a CalendarInterval wherever it is used. Let's see how to make this default intrinsic to the value type.

7.4 Specifying Defaults and Other Characteristics

For some value types there will be a sensible default value. A numeric value might default to 0 (or perhaps 1), a date might default to today (or perhaps an epoch value like Unix's 1-Jan-1970), and a color might default to white (or perhaps black). Rather than specify this default everywhere that we use the value, we can instead specify this once and only once for the value type.

As we've seen, the @Value annotation tells Naked Objects to use the nominated ValueSemanticsProvider to interact with the value type, which in turn supplies a Parser to parse and rerender the string representations of the object. This provider class can also supply a DefaultsProvider (in the applib):

```
public interface DefaultsProvider<T> {
    T getDefaultValue();
}
```

Let's refactor CarServ to exploit this capability by deleting the default-BookedInAndReady() supporting method and moving its logic into the provider:

```
chapter07/CalendarIntervalValueSemanticsProvider-defaultsProvider.java

@Override
public DefaultsProvider<CalendarInterval> getDefaultsProvider() {
    return new DefaultsProvider<CalendarInterval>() {
        public CalendarInterval getDefaultValue() {
            CalendarDate start = CalendarDate.from(
                    todayPlus(1).toString(), "yyyy-MM-dd");
```

```
            return CalendarInterval.startingFrom(
                    start, Duration.days(1));
        }
        private static final long MILLIS_PER_DAY = 24 * 60 * 60 * 1000;
        private Date todayPlus(final int days) {
            Date midnight = new Date(Clock.getTime());
            return new Date(midnight.getTime() + MILLIS_PER_DAY * days);
        }
    };
}
```

Run the application again, and make sure it still works as expected.

In addition to defining a Parser and a DefaultsProvider, the ValueSemanticsProvider also allows us to optionally return an EncoderDecoder. This is used by some of the object stores (see Chapter 16, *Integrating with the Database*, on page 287) and for client-server remoting (Chapter 18, *Deploying the Full Runtime*, on page 333).

The ValueSemanticsProvider also allows us to specify whether the class is immutable and has equals-by-content semantics. This information isn't used by Naked Objects v4.0 but may be in the future. The default is true in both cases.

We've now seen how to implement and support both our own and third-party value types. Although some of that implementation might have seemed a little complex, it really just boils down to three things:

- Either write the value type to define the concept or locate a preexisting third-party implementation of the value type.

- Write an implementation of a ValueSemanticsProvider that provides parsing and other related capabilities.

- Tell Naked Objects about this provider using either a @Value annotation or the nakedobjects.properties file (with the latter being the only option if you are using a third-party value type).

As I said in the introduction, value types tend to be underused, but as we've now seen, they are a great way of pushing complexity out of the domain objects. So, please, do try to use them.

Coming Up Next

In this chapter, we spent some time untangling what a *value type* is, and we saw how to write our own value types and use preexisting third-party values.

Although CarServ still isn't very large, we now have the ability to build a very rich domain model, with the ability to define business rules all the way down to value types. In the next chapter, we're going to shift focus and see how to enable our domain objects to use the services of lower-level infrastructure technology.

Exercises

Another chapter, and another version of CarServ for you to load up (***chapter07-02***). Note that this version uses the timeandmoney library, so you'll need to download the library and install into your local Maven repository, as discussed in Section 7.3, *Adding a Third-Party Value Type*, on page 114.

As a hands-on exercise, we now have both RegistrationNumberSpecification and Registration. There's only one concept here, so we should have only a single class. Have a go at removing the *specification*, writing it instead as a validate() method on RegistrationNumber.

You might also have noticed the first context parameter in the parseText-Entry() method. This allows for more sophisticated parsing. For example, with our CalendarInterval value type, we might imagine that +1 means extending the date range by an extra day. This would be a nice little enhancement to try.

For your own application, you might want to start by reusing the CalendarInterval value type that we set up. Once you have that working, have a go at putting together your very own value type.

Isolating Infrastructure Services

Up until now we've focused exclusively on coding the core *entity object*s and their supporting *value object*s. But there comes a point when, to get things done, our shiny new domain application needs to use functionality provided by lower-level infrastructure technology.

For example, in the case of CarServ, we might want to send out stock emails to a customer, which means somehow integrating with an email API. Or we might want to print details of a customer, which means somehow being able to submit jobs to a print queue.

We might also want to isolate our application from environmental dependencies—such as the time—so that it is easier to test. Or, we might want to get Naked Objects itself to do something for us, such as display a warning message box.

In Naked Objects, the solution is the same in all cases. We represent the required functionality in terms of a *service* (not to be confused with CarServ's Service domain object), and then we provide that service to the domain objects that need to use it.

In this chapter (**chapter08-01**[1]), we're going to extend CarServ to use a couple of such services. But before we do, let's just clarify some terms.

---

1. Includes solutions to Chapter 7's exercises

> **DDD in Context: Services**
>
> Sometimes know-how-to responsibilities aren't natural to assign to domain objects, typically when the behavior is stateless (holds no state on behalf of its clients). Such behavior should be modeled as services, available to be called by any domain object that requires it.

8.1 A Taxonomy of Services

In the world of DDD, the term *service* is rather overloaded. But things get clearer when we distinguish *domain services* from *infrastructure services* from *application services*. Let's see what each of these mean.

Domain Services

A *domain service* is a place to put functionality that doesn't naturally fit into any domain object. A domain service can invoke (be a client of) the domain object, or the domain object can invoke the domain service.

In Naked Objects, repositories are examples of domain services (which is why, incidentally, we register them in the nakedobjects.properties file with a *nakedobjects.services* property key). They act as the natural starting point for the user to locate existing domain objects (the icons/ links on the user interface), and those repositories are free to call *to* the domain objects if required. Equally, though, repositories can be called *by* domain objects.

Factories are also domain services: they can both call to domain objects (for example, to set up their initial state) or can be called by a domain object. In CarServ, we don't have any stand-alone factories because we've folded the factory functionality we need into our repositories by subclassing from AbstractFactoryAndRepository. This is common; from a user's point of view, the responsibilities of creating a new instance and finding an existing instance are related.

Infrastructure Services

Another category of service is an *infrastructure service*. Infrastructure services are called by domain objects, but the dependency is strictly one way; an infrastructure service should never call a domain object.

Infrastructure services act as adapters to, or encapsulate, some external API, filtering out the irrelevant technical detail and translating it into our domain model's own *ubiquitous language*. Examples of infrastructure services include the following:

- An EmailService for sending out emails

- A CalendarService to obtain the date

- A BarCodeManager to add bar codes to PDFs

- A RulesService to encapsulate a rules engine such as Drools

And, indeed, these are the main focus of this chapter.

Application Services

Although domain services are part of the domain layer (they may call and may be called by domain objects) and infrastructure services are "underneath" the domain layer (solely called by domain objects), *application services* sit on top of the domain layer and solely call domain services and domain objects.

We can think of application services as controllers, managing the current state for a particular user's use case and interpreting requests from the presentation layer to the domain layer.

A wizard in a word processing application is a good metaphor for, or example of, an application service. The wizard itself represents the use case (of performing a mail-shot, say). The dialog we fill in (to specify the contacts to send to) captures state for the use case. We click Next, and the wizard collects further information (such as the template to merge to). When we click Finish, the wizard interacts with the domain services and domain objects (to actually perform the mail-shot).

So, that's what an application service is. Naked Objects, though, very deliberately does *not* require you to explicitly code any application services; this layer (and the presentation layer itself, of course) is handled automatically by the framework. Instead, the user interacts directly with the domain layer.

That said, you can explicitly code these layers if you want, which is something we look at in Chapter 15, *Integrating with Web Frameworks*, on page 269. And you can if you want write domain objects that are akin to a wizard, something we'll look at in Chapter 10, *Applying Domain Patterns*, on page 163.

Another way to think of services is as adapters to some underlying technology. When we do this, the distinction between infrastructure services and domain services starts to blur. We could, after all, think of a repository as an adapter that hides the retrieval API of some underlying persistence technology. And a factory service also hides the fact that returned objects are registered with Naked Objects itself through using the inherited newTransientInstance() method (we'll see the significance of this in Section 8.3, *Dependency Injection*, on page 130).

As well as making technology available to domain objects, we can also use services to access functionality of other systems in the enterprise. There are, after all, probably a number of existing applications that CarServ might need to integrate with, such as invoicing, stock purchases, or the general ledger. We'll leave this for now and pick up on it in Chapter 17, *Integrating Within the Enterprise*, on page 311.

In addition to repositories and factories that we explicitly write, Naked Objects also provides an additional service, the DomainObjectContainer. We've used this implicitly already, but let's now look at its full set of functionality.

8.2 The Domain Object Container

You can think of the DomainObjectContainer as the single "touch point" between your domain objects and the framework itself. Our domain classes haven't used it directly, but if you have explored the implementation of the helper methods in the AbstractDomainObject convenience superclass, you'll see that they all just delegate to one or another of the DomainObjectContainer's methods:

- newTransientInstance() is used to create a new instance of some domain object. Normally this is called by way of a factory.

- allInstances(), allMatches(), firstMatch(), and uniqueMatch() allow retrieval of objects. Again, we normally use a repository for this, but behind the scenes in-memory repositories use these methods.

- persist() is used to save objects to the persistent object store, while isPersistent() checks whether a given object is already persistent.

- remove() allows persistent objects to be removed (deleted).

- informUser(), warnUser(), and raiseError() allow the domain object to explicitly inform the user of something, at three different severity

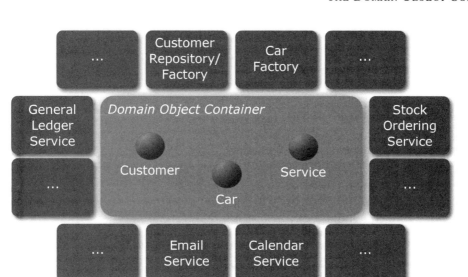

Figure 8.1: SERVICES ACT AS BOUNDARIES TO THE DOMAIN.

levels. The Naked Objects viewer then renders the message in the UI.

- getUser() returns a representation of the currently logged in user, using the UserMemento and RoleMemento classes from the applib.

Since we can call any of these methods from any domain object, another way of thinking about the DomainObjectContainer is as an all-purpose (or generic) factory or repository. During early prototyping, for example, it can be useful to directly call the creational and retrieval methods (newTransientInstance(), allMatches(), firstMatches(), and so on) from domain objects. But later you should look to refine this and replace those calls with factories and/or repositories. Introducing a factory helps us explain the intent of the code and can be important when we consider modularity, the topic of Chapter 11, *Keeping the Model Maintainable*, on page 193. For repositories there's a similar argument, and having repositories also allow us to easily substitute their implementations when we integrate the application, as discussed in Chapter 16, *Integrating with the Database*, on page 287.

Collectively, the various types of services act as a boundary to our domain application, as shown in Figure 8.1.

So far, so good, but how does the domain object get hold of a (domain or infrastructure) service in order to call it? The answer is dependency injection.

8.3 Dependency Injection

Dependency injection separates the responsibility of locating the service from that of using it. Rather than the domain object looking up a service from some central registry of services, it instead simply declares its dependency on that service. The runtime environment then injects the service into the domain object automatically.

Naked Objects provides this capability. It automatically performs *setter*-based dependency injection of services directly into domain objects. So, as a sketch (don't bother to add this to CarServ), suppose we wanted to allow our Customer to trade up by searching for Cars that are the same Model as those already owned by that Customer. CarRepository could have a method to find a number of new Cars of a given Model.

```
public class CarRepository extends AbstractFactoryAndRepository {
    ...
    @Hidden
    public List<Car> findNewerCarsOfSameModelAs(final Car car) {
        ...
    }
}
```

All the Customer class needs to do is provide a place for the CarRepository to be injected, that is, a *setter*:

```
public class Customer {
    ...
    private CarRepository carRepository;
    public void setCarRepository(CarRepository carRepository) {
        this.carRepository = carRepository;
    }
}
```

We would then write our action on Customer, delegating to the CarRepository as required:

```
public List<Car> suggestTradeUps() {
    List<Car> newerCars = new ArrayList<Car>();
    for(Car car: getCars()) {
        newerCars.addAll(
            carRepository.findNewerCarsOfSameModelAs(car);
    }
    return eliminateDuplicates(newerCars);
}
```

And that's all there is to it. If your domain object needs a service, it just asks for it by providing a public *set*ter.

You might be wondering how the magic happens, though. Well, for persistent objects, the framework is responsible for instantiating and initializing these instances. At the same time, it looks to see whether the object has any *set*ters for the services that the framework knows about and, if so, injects those services before returning the object. For transient instances, a similar process happens when we use the newTransientInstance() method to instantiate our objects. And just to reiterate, one of the services injected is the DomainObjectContainer discussed previously.

By the way, every service is injected into every other service if they declare a dependency, meaning that services can be layered. Services are also automatically injected into fixtures. Let's see how we can use this to simplify them.

8.4 Using Services in Fixtures

If we look at CarServ's fixtures, they all create objects, and between them there are searches of Makes, Models, Titles, and Customers. Creating and finding objects are the responsibilities of factories and repositories, so we could inject repositories into our fixtures and have the fixtures delegate to those repositories if we wanted.

That said, there's no point writing repositories if they are only to be used by fixtures. But we should use a repository if the functionality we need already exists.

The only case in CarServ where we have duplicated functionality is in AbstractCarFixture, which currently does a search for Customers using their LastName and FirstName. Let's remind ourselves of that code:

`chapter08/AbstractCarFixture.java`

```java
protected Customer findCustomer(
        final String lastName, final String firstName) {
    return firstMatch(Customer.class, new Filter<Customer>() {
        public boolean accept(Customer customer) {
            return customer.getLastName().equals(lastName) &&
                    customer.getFirstName().equals(firstName);
        }});
}
```

Let's refactor to use CustomerRepository instead:

chapter08/AbstractCarFixture-usingRepositories.java

```
protected Customer findCustomer(
        final String lastName, final String firstName) {
    List<Customer> customers =
        customerRepository.findByName(lastName, firstName);
    return customers.size() > 0 ? customers.get(0): null;
}
private CustomerRepository customerRepository;
public void setCustomerRepository(
        final CustomerRepository customerRepository) {
    this.customerRepository = customerRepository;
}
```

Run the application to double-check everything still works.

So much for using existing services such as repositories. Let's now see what it takes to write new services for use by our CarServ domain objects.

8.5 Requirements for Writing Services

Pretty much any vanilla JavaBean (or pojo) can be used as a service. There are a few rules that you should follow, though.

Write an Interface

Strictly, this is an optional step but is highly recommended. For each service, you should write a Java interface that defines the functionality available to the domain object. This allows different implementations to be used during development and testing.

Although the implementation of this interface is not part of the domain model, the interface itself is and so should live somewhere in the dom project.

Provide a Public No-Arg Constructor

So that our service can be instantiated by the framework, it should provide a no-arg constructor. The framework will instantiate each registered service only once, however, so effectively the services are singletons. There is *no need*, though, to explicitly implement the service as a singleton (that is, no need for a **static** getInstance() method).

Register in nakedobjects.properties

With the service class defined, it then needs to be registered in the nakedobjects.properties file using the *nakedobjects.services.prefix* and *nakedobjects.services* property keys.

Either Write an iconName Method or Annotate as @Hidden

By default, all services will be rendered as icons on the desktop, using the fully qualified class name of the service to determine the icon to use. We usually do want repositories and factories to appear, and since they are normally for a particular entity, they should have the same icon as that entity. To save us from having two copies of the same icon, we can (as we've seen) use the iconName() method to indicate which icon to use.

If a service object is to appear as an icon, then it is subject to the same programming conventions as any other domain object. So, if you want to use business rules (such as the validateXxx() supporting method) for your actions, then you can.

For infrastructure services, though, it usually doesn't make sense to allow these to be used directly by the user; they are there to be injected into the domain objects. These services should therefore be annotated as @Hidden. This isn't a hard-and-fast rule, however. You might have a service to allow domain objects to send instant messages; by not hiding the service, it will appear as an icon and let the end user send instant messages too.

Provide Public Methods for the Domain Object to Invoke

This is the guts of the service, and the methods will depend on what the service is there for. So, for example, the CarRepository provides (among others) a findByModel() method. An EmailService, on the other hand, would probably have a method such as sendEmail().

Your implementation can if you want inherit from AbstractService (in the applib), and if writing an in-memory repository, then you can subclass from AbstractFactoryAndRepository, as we have already done.

Now that we know a little more about the anatomy of services, we should refactor our repositories to reflect best practices.

8.6 Using Interfaces for Repositories

As discussed in the previous section, all services should have a corresponding interface. In CarServ, our repositories don't yet follow this rule, so let's fix them. First, copy the existing implementations into the (until now, empty) *services* project. Then, rename them to indicate that these are implementations that use the in-memory object store:

From dom **project**	**To service project**
dom.customer.CustomerRepository	inmemory.customer.CustomerRepositoryInMemory
dom.vehicle.CarRepository	inmemory.vehicle.CarRepositoryInMemory

These are both relative to the com.pragprog.dhnako.carserv package. You will need to fix up some **import**s, but otherwise the code should compile with no problems.

Now, convert the original repositories into interfaces, either by using Eclipse's *extract interface* refactoring or doing it by hand. For example:

chapter08/CustomerRepository.java

```
@Named("Customers")
public interface CustomerRepository {

    public Customer newCustomer();

    public List<Customer> findByName(
            @Optional
            @Named("Last Name")
            final String lastName,
            @Optional
            @Named("First Name")
            final String firstName);

    @Exploration
    public List<Customer> allCustomers();

    @Debug
    public UserMemento currentUser();
}
```

Then, make the in-memory implementations implement the interfaces:

chapter08/CustomerRepositoryInMemory.java

```
public class CustomerRepositoryInMemory
        extends AbstractFactoryAndRepository
        implements CustomerRepository {
```

```
    public String iconName() {
        return "Customer";
    }

    public Customer newCustomer() {
        Customer customer = newTransientInstance(Customer.class);
        return customer;
    }

    public List<Customer> findByName(
            final String lastName,
            final String firstName) {
        return allMatches(Customer.class, new Filter<Customer>() {
            public boolean accept(final Customer customer) {
                return customer.matches(firstName, lastName);
            }});
    }
    public String validateFindByName(
            final String lastName,
            final String firstName) {
        if (lastName == null && firstName == null) {
            return "Must specify at least one name";
        }
        return null;
    }

    public List<Customer> allCustomers() {
        return allInstances(Customer.class);
    }

    public UserMemento currentUser() {
        return getUser();
    }
}
```

Note that we have annotations in the interfaces but not in the implementations; they will be inherited. Finally, update the registration of these services in nakedobjects.properties:

chapter08/nakedobjects.properties

```
nakedobjects.services.prefix = com.pragprog.dhnako.carserv.inmemory
nakedobjects.services = customer.CustomerRepositoryInMemory,\
                        vehicle.CarRepositoryInMemory
```

Run the application, and confirm that everything is still hunky-dory.

In the previous refactoring, I've chosen to keep allCustomers() on the interface and annotated it as @Exploration. There's also an argument for keeping this method only in the in-memory implementation; after all, it's unlikely to be supported for a repository implementation that delegates to an RDBMS, for example.

In the introduction to this chapter, we identified a couple of scenarios where we might want to extend CarServ using services, so let's look at how to implement one of these nonrepository services in practice.

8.7 Implementing a Calendar Service

In the previous chapter, we refactored the Service's bookedInAndReady property to use a CalendarInterval value type. This is defaulted using its DefaultsProvider:

```
chapter07/CalendarIntervalValueSemanticsProvider-defaultsProvider.java

@Override
public DefaultsProvider<CalendarInterval> getDefaultsProvider() {
    return new DefaultsProvider<CalendarInterval>() {
        public CalendarInterval getDefaultValue() {
            CalendarDate start = CalendarDate.from(
                    todayPlus(1).toString(), "yyyy-MM-dd");
            return CalendarInterval.startingFrom(
                    start, Duration.days(1));
        }
        private static final long MILLIS_PER_DAY = 24 * 60 * 60 * 1000;
        private Date todayPlus(final int days) {
            Date midnight = new Date(Clock.getTime());
            return new Date(midnight.getTime() + MILLIS_PER_DAY * days);
        }
    };
}
```

The call to Clock.getTime() (which ultimately traces back to Section 4.2, *Fixtures for Setting Up the Clock*, on page 67) returns the time according to applib Clock singleton. The default implementation set up for us in exploration or prototype mode is the settable FixtureClock; otherwise, we are given an implementation that uses the system time.

We can write a CalendarService to bootstrap a different implementation for the applib. Our domain objects then either can continue to use the applib's Clock system clock or, to make their dependencies more obvious, can have the CalendarService injected into them. Let's go work through the latter approach and use it to "mock the clock."

Define the Interface

As for our previous example, we start off with an interface.

Here's CalendarService:

```java
public interface CalendarService {
    public CalendarDate today();
}
```

Since we already have a precedent, I've chosen to use the timeand-money library's CalendarDate class to represent a date. Note since we want it to appear as an icon, it is *not* annotated as @Hidden.

Write the Implementation

Next we need an implementation. While in exploration or prototype mode, we get a FixtureClock by default, but let's write an implementation that actually explicitly initializes FixtureClock. We'll also expose the ability to change the clock:

```java
public class CalendarServiceDemo
        extends AbstractService
        implements CalendarService {

    static {
        FixtureClock.initialize();
    }

    public CalendarDate today() {
        Calendar cal = Clock.getTimeAsCalendar();
        int year = cal.get(Calendar.YEAR);
        int month = cal.get(Calendar.MONTH) + 1;
        int day =  cal.get(Calendar.DATE);
        return CalendarDate.date(year, month, day);
    }

    public void turnTo(
            @Named("Year") int year,
            @Named("Month") int month,
            @Named("Day") int day ) {
        getFixtureClock().setDate(year, month, day);
    }
    public int default0TurnTo() {
        return Clock.getTimeAsCalendar().get(Calendar.YEAR);
    }
    public int default1TurnTo() {
        return Clock.getTimeAsCalendar().get(Calendar.MONTH)+1;
    }
    public int default2TurnTo() {
        return Clock.getTimeAsCalendar().get(Calendar.DATE);
    }
```

```
    private FixtureClock getFixtureClock() {
        return (FixtureClock) Clock.getInstance();
    }
}
```

The static initializer does the required magic, explicitly installing Fixture-
Clock as the Clock singleton. Meanwhile, the turnTo() action gives us the
ability to change the time if we want.

Register, Inject, and Use the Service

Next we need to register the CalendarServiceDemo into nakedobjects.prop-
erties. This is straightforward, so I'll leave you to complete this step.

Most of the time we inject services into domain objects. For CalendarService, though, we actually need to inject into the CalendarInterval's Value-
SemanticsProvider:

chapter08/CalendarIntervalValueSemanticsProvider-defaultsProvider.java

```
public static final class CalendarIntervalDefaultsProvider
            implements DefaultsProvider<CalendarInterval> {
    public CalendarInterval getDefaultValue() {
        return CalendarInterval.startingFrom(
                calendarService.today().plusDays(1), Duration.days(1));
    }
    private CalendarService calendarService;
    public void setCalendarService(
            final CalendarService calendarService) {
        this.calendarService = calendarService;
    }
}
@Override
public DefaultsProvider<CalendarInterval> getDefaultsProvider() {
    return new CalendarIntervalDefaultsProvider();
}
```

One slight subtlety here; it is no longer possible to use anonymous
inner classes because the *setter* would not be visible. Instead, we've
refactored the class to be a **public** nested **static** class.

Run the application again. The CalendarService should be shown as an
icon, as in Figure 8.2, on the next page (I've copied over an icon image),
but the application should behave just the same. Now set the CalendarService to a different date. When you next create a Service, the date
defaulted for the BookedInAndEstReady property should be this new date.

Let's finish off this chapter with a few more general observations on
writing services.

Figure 8.2: CALENDARSERVICE LETS THE DATE BE MODIFIED.

8.8 Hints and Tips for Writing Services

Writing services is pretty straightforward, but there are a couple things worth emphasizing.

Use Coarse-Grained Interfaces

Sometimes service implementations are actually thin proxies for a web service that's implemented elsewhere. If there's a chance that an implementation may need to make RPC calls across the network, then the service interface should be relatively coarse-grained. A too "chatty" interface will have a negative impact on performance. For example, if we wanted to use an RPC-based spell-checking service, then we might call it with a paragraph or an entire document; we probably wouldn't call it to check each word or on each keystroke.

In our implementation of CalendarService, we just got the time from our computer's system clock. However, we could equally have written an implementation that used the Network Time Protocol (NTP) to obtain the time from some time server running either within our enterprise or up on the Internet. In other words, our service's implementation is a proxy to the "real" implementation running remotely.

Keep the Service Stateless

Services should not hold state, except perhaps for implementation reasons such as caching. Any state held should most definitely not relate to their callers (for example, the domain objects).

For example, to minimize network traffic, it would be permissible for a CalendarService to check against NTP once a minute and to service the request using the system clock in between. Such an implementation would need to remember how long since the NTP service was called, but such state would not relate to callers so would be OK.

Even then, the state should be persisted rather than being held in-memory. Although in prototyping mode services are long-lived, in contrast when running in client-server mode, any services on the server-side are very short-lived, re-created for each action invocation. This also allows for more complex deployment scenarios, such as clustering.

For similar reasons, it would be a very unwise for a service to provide a callback mechanism by holding a reference to domain objects. On the server side, the domain objects are similarly short-lived and may have been garbage collected before any callback could be called. But an alternative is to use an enterprise service bus, which is something we discuss in Chapter 17, *Integrating Within the Enterprise*, on page 311.

Shadow Persistent State

Another reason for keeping your services stateless is to prevent domain logic from "leaking" into your services. If you find yourself wishing you could add some state to an existing service, then step back and think what that state represents in the wider domain and introduce a new domain object to capture that state, possibly "shadowing" state held in the remote service's own underlying persistence store.

For example, an Employee domain object is in a sense a shadow of a user held by a security authentication mechanism. Similarly, a Document or Communication domain object could act as a domain model representation of some sort of a document URI provided for a DocumentManagementService.

Coming Up Next

In this chapter, we identified different types of services, refactored our existing domain services (repositories), and saw how to use and write infrastructure services. And it brings us to the end of Part I of the book.

We've now pretty much covered most of the features that Naked Objects has, and CarServ is perfectly presentable. We can locate Customers and Cars from the repositories, bidirectional relationships are automatically maintained, we have used value types to centralize value-related business rules, and we have actions (with user-friendly choices and defaults) so that we can implement behaviorally complete objects. However, our design is not particularly sophisticated or necessarily insightful. So, in the next part of the book, we're going to look at various approaches to deepen the design.

Exercises

If you weren't coding along, then load up the latest version of CarServ (**chapter08-02**) with the service we defined in this chapter, and give it the once-over.

Then, have a go at writing a new EmailService so that we can send email reminders to Customers. Add a new emailAddress property to Customer, and add a remind() action that sends a fixed message using the injected service. In the EmailService, define a single method sendEmail() accepting four string parameters (from, to, subject, and body).

You might want to have a go at writing a new implementation of CalendarService that acts as an NTP client to a time server. To get you going, you'll find that the timeandmoney library (that we used in Chapter 7, *Using Value Types*, on page 109) has a class called NISTClient that should help.

With your own application, you might want to reuse the services that we have defined or CarServ. Or, you could use some of the other ideas for services that were mentioned and have a go at writing them.

Part II

Techniques

Distributing Class Responsibilities

In the first part of this book, we've seen how Naked Objects can be used to develop a simple domain model, bringing in many of the fundamental DDD concepts. We've identified and associated domain *entities*, composed those entities out of *value objects*, and developed a number of *services* and *repositories* for them to call upon. We've also seen how fixtures enable rapid prototyping with an in-memory object store.

In mastering the Naked Objects programming model, we now have the *tools* to build a domain model, and we've used them to build a version of CarServ that's usable, if basic. Right now it's also pretty easy to understand how CarServ fits together, but that's probably only because it is so small. Back in the real-world, though, our domains are going to have considerably larger scope. If we just start coding away, then we're likely to end up with a domain model that's a tangled mass, hard to understand, and almost impossible to maintain.

The overall goal for Part II of this book is to focus on the *techniques* to help us deal with larger, more complex domains. But there's nothing new under the sun. The object-oriented paradigm has been around since the 60s, so there's a wealth of ideas and literature already out there that we can mine for inspiration. By the end of Part II, we'll have added a whole bunch of techniques to our tool set, and that will set us up well for Part III when we discuss how to put all this into practice.

We're going to keep with CarServ to illustrate the ideas, refactoring it as we go. In the ideal world, we would want to apply the techniques in

Part II from the outset, involving our domain experts as we go, so in a sense we're starting from a less-than-perfect situation. But applying the refactorings themselves will also be useful.

I'm also going to up the pace a little so that there's room to get through as many techniques as possible. To compensate, there'll be more versions of CarServ to download so you can pick up the story wherever you want.

So. . . that's the plan for Part II of this book; what of this chapter? Well, we've already had a couple of chapters focusing on identifying class responsibilities. In this chapter (**chapter09-01**[1]), we're going to use techniques that help us distribute those responsibilities appropriately across the domain classes. Some of the techniques you may recognize, and we'll note any "prior art" as we go. But one at least is specific to Naked Objects, and we'll get to that at the end.

Let's kick off with a nice little technique from Peter Coad.

9.1 Applying Coad Colors

When faced with a large domain model, the immediate question is, "Which bits are the most important?" What we need is a *highlighted core*.

Coad's technique is to use colors, described in *Java Modeling in Color* [CLL99]. It grew out of using class-responsibility-collaboration (CRC) cards as a way of identifying or initially modeling domain classes. These are usually captured on 6x4-inch index cards. Rather than use plain cards, Coad uses colored cards. So, we have red ones, yellow ones, green ones, and blue ones. However, reading black text on dark colors can be tricky, so instead we add a dash of white to each and end up with pink, light yellow, light green, and light blue. Coad calls these *archetypes*:

- Pink (red) is the most important (the color of stop on a traffic light or the color of a fire engine), and we use this for classes that represent a moment of time or an interval of time—a *moment-interval*. Pink classes often represent transactions, which are the lifeblood of the enterprise.

---

1. This version has a solution to the EmailService exercise from Chapter 8, though none of the other exercises.

in context...

Highlighted Core

A *highlighted core* is a means to identify the most significant domain concepts within a domain model. This is useful when the most significant classes aren't immediately obvious from the structure or partitioning of the model itself.

- Yellow is next (after red in the traffic light) and indicates a *role* that an object plays with respect to some other object.

- Green comes next (bottom of the traffic light) and represents a *party, place, or thing.* Greens tend to be concrete—something you could stub your toe on.

- Blue is the last of the Coad archetypes and is the most neutral (the color of your bathroom?). Blues are used to describe or catalog other objects; they are *descriptions.*

If you use these colors, then you'll find your eye naturally drawn to the pinks first and then to the yellows, then to the greens, and finally to the blues.

Coad's colors might seem trite, but they can be very handy. For example, if we were developing a library application (sorry, hackneyed example), then what color should Book be? If you said blue, then you are probably thinking of Book in the sense of Title, with an ISBN number. If you said green, then you are probably thinking of a particular Copy of a book, perhaps that one with a torn cover page.

As another example, an Airbus A318-100 is a type of plane (a PlaneType); the aircraft with the marking "F-GUGJ" identifies a instance of a Plane. PlaneType is blue, and Plane is green.[2]

Or much more generally, a CatalogItem is blue, and a StockItem is green.

Coad archetypes also tend to follow well-defined relationships. Pinks play or use a role (yellow) with respect to greens, which are in turn

---

2. The correct term for a Plane—as used by domain experts—is apparently Tail, because the aircraft's number was traditionally painted on the tail. This is part of the *ubiquitous language* for air-traffic control.

described by blues. So, if we go to the library and borrow a book, then we'll create a Loan (pink) of a Loanable (yellow) Book (green), which is of a Title (blue). This is by no means an exact science; I've observed that pinks are also sometimes described by blues too. But it can help determine which way dependencies "ought" to go.

Let's try applying Coad's colors to CarServ:

- The most important object in CarServ is Service. It's a car-*servicing* application after all; its raison d'etre is to manage the servicing of cars. Since Service represents an interval of time, we color it pink.

- Both the Customer and the Car classes are green, falling into the concrete party/place/thing category. These are very much things you could stub your toe on.

- Both the Model and the Make classes are blue; both are used to describe Car. And Title describes Customer, so it is blue too. When we first met these in Chapter 3, *Relating Objects Together*, on page 47, I called them *describing*; now you know why.

There are no yellows yet in CarServ, but we'll add some in time.

Unlike Coad's book, unfortunately this one isn't in color. But we can at least indicate the Coad archetypes, as shown in Figure 9.1, on the next page.[3]

Enough on colors (for now at least). I fancy doing a bit more coding, so let's get our hands dirty.

9.2 Factoring Out Objects

If we want our domain model to be understandable, then any single domain class must be understandable too. But when modeling domain classes, it's quite possible to suddenly find oneself staring at a class of 1,000 lines or more, and that's too large for comfort.

One reason is that in Naked Objects all our business logic lives only in domain objects; there are no other layers to hide the business rules. That's a benefit, of course, because we'll more quickly realize that we've heaped too many responsibilities on a single class. But we still need to do something about it.

---

3. This diagram was created using the freeware edition of Omondo, http://www.omondo.com. Another similar commercial tool is Borland Together, http://www.borland.com.

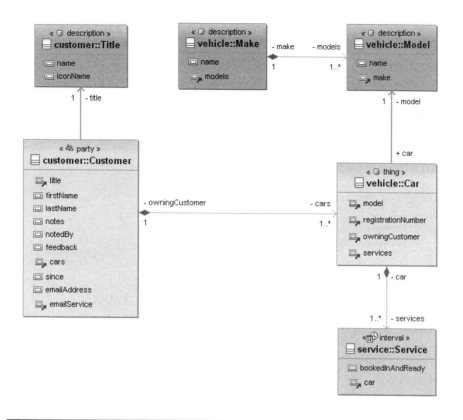

Figure 9.1: CARSERV WITH COAD ARCHETYPES APPLIED

It's time to draw on a little more "prior art." Back in the 90s Robert Martin's (alias "Uncle Bob") wrote a series of articles for *C++ Report* magazine, collectively called the "Principles of OO Design." He's since written them up in his book *Principles, Patterns and Practices* [Mar02].

The one we care about right now, though, is his *single responsibility principle*, which states that there should never be more than one reason for a class to change. In other words, the need to change any of a class's more fine-grained know-what or know-how-to responsibilities should be equally likely.

The corollary of this is that if one of these responsibilities is more (or indeed less) likely to change than another, then it should be factored out into its own class.

A good example in CarServ is a Customer's name. We can envisage that
new properties or actions might be added to a Customer, but it's pretty
unlikely that the set of properties making up its name—title, firstName,
and lastName—are likely to change.

Let's therefore introduce a new Name class to hold these three properties and cut and paste them out of Customer. Then, make the Customer
reference the Name:

`chapter09/Customer-Name.java`

```
public class Car extends AbstractDomainObject {
    ...
    public void created() {
        setName(newTransientInstance(Name.class));
    }

    public String title() {
        return getName() != null? getName().title(): null;
    }
    public String iconName() {
        return getName() != null?
            getName().getTitle().getIconName(): null;
    }

    private Name name;
    @MemberOrder(sequence="1")
    @Disabled
    public Name getName() { ... }
    public void setName(final Name name) { ... }

    @Hidden
    public boolean matches(String firstName, String lastName) {
        return getName() != null?
            getName().matches(firstName, lastName): false;
    }
    ...
}
```

The most important method here is created(), one of the callback methods (we saw another one in Section 6.5, *Validating the Entire Object*,
on page 105, and all are summarized in Appendix A, on page 365). It
is called once the object has been instantiated; this is where Customer
should create its Name object. The changes to the title(), the iconName(),
and the helper matches() method are all pretty mechanical.

The result of the refactoring is shown in Figure 9.2, on the facing
page. In addition to the previous refactoring, you'll also need to change
CustomerRepository and AbstractCustomerFixture. Again, the changes are

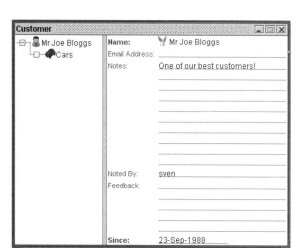

Figure 9.2: NAME FACTORED OUT FROM CUSTOMER

straightforward, so I won't detail them here; or, you can load up the examples from the book's download (***chapter09-02***).

An alternative might have been to factor out the Name class as an (immutable) value object. However, it doesn't really have value semantics; there's no closed set of operations, it doesn't act as an identifier to a Customer, and it's not necessarily immutable. We might also want to subclass for cultures dealing with different ways of addressing someone. In fact, Name is an *aggregated object*, with Customer as its root.

Unlike regular *entities*, aggregated objects should not be shared by roots. In UML terms, the relationship between a root and an aggregated object is one of composition or containment (in a UML class diagram you would fill in the black diamond on the relationship's line). Compare: two Cars may reference the same Model, but two Customers should not reference the same Name. The Naked Objects applib provides an @Aggregated annotation to document that a class is intended to be aggregated within a root, and if you use the @Disabled annotation on the reference, it will at least ensure that the reference cannot be modified through the UI.[4]

---

4. Note, though, that Naked Objects isn't smart enough (at least, not in v4.0) to enforce the nonshareable semantic for us.

in context...

Aggregates

Aggregates are used to restrict the number of references allowed between entities, defining a boundary within which invariants can be enforced while reducing the overall intellectual weight of a model.

A root entity contains aggregated objects, and the only permanent references allowed to aggregated objects are by the root or by other aggregated objects. Objects outside the aggregate interact only through the root.

I've seen objections to Naked Objects itself on the basis that it gives rise to monstrous, barely intelligible forms in the user interface. That isn't the case if you factor out objects wherever you see them. In fact, I could argue it the other way: when you see a monstrous, barely intelligible form in the UI, then that's a sure sign that you need to tease out the root object into some *aggregate*s.

Not only does factoring out objects make the original object more easily understood (by reducing its size), it also extends our *ubiquitous language*. For example, in CarServ we just introduced the concept of Name. And although for now we only moved out know-what responsibilities, we now have a class where we could start to introduce know-how-to responsibilities. So in the future, the Name object might know how to create an AddressLabel, for example.

So, that's useful. In the next section, what is under consideration is not where the responsibility should live but what type of responsibility it should be. Read on, MacDuff.

9.3 Balancing Responsibilities

Here's a well-known OO antipattern: the *anaemic domain model*.[5] The domain objects hold lots of data, sure, but they just sit there, inert, doing nothing. They have plenty of know-what responsibilities (properties and collections), but no know-how-to responsibilities (actions).

---

5. See, for example, http://martinfowler.com/bliki/AnemicDomainModel.html.

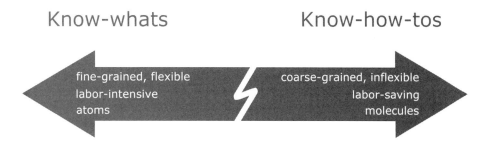

Figure 9.3: KNOW-WHATS VS. KNOW-HOW-TOS

In conventional *layered architectures*, *anaemic domain models* are rather common. The know-how-tos tend to shift into an explicitly coded application layer that takes responsibility for mediating between the dumb data objects. From the end users' point of view, the application broadly has the functionality it requires, but the application is in effect procedural rather than object-oriented, separating function (in the app layer) and data (in the domain layer). Such architectures throw away lots of the goodness of object orientation.

Naked Objects deliberately has no explicitly coded application layer, so we can't fall into the *anaemic domain model* trap by accident. If our objects are too dumb and expose no useful actions, our end users will be sure tell us! On the other hand, we don't want to go too far the other way either by having objects that can be used and modified only through a very restricted number of actions.

We could think of this as a spectrum, as shown in Figure 9.3. Domain objects that consist only of know-whats are flexible and support many business processes but are relatively fine-grained and thus labor intensive for the end user to work with. On the other hand, domain objects that have more know-how-tos are easier for the end user to use (they can do more), but the actions are necessarily hard-coded to specific business processes requirements and can't (without recompiling the application) be changed to do something else.

This tells us that for business processes that are new or are changing, we should keep left; but as the business activity becomes more well-defined and common (and probably as transaction volumes increase), the further to the right we want to be. Put another way, we only reify the business activities into domain object actions as the business

Figure 9.4: CAR CAN TELL US ITS MOST RECENT SERVICE.

processes that they support mature. The know-whats are the atoms, and the know-how-tos are the molecules made up of those atoms.

So, let's see a small example of this. Suppose in CarServ that there was a requirement to find the most recent Service for a Car so that a reminder letter could be sent out for those Cars overdue a Service. We could just let the user navigate through the collection of Services for the Car and inspect each one individually, but that would be too far to the left on our spectrum. Better would be if a Car could simply return the most recent Service automatically:

```
chapter09/Car-mostRecentService.java
@MemberOrder(sequence = "1.3")
@Disabled(When.UNTIL_PERSISTED)
public Service mostRecentService() {
    TreeSet<Service> sortedServices =
        new TreeSet<Service>(new Comparator<Service>() {
            public int compare(Service s, Service t) {
                return s.getBookedInAndReady().compareTo(
                    t.getBookedInAndReady());
            }
        });
    sortedServices.addAll(getServices());
    return sortedServices.size() > 0? sortedServices.last(): null;
}
```

In Figure 9.4, we can see this new know-how-to responsibility.

This new responsibility (***chapter09-03***[6]) can of course be called programmatically by other objects as well as by the user. Indeed, we'll use it in the next section, which also looks at different ways to implement the same general responsibility.

---

6. Includes fixtures to set up some Services

> ### Behaviorally Complete != Bloated
>
> A *behaviorally complete* domain object is one that exposes a know-how-to set of actions for the end user (or other objects) to call.
>
> However, it doesn't mean that the implementation of those actions needs to be in the domain object. There's nothing to prevent the domain object from delegating to other objects—possibly not visible in the user interface—that implement the actual behavior required.
>
> A good example is the *state* pattern, which uses a different object to represent each state.* These *state* objects are internal but hold the knowledge as to the valid state transitions and may also implement behavior that varies polymorphically by state.
>
> _____
>
> *. More on patterns in the next chapter; the *state* pattern is described in the classic *Design Patterns* (GHJV95) book.

9.4 Representing Large Collections with Finder

When starting out with a new and unfamiliar domain, our goal as we identify likely looking domain concepts is then to figure out how they relate. However, just because there is a relationship between two concepts in the "real world," it doesn't follow that there should be a corresponding relationship between the classes in our domain model. Or more to the point, it doesn't follow that there should be a *navigable* relationship. One case in particular where we should remove the relationship is when the number of objects in that collection is large.

For example, in CarServ a Customer has a collection of Cars, and a Car has a collection of Services. Neither is likely to get too large, so using a collection is reasonable. We also have a relationship between Car and Model: every Car is of a particular Model, and for a given Model, there could be many Cars. Here, though, there could be thousands of Cars for a given Model. If we naively added this collection and then ran the application, we'd quickly realize (as the user waded through those Car instances) that the collection shouldn't be there. Instead, we should model this responsibility as a finder action, with some additional criteria to restrict the results.

> ### ⚡ Joe Asks...
>
> #### Does Naked Objects Support Paging of Collections?
>
> No, Joe, the standard Naked Objects viewers don't support paging. Although we've thought several times of adding such a capability, we've always done fine without. The lack of this functionality in the viewer means we think more deeply about the domain model, specifically, to consider the maximum cardinality of each of our collections. If the collection is too big, we model the relationship with a finder.

Continuing the example of the previous section, suppose that on occasion a manufacturer issues a recall for Cars of a certain Model. We might want to support that by finding those Cars of a certain Model without a Service in the last year.[7] The usual pattern for finder actions such as this is to delegate up to a repository, so let's add an action and inject the CarRepository into the Model class:

chapter09/Model-findCarsWithoutRecentService.java

```
public class Model extends AbstractDomainObject {
    ...
    public List<Car> findCarsWithoutRecentService(
            @Named("Months since")
            final Integer monthsSince) {
        return carRepository.findCarsWithoutRecentService(
                                            this, monthsSince);
    }
    ...
    private CarRepository carRepository;
    public void setCarRepository(final CarRepository carRepository) {
        this.carRepository = carRepository;
    }
}
```

In the CarRepository interface as well as in the CarRepositoryInMemory implementation, we add the new finder that in turn uses an injected CalendarService.

---

7. This is, admittedly, slightly contrived.

```
chapter09/CarRepositoryInMemory-findCarsWithoutRecentService.java
```

```java
public class CarRepositoryInMemory
        extends AbstractFactoryAndRepository
        implements CarRepository {
    ...
    @Hidden
    public List<Car> findCarsWithoutRecentService(
            final Model model, final Integer months) {
        final CalendarDate earlierDate =
            calendarService.today().plusMonths(-months);
        return allMatches(Car.class, new Filter<Car>() {
            public boolean accept(Car car) {
                if (car.getModel() != model) return false;
                Service service = car.mostRecentService();
                return service != null &&
                        service.getBookedInAndReady()
                                .start().isBefore(earlierDate);
            }});
    }
    ...
    private CalendarService calendarService;
    public void setCalendarService(
            final CalendarService calendarService) {
        this.calendarService = calendarService;
    }
}
```

Since this is an in-memory implementation of the CarRepository, it simply checks every Car using the mostRecentService() method we added previously. An RDBMS implementation would use some clever SQL, but the end result would be the same. Note also the @Hidden annotation on this method; it is designed to be called programmatically, so we suppress it from the view. In Figure 9.5, on the next page, we see the ModelRepository and Model's new behavior.

There's also one thing missing here: how to get hold of the Models in the first place. We should also add a new ModelRepository and ModelRepositoryInMemory implementation and register it in nakedobjects.properties:

```
chapter09/ModelRepositoryInMemory.java
```

```java
public class ModelRepositoryInMemory
        extends AbstractFactoryAndRepository
        implements ModelRepository {

    public String iconName() {
        return "Model";
    }
```

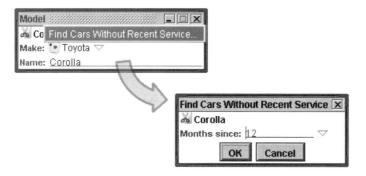

Figure 9.5: MODEL HAS A FINDER INSTEAD OF A LARGE COLLECTION.

```
    @Exploration
    public List<Model> allModels() {
        return allInstances(Model.class);
    }
}
```

To summarize, if the number of instances in a collection is large, we should remove that collection and if necessary replace it with a finder that restricts the number of instances using some criteria (**chapter09-04**).

To implement this finder, we needed to inject the CarRepository into Model. However, it turns out that we can remove that dependency completely. Let's see how.

9.5   Contributing Actions from Services

Now pay attention, because our last technique is specific to Naked Objects, so you probably haven't seen it before!

In the previous section, we added a new findCarsWithoutRecentServices() action to the Model domain class. But the price we paid for that new functionality was to add a dependency from Model to CarRepository.

The trouble with dependencies, of course, is they make the domain model more difficult to understand. If that dependency is closely related, then that's probably OK. But if the dependency is off to a far-flung corner of the model, then perhaps not. For example, if you saw a relationship between the Model class and Customer, you might be scratching your head as to what it represented (I know I would be).

So, a key weapon in battling complexity is to decouple wherever possible, something we'll look at in detail in Chapter 11, *Keeping the Model Maintainable*, on page 193. By adding that dependency into the Model class, we seem to have been going in the wrong direction. However, Naked Objects has a trick up its sleeve. Let's look again at how the Model class uses its injected CarRepository:

```
chapter09/Model-findCarsWithoutRecentService.java
public class Model extends AbstractDomainObject {
    ...
    public List<Car> findCarsWithoutRecentService(
            @Named("Months since")
            final Integer monthsSince) {
        return carRepository.findCarsWithoutRecentService(
                                            this, monthsSince);
    }
    ...
    private CarRepository carRepository;
    public void setCarRepository(final CarRepository carRepository) {
        this.carRepository = carRepository;
    }
}
```

The called method on CarRepository is annotated @Hidden because it is intended to be invoked only programmatically:

```
chapter09/CarRepository-findCarsWithoutRecentService-Signature.java
@Hidden
public List<Car> findCarsWithoutRecentService(
        Model model,
        @Named("Months since")
        Integer months);
);
```

Let's remove that @Hidden annotation and run the application. As we see in Figure 9.6, on the next page, if we bring up a Model instance, there is now a submenu called Cars, which has a findCarsWithoutRecentService() action. Although in the UI this action appears to belong to the Model, the implementation still lives on the CarRepository.

This submenu action is called a *contributed action*, because it is seemingly *contributed* to the object by the repository. The framework does

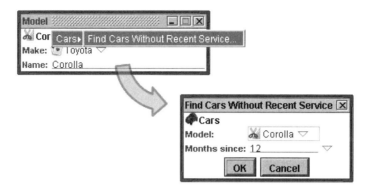

Figure 9.6: THE CARREPOSITORY CONTRIBUTES AN ACTION TO MODEL.

this for us because the CarRepository's findCarsWithoutRecentService()
action accepts a Model as one of its parameters.

Since we now have the contributed action, we can just remove the
findCarsWithoutRecentService() action from the Model class and indeed
remove the dependency injection of CarRepository. We still have the functionality we want but no longer any dependency (**chapter09-05**).

Contributed actions are reminiscent of extension methods in .NET or
introduced methods in AspectJ. It would theoretically be possible to
accomplish the same effect using aspects, but why bother? Naked Objects combines the domain object and the related service actions dynamically in the UI for you, with no effort at all.

So, that's quite a nice trick, but why did I start off this section claiming
it is so important? Well, it's because contributed actions also apply to
interfaces too, and it's *that* which lets us decouple further.

For example, right now in CarServ, Car and CarRepository depend on the
Model class, which does make sense (green depends on blue). But if we
had a reason to, we could decouple these classes through an interface.
As a sketch:

1. We would introduce a CarClassifier interface.
2. We would make Car and CarRepository reference CarClassifier instead
   of Model.
3. We would make Model implement CarClassifier.

In the UI, we'd still see the CarRepository's action contributed into the Model class, because Model would-be-a CarClassifier. However, Car and CarRepository would no longer depend on the Model class directly. This change isn't needed for the tutorial, but you can see how it would work.

As I said, we'll come back to the topic of decoupling in Chapter 11, *Keeping the Model Maintainable*, on page 193. But that wraps it up for this chapter.

Coming Up Next

In this chapter, we used a number of techniques to help us reduce both the size of our domain objects and the coupling between those objects. We also saw how Coad's colors help us rationalize about dependencies. Applying these techniques to larger-scale domain models than CarServ will help keep them understandable.

Some of these techniques we could call implementation patterns. Patterns have been enthusiastically adopted by the software community, which is no surprise, because they provide us with a vocabulary to explain how objects interact. In our next chapter, we're going to work through a number of higher-level design and analysis patterns and see how they too let us deepen the design.

Exercises

Download the various versions of CarServ, and check that you understand what each of the refactorings has done to the model.

As a bit of revision, in Chapter 8, *Isolating Infrastructure Services*, on page 125, we talked about how services are injected into fixtures and how fixtures should use repositories if available. Now that we have a ModelRepository, go back and move any finder logic from the fixtures and into the ModelRepository. Since Make and Model are so closely linked, you might also want to introduce a MakeRepository too.

In your own application, try the following:

- Identify the Coad colors of each of your domain objects. See if they fit the general pattern of pink – yellow – green – blue.
- Factor out new (aggregated) objects.
- Replace large collections with finders on repositories.
- Ensure that finder actions are contributed to their parameters.

Then go to bed. It's late, you know.

Chapter 10

Applying Domain Patterns

Design patterns are named solutions for certain common design problems, and what makes them so useful is that they provide a vocabulary that raises the level of abstraction of the discussion. So, assuming that you and I both know what, say, the *composite* pattern is for, then I could say, "I think we've got a hierarchical relationship going on here, so why don't we apply the *composite*?" You would immediately know the solution I'm envisaging, so the discussion can focus on the important stuff: whether my analysis is correct.

The original seminal *Design Patterns* [GHJV95] book catalogued twenty-one such patterns, but there are many more than this (and indeed many more pattern books have followed). Evans mentions a couple of design patterns in his book, specifically *composite* (mentioned already) and *strategy*. These two in particular do seem to be applicable to most domains. But as Evans says, it's possible that other design patterns might also work at the domain level. . . it depends what your domain is.

Patterns aren't applicable to only design. They can also apply down at the implementation level (when they are sometimes called *idioms*) and up to larger-scale analysis patterns, where the intent is to provide a precanned and reusable object model, sometimes targeted at a specific domain. A couple of good books with this ambition are Martin Fowler's *Analysis Patterns* [Fow96] and also David Hay's *Data Model Patterns* [Hay96]. The latter of these is targeted at data modelers rather than OO developers, but both are good places to hunt for inspiration.

In this chapter (***chapter10-01***[1]), we're going to continue refactoring CarServ using design patterns and analysis patterns. All but one of the patterns have been documented before (some of them many times before), and so for these I've provided references to further reading.

Again, I don't have space to do a detailed walk-through of every pattern in this chapter, but I'll try to compensate with plenty of diagrams. If there's not quite enough detail for you, remember you can always download the refactored code from the book's website.

Let's begin with a pattern that aptly enough has to do with creation.

10.1 Type as Factory Pattern

One of the most powerful features of OO languages is of course polymorphism, giving us the ability to extend a model without needing to know what those extensions might be at the outset. This is key to the *open-closed principle*, another of Robert Martin's principles. (See *Principles, Patterns and Practices* [Mar02].)

The *open-closed principle* says that classes should be open for extension and closed for modification. In practice, this means we can extend the model by implementing an interface or subclassing an abstract class. But we also need to be able to create instances of these new types: polymorphic constructors, in effect.

The objective of the *type as factory* pattern is to do just this.[2] As usual, let's make this concrete with an example from CarServ.

Create New Vehicle Hierarchy

Suppose we wanted CarServ to support vehicles other than Cars. For example, we might want to service Vans and Motorcycles as well, in other words, Vehicles. If we were building CarServ for real, then we'd only do this once we'd identified some actual responsibilities (properties, collections, and actions) that were specific to one of the Vehicle subtypes; otherwise, we could make do simply by renaming Car to Vehicle.

---

1. Includes solutions to Chapter 9's exercises
2. The *type as factory* pattern is a variation on the *type object* pattern, described for example in *Pattern Languages of Program Design, vol3* [MRB97].

But for the purpose of the book, let's continue to make these changes:

- Use the refactoring support in your IDE to globally rename Car to Vehicle. Then mark Vehicle as **abstract** since it is our base class. Similarly, rename CarRepository and CarRepositoryInMemory, and update nakedobjects.properties.
- Change all uses of Car to Vehicle throughout. For example, rename the methods in Customer that make up its Cars collection: getCars() to getVehicles(), addToCars() to addToVehicles(), and so on. Do the same for Service and for VehicleRepository.
- Reintroduce Car as a new subclass of Vehicle, and add the Van subclass and the Motorcycle subclasses. Add icons for the new classes.
- Update fixtures to create concrete Cars, not abstract Vehicles.

So far, so good. Let's now get to the guts of this pattern and consider how we create new Vehicles.

Introducing the VehicleType Power Type

We currently create Cars using the newCar() action on Customer. We want to replace this with the ability to create any type of vehicle. Put another way, we want to create a Vehicle of a specified VehicleType.

Here's the plan. We're going to have VehicleType (in the vehicle package) as a factory to create instances of the subclasses of Vehicle. There will be one instance of VehicleType for each of the subclasses of Vehicle. In his book *Advanced Object-Oriented Analysis & Design Using UML* [Ode98], James Odell calls such classes *powertypes*; Coad would color them blue. In Figure 10.1, on the following page, we can see the domain model we're aiming for.

To make these changes, you should do the following:

1. Create the VehicleType class like so:

   chapter10/VehicleType.java

```
@Bounded
@Immutable(When.ONCE_PERSISTED)
public class VehicleType extends AbstractDomainObject {

    public String title() {
        return vehicleSubclass().getSimpleName();
    }
    public String iconName() {
        return title();
    }
}
```

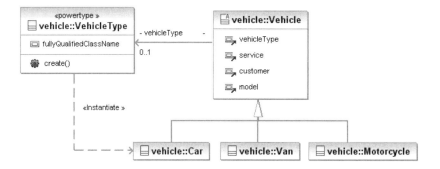

Figure 10.1: VEHICLETYPE ENUMERATES THE VEHICLE SUBCLASSES.

```java
private String fullyQualifiedClassName;
public String getFullyQualifiedClassName() { ... }
public void setFullyQualifiedClassName( ... }

@Hidden
public Vehicle create() {
    try {
        Vehicle vehicle = newTransientInstance(
                                    vehicleSubclass());
        vehicle.setType(this);
        return vehicle;
    } catch (Exception ex) {
        throw new ApplicationException(ex);
    }
}

@SuppressWarnings("unchecked")
private Class<? extends Vehicle> vehicleSubclass() {
    try {
        return (Class<? extends Vehicle>)
            Class.forName(getFullyQualifiedClassName());
    } catch (ClassNotFoundException e) {
        throw new ApplicationException("No such vehicle type");
    }
}
}
```

The FullyQualifiedClassName property is the key to the pattern, holding the fully qualified class name of a subclass of Vehicle. The (hidden) create() method then uses the container to instantiate the correct subclass.

2. Also create a VehicleTypeRepository and a VehicleTypeRepositoryIn-Memory implementation, and register in nakedobjects.properties.

3. Update MakesAndModelsFixture to set up the VehicleType instances:

`chapter10/MakesAndModelsFixture-VehicleTypes.java`

```java
public void install() {
    VehicleType carVehicleType =
        createVehicleType(Car.class);
    VehicleType vanVehicleType =
        createVehicleType(Van.class);
    VehicleType motorcycleVehicleType =
        createVehicleType(Motorcycle.class);
    ...
}
private VehicleType
        createVehicleType(Class<? extends Vehicle> subclass) {
    VehicleType vehicleType =
        newTransientInstance(VehicleType.class);
    vehicleType.setFullyQualifiedClassName(subclass.getName());
    persist(vehicleType);
    return vehicleType;
}
```

The reasons for updating the MakesAndModelsFixture fixture class will become apparent shortly.

4. Update Vehicle to reference its VehicleType so that it knows its type:

`chapter10/Vehicle-VehicleType.java`

```java
private VehicleType type;
@Disabled
public VehicleType getType() { ... }
public void setType(final VehicleType type) { ... }
```

Note the @Disabled annotation; a vehicle can't change its type.

5. Update the Customer's newVehicle() no-arg action to take a Vehicle-Type as a parameter:

`chapter10/Customer-newVehicle-VehicleType.java`

```java
public Vehicle newVehicle(final VehicleType vehicleType) {
    Vehicle vehicle = vehicleType.create();
    vehicle.setOwningCustomer(this);
    return vehicle;
}
```

6. Inject the VehicleTypeRepository into AbstractCarFixture so that cre-ateCar() can look up the VehicleType corresponding to the Car, and use the Customer's newVehicle() action to actually create the Car.

In Figure 10.2, on the next page, we can see how this action looks in the user interface.

Figure 10.2: THE USER CAN SELECT WHICH TYPE OF VEHICLE TO CREATE.

We can now polymorphically create subtypes of Vehicle. Have a go at making these changes, or just download the latest version of CarServ (***chapter10-02***).

Deepening the Design

The previous steps outline the general form of the *type as factory* pattern. The powertype drop-down both enumerates the subclasses and is responsible for creating instances of them.

In our particular case, we can go a little further, though. When we create a new Car, we at some point must specify its Model. Thinking this through, the Model in fact determines the VehicleType. In Figure 10.3, on the facing page, we can see the relationship between these two classes.

And now, we suddenly get (what Evans called) a *cascade of insights*: we don't need that reference from Vehicle to VehicleType after all, because there is already a reference up to Model from which we can infer the VehicleType. Similarly, the argument to the newVehicle() action shouldn't be a VehicleType; it should be a Model. We can then delegate to the Model to have it create the correct subclass of Vehicle.

To make these changes, you should do the following:

1. In Model, add a VehicleType reference, and add a create() action:

```
chapter10/Model-VehicleType.java

public class Model ... {
    ...
    private VehicleType vehicleType;
    public VehicleType getVehicleType() { ... }
    public void setVehicleType(VehicleType vehicleType) { ... }

    public Vehicle create() {
        return getVehicleType().create(this);
    }
}
```

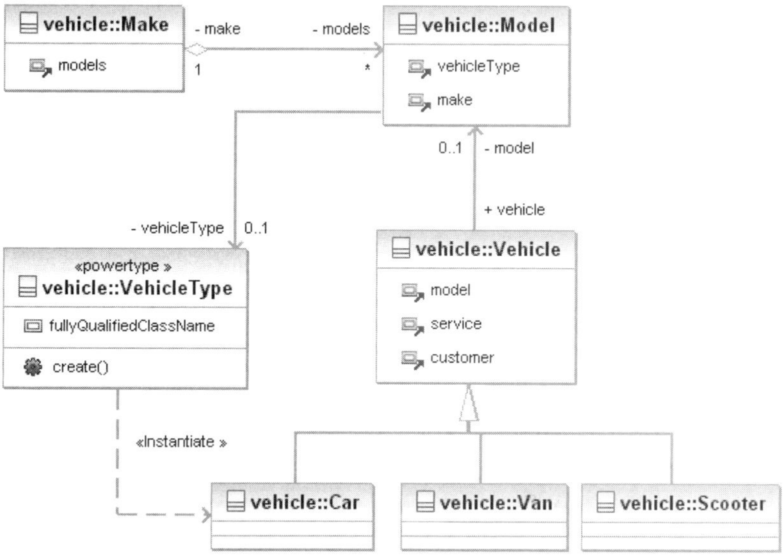

Figure 10.3: VehicleType is determined by Model.

2. In VehicleType, update its create() action to take the Model:

```
chapter10/VehicleType-create.java
@Hidden
public Vehicle create(final Model model) {
    try {
        Vehicle vehicle = newTransientInstance(vehicleSubclass());
        vehicle.setModel(model);
        return vehicle;
    } catch (Exception ex) {
        throw new RuntimeException(ex);
    }
}
```

3. Update MakesAndModelsFixture to set up the reference from Model to VehicleType. (Now you see why we used this fixture earlier.)

4. In Vehicle, remove that reference to VehicleType; we can infer it from the Model.

5. In Customer, modify the newVehicle() action to take a Model rather than a VehicleType:

`chapter10/Customer-newVehicle-Model.java`

```java
public Vehicle newVehicle(final Model model) {
    Vehicle vehicle = model.create();
    vehicle.setOwningCustomer(this);
    return vehicle;
}
```

6. Finally, in AbstractCarFixture's createCar() method, there's no longer any need to look up the VehicleType, so remove that logic and indeed the injected VehicleTypeRepository.

The previous example (**chapter10-03**) nicely demonstrates how applying some standard patterns, such as *type as factory*, can lead us to deeper insights into our domain model. Previously the Model class was a pretty boring bit of reference data, whereas now it is integral to our approach for supporting different types of vehicles.

The next design pattern we're going to look at will also get our boring blue reference data classes working harder for us. Let's see how.

10.2 Knowledge Level Pattern

These days, when you buy a new car, a little warning light might appear after six months or so telling you it's due for a service. But a different car might warn you after twelve months or some other period. Or, you might get a warning after you've driven 10,000 miles or so. For another car, perhaps it's some other distance. But it's not so much the Car that is determining the interval between Services; it's the Car's Model.

The *knowledge level* pattern is about splitting responsibilities between those objects that know how things *should be* and those objects that capture how things *are*.[3] The former objects constitute the *knowledge level*, and the latter objects constitute the *operational level*. Using Coad's colors, knowledge-level objects are usually blue; operational-level objects are the greens and pinks. The operational-level objects reference the knowledge-level objects.

Separating these responsibilities is in line with the Robert Martin's *single responsibility principle* mentioned in Section 9.2, *Factoring Out Objects*, on page 148. Rather than a single domain object with a tan-

---

3. The *knowledge level* pattern is described both in Evans' *Domain Driven Design* [Eva03] and in Fowler's *Analysis Patterns* [Fow96].

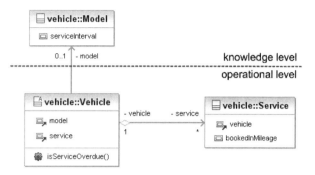

Figure 10.4: MODEL HOLDS THE KNOWLEDGE ABOUT SERVICE INTERVALS.

gle of responsibilities, we end up with two smaller objects with a well-defined relationship between them; our model should be easier to understand.

In CarServ, let's formalize Model as the *knowledge level* for Vehicle, as shown in Figure 10.4. The Model class captures the knowledge about how often Services should occur. The Vehicle and Service classes meanwhile capture what is happening "on the ground." If we consider the other classes in our model, then Customer (green) will also be at the operational level, while Make and VehicleType (both blues) will be in the *knowledge level*. To make these changes, you should do the following:

1. Update the Model class with a new serviceInterval property to represent the number of months between Services. Also update the MakesAndModelsFixture with suitable values.

2. Add a new action to Vehicle so it can tell us whether it is overdue for servicing with respect to its Model:

chapter10/Vehicle-isServiceOverdue.java

```java
@Hidden
public boolean isServiceOverdue() {
    if (mostRecentService() == null) return false;
    final CalendarDate lastService =
        mostRecentService().getBookedInAndReady().start();
    final CalendarDate serviceDue =
        lastService.plusMonths(model.getServiceInterval());
    return calendarService.today().isAfter(serviceDue);
}
```

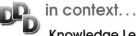 in context...
Knowledge Level

A *knowledge level,* according to *Fowler* (Fow96), is a group of objects that describes how another group of objects should behave. Evans notes that it is an application of reflection for domain models.

This also needs CalendarService to be injected into Vehicle.

3. Refactor our findVehiclesWithoutRecentService() action on VehicleRepository. Currently it takes a parameter for the number of months, so remove this parameter (and its defaults and choices) and instead use the Vehicle's new isServiceOverdue() action:

```
chapter10/VehicleRepository-findCarsWithoutRecentService-isServiceOverdue.java
public List<Vehicle> findVehiclesWithoutRecentService(
        final Model model) {
    return allMatches(Vehicle.class, new Filter<Vehicle>() {
        public boolean accept(Vehicle vehicle) {
            if (vehicle.getModel() != model) return false;
            return vehicle.isServiceOverdue();
        }});
}
```

The CalendarService no longer needs to be injected into VehicleRepository, so remove the *setter.*

In Chapter 9, *Distributing Class Responsibilities*, on page 145, we decided that a Model should not have a collection of Vehicles; instead, we should use a finder. Our argument then was pragmatic: there would have been too many Vehicles in the collection. Considering knowledge levels and operation levels gives us another (better?) reason not to have this collection; the knowledge level should not know about the operational level. You shouldn't navigate from blues to greens (**chapter10-04**).

The next pattern we're going to look at shows that inspiration can come from the code itself.

10.3 Null Object Pattern

In the preceding pattern, we refactored findCarsWithoutRecentService()
several times, but in every implementation we have a **null** check within
isServiceOverdue():

`chapter10/Vehicle-isServiceOverdue-abbreviated.java`

```
@Hidden
public boolean isServiceOverdue() {
    if (mostRecentService() == null) return false;
    // ... remainder of the method ...
}
```

That bothers me. Why should we have a special case processing for the
very first Service? And how would we know when the first Service is due,
anyway?

If we could guarantee that there would always be a Service, then we
wouldn't need any special processing at all. What we want is a sort of
do-nothing marker Service, created automatically when the Vehicle itself
is created. This is the *null object* pattern.[4]

The user will need to be able to distinguish between this null service
and a regular service, and there are a couple of ways we could model
this. The simplest approach would be to just have a boolean isNull property. Slightly more sophisticated (and the discussion that follows provides some justification for this) would be to create an inheritance hierarchy so that Service becomes **abstract** with subclasses to represent the
different service types. As shown in Figure 10.5, on the following page,
we can start off with just two.

To make these changes, you should do the following:

1. Create a new RegularService and subclass from Service. Mark Service
   as **abstract**.
2. Similarly, create a new NullService and subclass from Service.
3. Add icon images for both, and provide a title() for NullService to
   easily distinguish from RegularService:

   `chapter10/NullService-title.java`

   ```
   public String title() {
       return super.title() + " (null)";
   }
   ```

---

4. The *null object* pattern is described in *Pattern Languages of Program Design, vol3*
[MRB97].

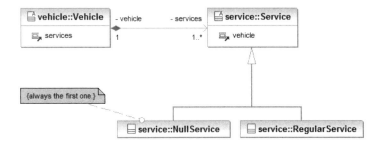

Figure 10.5: SERVICE BECOMES A HIERARCHY.

4. In Vehicle's bookService() action, change the implementation to instantiate a RegularService rather than the (now **abstract**) Service.

5. Also in Vehicle, add a created() life-cycle method to create a new NullService:

`chapter10/Vehicle-created.java`

```java
public void created() {
    addToServices(newTransientInstance(NullService.class));
}
```

6. Update the AbstractCarFixture subclasses so that the effective date when each Vehicle is first created is prior to its first RegularService booked (if any).

Now we get to the payback. Since we know there will always be at least one Service, we can simplify that isServiceOverdue() method and remove that if (mostRecentService() == null) return false; check.

My problem with this pattern is in explaining it to the domain expert; just what does a "null" service mean in our *ubiquitous language* anyway? And yet it feels like we're going in the right direction, because we can now determine when the first regular Service is due, whereas we couldn't before.

The question to ask our domain expert is, how do they determine when a vehicle's first service is due? It might be that there's special-case processing where the vehicle's initial registration date is used, rather than the previous service. In that case, we should update our model to reflect this business process. Alternatively, it might be that there *is* such a thing as our initial "null" Service, except it is actually a predelivery service (if a new car) or an initial assessment service (if the customer just

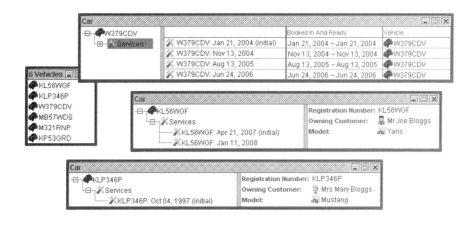

Figure 10.6: EVERY VEHICLE HAS AT LEAST ONE SERVICE.

bought a secondhand car). The introduction of a hierarchy for Services now looks like a good idea; we can start to vary charging policies and other matters based on service type.

To close off this discussion, let's go with the second of these alternatives and rename NullService to InitialService. In Figure 10.6, we see this version of CarServ (**chapter10-05**).

Our next pattern is from the other end of the spectrum; it's really an analysis pattern.

10.4 Role Object Pattern

Sometimes we come across two domain concepts that seem to share a lot in common but feel distinct. It often turns out that they are the same concept but playing different roles with respect to other parts of the model. In this case, we can model the role as a simple (Java) **interface**.

But on occasion the role itself is important (has its own know-what or know-how-to responsibilities), meaning that it needs to be modeled separately. This is the *role object* pattern.[5] What's nice about this pattern is that it allows the roles that an object plays to change over time.

---

5. The *role object* pattern is described in *Pattern Languages of Program Design, vol4* [HFR00].

Whereas with a role modeled by an **interface**, the relationship is permanent (SomeClass implements SomeInterface), with a role object we can attach and detach roles over time. We can also keep a history of roles as an audit trail.

Let's make this concrete again. Suppose in CarServ we want to keep track of the time spent per Service per employee so we can charge for labor. The rate depends on the experience of the mechanic, so we'll need an Employee class with an hourlyChargeRate property. We'll also identify each Employee by Name.

Noticing that Name is shared with Customer, we might be tempted to create a superclass Person to hold the Name reference and have both Customer and Employee inherit from it. Not so fast, though! Suppose we also had a requirement that Employees get a 10 percent discount. We would need to start associating each Employees with their corresponding Customers. But what then if an Employee/Customer changes their Name? We'd need to update that Name twice over.

The problem with the previous design is that we have two different instances of a Person entity (one a Customer and one an Employee) when "in the real world" there's only a single person. It was the right idea to introduce a Person entity, but Employee isn't a subclass of Person. Instead, it's a role that a Person plays. Likewise for Customer.

In Figure 10.7, on the facing page, we see the relevant classes and properties in our revised domain model. To get here, you'll first need to refactor Customer into a role:

1. Create a new person package, and move Name and Title into it.
2. Create a Person class in the new person package, and add a reference to Name class (or copy Customer and remove the unwanted stuff). Implement title() and iconName() as follows:

   chapter10/Person-title-iconName.java

```java
public String title() {
    TitleBuffer buf = new TitleBuffer();
    if (getName() != null) {
        buf.append(getName().title());
    }
    buf.append(" (Person)");
    return buf.toString();
}
public String iconName() {
    return getName() != null?
                getName().getTitle().getIconName(): null;
}
```

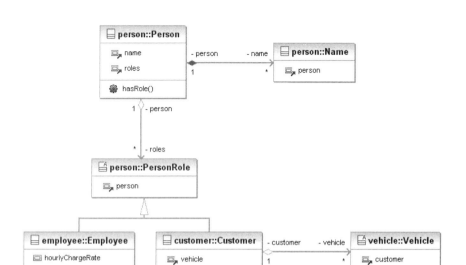

Figure 10.7: EMPLOYEE AND CUSTOMER BECOME ROLES OF PERSON.

3. Create an **abstract** PersonRole class (again in the person package). Choose an icon for the class. Add a bidirectional unmodifiable one-to-many relationship between Person and PersonRole, and implement title() as follows:

chapter10/PersonRole-title.java

```java
public String title() {
    return getPerson() != null?
        getPerson().title() + " (" + roleName() + ")": null;
}
public String iconName() {
    return getPerson() != null? getPerson().iconName() : null;
}
protected abstract String roleName();
```

In PersonRole, add a persisting() life-cycle method so the role is added to the Person when it is saved:

chapter10/PersonRole-persisting.java

```java
public void persisting() {
    getPerson().addToRoles(this);
}
```

4. Add helper hasRole() and getRole() methods to Person:

`chapter10/Person-getRole-hasRole.java`

```java
@SuppressWarnings("unchecked")
@Hidden
public <T extends PersonRole> T getRole(Class<T> roleType) {
    for(PersonRole role: getRoles()) {
        if (roleType.isAssignableFrom(role.getClass())) {
            return (T) role;
        }
    }
    return null;
}
@Hidden
public boolean hasRole(Class<? extends PersonRole> roleType) {
    return getRole(roleType) != null;
}
```

5. Make Customer subclass PersonRole. Remove its Name property and title(); also implement roleName();

6. Rework the CustomerRepository's newCustomer() action so that it returns a still-transient Person object with a Customer role attached. Leave the finders alone, though.

7. Rework AbstractCustomerFixture to use CustomerRepository's newCustomer() action.

With those changes done, add the Employee role also:

1. Add an Employee class as a subclass of PersonRole in a new employee package. Add the hourlyChargeRate property, implement roleName(), and choose an icon for the class.

2. Create a new EmployeeRepository, similar to CustomerRepository, and register in nakedobjects.properties.

3. Create a new AbstractEmployeeFixture, and then create a FredSmith-EmployeeFixture subclass and for other employees too. Make sure the logic copes with creating a new Employee who is already a Customer. Add to CustomerCarsMaintenanceFixture.

In Figure 10.8, on the next page, we can see what our application now looks like (the icons distinguish the role types).

You can load up a version of CarServ with these changes applied (**chapter10-06**). With this refactoring done, it would now be easy to start implementing some of our requirements. For example, for the 10 percent employee discount, it'd be easy to find out whether the Person of the Customer in question also has an Employee role (this is just a sketch).

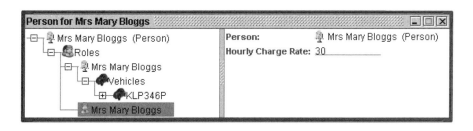

Figure 10.8: CUSTOMER AND EMPLOYEE ARE ROLES OF PERSON.

```
public class Service ... {
    ...
    public void calculateTotal() {
        this.total =
            (sumParts() + sumLabor()) * (1.0 - employeeDiscountIfAny());
    }
    private double employeeDiscountIfAny() {
        return getCar().getCustomer().getPerson()
                    .hasRole(Employee.class)) ? 0.1: 0.0;
    }
}
```

Before we move on, we ought to note one of the downsides of this pattern, which is that it is quite complex for the end user. There is no is-a-kind-of relationship between the *role object*s (Customer and Employee) and the object that has the roles (Person). So, although the end user might informally talk about a Customer's Name, strictly speaking what we now have is the Name of the Person that happens to be a Customer. If the end user wanted to modify a "customer's name," then they would need to walk the graph (click through) from Customer up through Person to get to Name.

That said, if the Customer's Name (or some other property that belongs to Person) changes frequently, then there's nothing to prevent us from providing a convenience action to modify the Name from the Customer. Indeed, if we put the action in the PersonRole superclass, then any subclass role would inherit this convenience action.

It's time to move on. Next we're going to consider the relationship between the newly introduced Employee object and the users of the application themselves.

10.5   User Peer Object Pattern

We spend a lot of time thinking about the domain objects with which the user of our application will interact. But for some systems, especially those with a workflow element, what also matters is *who* is doing the interacting, and that is the users themselves.

To model this, we need a representation of those users in the model, which we then need to integrate that with the system's own representation of the user (that is, their login).

In the case of CarServ, we already have an Employee object. So when our user logs in, how does that user quickly bring up "their" Employee object? What we need is some way of associating the system-level user identity (login) with the domain-level concept of Employee, which we can do using the *user peer object* pattern.[6] The Employee is the peer domain object of the system-level user identity, in a one-to-one correspondence.

This is a simple pattern to implement:

1. First, link the Employee to the user by adding an (unmodifiable) UserId string property.
2. Update the AbstractEmployeesFixture and its subclasses to specify the UserId. As we learned in Section 4.3, *Fixtures for Setting Up User Sessions*, on page 70, the current user depends on whether you have a logon fixture (as is the case in the CarServ downloads, specifically LogonAsFredSmithFixture) but otherwise depends on whether you log in using exploration or prototype mode.
3. Finally, provide a new me() action to search for the current user. Something like this:

```
chapter10/EmployeeRepository-me.java

public Person me() {
    return firstMatch(Person.class, new Filter<Person>() {
        final String currentUserId =
            getContainer().getUser().getName();
        public boolean accept(final Person person) {
            Employee employee = person.getRole(Employee.class);
            return employee != null &&
                    employee.getUserId().equals(currentUserId);
    }});
}
```

---

6. I couldn't find a description of this pattern in existing literature, so even though it's a well-known technique, this might be the first time it has been given a name.

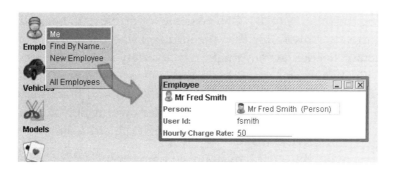

Figure 10.9: EMPLOYEE IS THE *user peer object*.

Remember, we can find the current user's name using the injected DomainObjectContainer; for a recap, see Section 8.2, *The Domain Object Container*, on page 128.

In Figure 10.9, we can see what the application should look like when you run it (**chapter10-07**).

Now that we have linked our Employee domain object to the system user—now that the application knows who's using it—we could start adding further functionality. For example, we could provide a workflow capability using different types of work items, where one work item type might represent the labor required on a Service. Other related functionality we could add might include auditing and quality control, but all of it follows on from this pattern.

Let's now look at one of the all-time classic design patterns.

10.6 Strategy Pattern

The *strategy* pattern, sometimes also called *policy*, allows us to represent pluggable behaviors as objects themselves.[7] These strategies effectively define the behavior of the object that references them.

The object acting as a *strategy* can be one of several Coad colors. If the *strategy* holds no intrinsic state, then it'll be blue, representing the know-how-to responsibilities for the operational know-what objects.

---

7. The *strategy* pattern is described in *Design Patterns* [GHJV95].

But going the other way, it's also possible for *strategy* to be pink, representing the interval of time that the *strategy* was attempted. For example, a debt collection agency might use a variety of strategies to recover a debt. Each *strategy* could keep track of when it was applied and whether it was successful. Or it might be green and hold just enough state to control the workflow for a particular owning object. Coad's colors can really help to tease out the nature of the *strategy*.

It's time to make this concrete again. At some point we're going to need to charge our Customers for Services, so let's add some functionality around that requirement. Most Customers will probably want to pay by credit card, so we can model that as one method of payment. But we might also allow our regular Customers to pay on account, and there will be those Customers who prefer to pay by cash.

Each of these are PaymentMethods, and they represent a *strategy* by which we charge for work done. The different ways—strategies—for paying (CreditCard, Cash, and Account) are subclasses of PaymentMethod. In Figure 10.10, on the next page, we can see this sketched out, once again using the *type as factory* pattern.

To get there from here, you'll need to do the following:

1. Create a PaymentMethodType powertype in a new payment package, and create a corresponding PaymentMethodTypesFixture fixture.

2. Create an **abstract** PaymentMethod superclass (also in payment) with an unmodifiable Type property to its PaymentMethodType. To make it a little more interesting, you could also add a Current flag.

3. Create CreditCard, Account, and Cash as subclasses of PaymentMethod in the customer package, with appropriate properties.

   For example, CreditCard would capture the cardNumber and expiryDate, Account might detail the current balance and a limit, and Cash perhaps has no additional properties.

4. Add a bidirectional unmodifiable collection of PaymentMethods to Customer, and in PaymentMethod add a corresponding Owner.

5. In Customer again, write a newPaymentMethod() action taking PaymentMethodType as a parameter. This should return a still-transient instance of the appropriate subclass of PaymentMethod. In the PaymentMethod's persisting() life-cycle method, it should add itself to its owning Customer's paymentMethods collection.

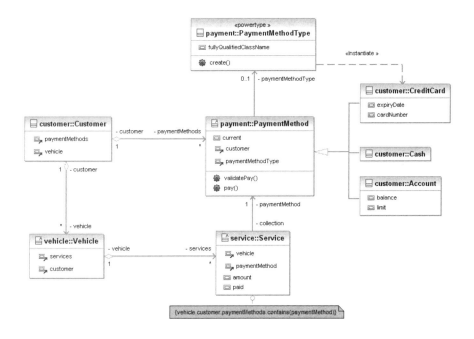

Figure 10.10: PAYMENTMETHOD PROVIDES STRATEGIES FOR PAYING.

6. Update the AbstractCustomerFixture and subclasses to create some initial PaymentMethods for each.

7. Add icons for all new domain classes (PaymentMethodType, PaymentMethod, Cash, CreditCard, and Account).

With this scaffolding out of the way, we can implement the payment functionality. The PaymentMethod is going to act as the pluggable *strategy*, providing two responsibilities. First, validatePay() will make sure that the amount to pay is within the limit, and second, pay() will actually process the payment. Therefore:

1. In PaymentMethod, add **abstract** pay() and validatePay() methods, each taking a Service.

2. In Service, add an Amount property (ultimately this would be calculated; for now we'll make do with an editable property). Also add an unmodifiable Paid flag.

3. Also in Service, add a payUsing() action that accepts a Payment-Method:

chapter10/Service-payUsing.java

```java
public void payUsing(final PaymentMethod paymentMethod) {
    paymentMethod.pay(this);
}
public String validatePayUsing(PaymentMethod paymentMethod) {
    final ReasonBuffer buf = new ReasonBuffer();

    buf.appendOnCondition(
        paymentMethod.getOwner() !=
                        getVehicle().getOwningCustomer(),
        "Payment method must belong to this customer");

    buf.appendOnCondition(
        !paymentMethod.getCurrent(),
        "Payment method must be current");

    buf.append(paymentMethod.validatePay(this));
    return buf.getReason();
}
public List<PaymentMethod> choicesOPayUsing() {
    return getVehicle().getOwningCustomer().getPaymentMethods();
}
public String disablePayUsing() {
    final ReasonBuffer buf = new ReasonBuffer();
    buf.appendOnCondition(getAmount() == 0, "Nothing to pay");
    buf.appendOnCondition(getPaid(), "Already paid");
    return buf.getReason();
}
```

4. Finally, in the PaymentMethod subclasses, implement the pay() and validatePay()*strategy* methods. The Cash implementation probably just needs to use warnUser() to pop up a message and then mark the Service as paid:

chapter10/Cash-pay.java

```java
public void pay(Service service) {
    warnUser("Paid in Cash");
    service.setPaid(true);
}
```

The CreditCard implementation would most likely use an infrastructure service (as discussed in Chapter 8, *Isolating Infrastructure Services*, on page 125), but for now we can just write a stub.

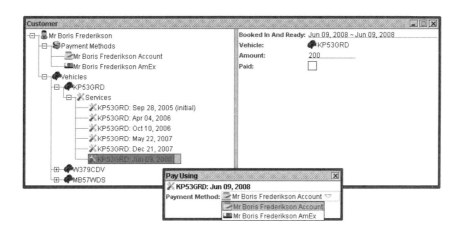

Figure 10.11: SERVICE CAN BE PAID FOR USING ANY PAYMENTMETHOD.

```
chapter10/CreditCard-pay.java
```
```java
@Override
public void pay(Service service) {
    // stub implementation, would probably delegate to
    // a CreditCardService.
    warnUser("NOT YET IMPLEMENTED - ignoring");
}
```

The Account implementation would add the Service's Amount to its Balance, again marking the Service as paid:

```
chapter10/Account-pay.java
```
```java
@Override
public void pay(Service service) {
    warnUser("Put onto Account");
    setBalance(getBalance() + service.getAmount());
    service.setPaid(true);
}
@Override
public String validatePay(Service service) {
    int available = getLimit().intValue() - getBalance().intValue();
    return service.getAmount() > available?
        "Amount exceeds available credit": null;
}
```

With all that done, we can see the application in use in Figure 10.11.

Thanks to the *type as factory* pattern we saw earlier, adding other payment strategies will be straightforward.

Note that in this implementation (***chapter10-08***), the *strategy* object is green; it's a thing belonging to the Customer. To finish off this chapter, let's look at a pattern designed to support labor-intensive business processes.

10.7 Process Object Pattern

Sometimes we have use cases that need to create or update a whole graph of objects together in a single go. For example, in an expense system, this would be entering a week's expenses. It would be frustrating for the user to have to navigate around the object graph and enter each expense item in turn. Instead, our system should provide the ability to bulk upload the week's expenses in a single hit.

With the *process object* pattern, we introduce a domain object whose purpose is solely to make such bulk updates easier.[8] This domain object is never persisted, so we annotate it using @NotPersistable. Instead of a save action, it provides a means to "take on" the update.

Another way of thinking about this is in terms of "problem spaces" and "solution spaces." The domain model we've developed belongs to the problem space: it organizes the concepts of the domain (Customers, Vehicles, Services, and so on) in a way that is useful for us. The *process object*, however, belongs to the solution space; it helps solve a particular use case in a particular way.

Let's see this in operation. In CarServ, it's a pretty reasonable bet that whenever we enter a new Customer, we'll also be entering details about their Vehicle(s), along with their PaymentMethods. We could combine all of these into a single CustomerTakeOn object, as shown in Figure 10.12, on the facing page.

To make these changes, do the following:

1. Create the CustomerTakeOn object, consisting of mandatory properties Title, FirstName, and LastName, and of the optional properties Vehicle1Model, Vehicle1RegNo, Vehicle2Model, Vehicle2RegNo, CreditCardNumber, CreditCardExpiryDate, AccountLimit, and SetUpCash.

   Annotate the class as @NotPersistable.

---

8. The *process object* pattern is a variation on the *transaction script* pattern; see *Patterns of Enterprise Application Architecture* [Fow03].

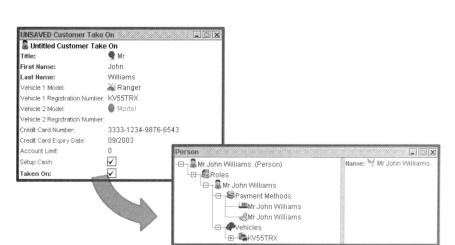

Figure 10.12: CUSTOMERTAKEON SIMPLIFIES THE COMMON USE CASE.

2. Also add a disabled TakenOn boolean property, which we'll use for state tracking. Add a disableXxx() supporting method for each of the properties to disable it when this boolean is set.

3. Create a PaymentMethodTypeRepository and in-memory implementation, annotated as @Hidden. Inject into CustomerTakeOn.

4. Add an ok() action to the CustomerTakeOn. This is the action that does the take-on itself:

`chapter10/CustomerTakeOn-ok.java`

```java
@Named("OK")
public Person ok() {
    Person person = customerRepository.newCustomer();
    person.getName().setFirstName(getFirstName());
    person.getName().setLastName(getLastName());
    person.getName().setTitle(getTitle());
    Customer customer = person.getRole(Customer.class);
    if (enteredAllOf(getVehicle1Model(),
                     getVehicle1RegistrationNumber())) {
        Vehicle vehicle = customer.newVehicle(getVehicle1Model());
        vehicle.setRegistrationNumber(
                    getVehicle1RegistrationNumber());
        customer.addToVehicles(vehicle);
    }
    if (enteredAllOf(getVehicle2Model(),
                     getVehicle2RegistrationNumber())) {
        Vehicle vehicle = customer.newVehicle(getVehicle2Model());
```

```
                    vehicle.setRegistrationNumber(
                            getVehicle2RegistrationNumber());
                    customer.addToVehicles(vehicle);
            }
            if (enteredAllOf(getCreditCardNumber(),
                            getCreditCardExpiryDate())) {
                    CreditCard creditCard =
                        (CreditCard) customer.newPaymentMethod(
                            findPaymentMethodType(CreditCard.class));
                    creditCard.setCardNumber(getCreditCardNumber());
                    creditCard.setExpiryDate(getCreditCardExpiryDate());
                    customer.addToPaymentMethods(creditCard);
            }
            if (enteredAllOf(getAccountLimit()) &&
                    getAccountLimit() > 0) {
                    Account account =
                        (Account) customer.newPaymentMethod(
                            findPaymentMethodType(Account.class));
                    account.setLimit(getAccountLimit());
                    customer.addToPaymentMethods(account);
            }
            if (getSetupCash()) {
                    Cash cash = (Cash) customer.newPaymentMethod(
                            findPaymentMethodType(Cash.class));
                    customer.addToPaymentMethods(cash);
            }
            persist(person);
            setTakenOn(true);
            return person;
    }
    public String disableOk() {
            String invalidReason = validate(this);
            if (invalidReason != null) {
                    return invalidReason;
            }
            return getTakenOn()?"Already taken on":null;
    }
```

At the end of the method, this sets the TakenOn flag when complete, thereby disabling the object once the take-on has occurred. Also, note the use of the validate() method, mentioned in Section 6.5, *Validating the Entire Object*, on page 105. This disables the ok() action if the object (which includes any property of the object) is invalid.

5. Add a new takeOnCustomer() action to CustomerRepository. This should instantiate and return the CustomerTakeOn. Also, mark the newCustomer() action as @Hidden.

With these changes made, try the application (***chapter10-09***).[9]

It's also possible to create more complex *process object*s that have collections, possibly prepopulated to create a grid-like form. For example, CustomerTakeOn might have had a Vehicles collection (of VehicleTakeOn objects). When the takeOn( ) action is invoked, any completed VehicleTakeOns would be used to create corresponding Vehicles.

I should point out that with the *process object* pattern, we're on a slippery slope. As we discussed in Section 9.3, *Balancing Responsibilities*, on page 152, Naked Objects' lack of an explicitly coded application layer helps prevent an *anaemic domain model*. But with the *process object* pattern, what we're doing is reintroducing that layer. We may end up duplicating validation logic in both our domain objects and our *process object*s, potentially introducing bugs. But more significantly, we are encouraging our business users to interact with our system in very narrow ways. One of the hallmarks of Naked Objects' applications is that they empower users by placing as few constraints on the usage of the system as possible. But if the domain objects are hidden beneath *process object*s, this flexibility gets lost.

However, *process object*s do have their place. You should start out providing the functionality in the domain objects. Then, you can add *process object*s where necessary; you're unlikely to need too many. There's an analogy here with database denormalization, where we start fully normalized and then denormalize for performance reasons. Except here we're not denormalizing data; we're "denormalizing" functionality.

Coming Up Next

In this chapter, we substantially enlarged the scope of CarServ, but it remains understandable because we can now think of it at a higher abstraction level as a collection of patterns. The overall number of concepts we need to hold in our heads is still manageable.

Admittedly, there's nothing in the Naked Objects approach that says where patterns have been applied or why. To help future developers honor the design decisions you make, you'll need to document their usage separately (see the sidebar on the next page). But at least we

---

9.   At the time of writing, the HTML viewer does not currently support the *process object* pattern.

Documenting the Usage of Patterns

When we apply a design pattern, the code represents the effect of applying the pattern; however, the pattern instance itself (the cause of the effect, if you like) has no direct representation in code. Future generations looking only at the code might not spot that the pattern was applied, so the design decision we took will be lost.

One option for documenting pattern instances is to represent the pattern in a class name. For example, a class named XxxComposite would presumably represent the *composite* pattern. However, this doesn't work if there are lots of participants in the pattern (it would be hard to determine the leaf objects in the *composite*). One could also argue we are polluting the *ubiquitous language* in choosing these names.

An alternative is to use humble Javadoc. And that is fine, except of course that (not being code) it may get ignored, either never read or never updated.

Another approach is to use a UML modeling tool that reverse engineers the code into UML class diagrams and then allows the patterns to be annotated over the top. TogetherJ was an early tool that did this (see *the book* (CH02) I coauthored from a few years ago), and there are similar tools around now that integrate with Eclipse and other IDEs. They still require the developer to load up the diagram to update it, though.

only have to look in the domain layer for them, not the other layers, and they will all work at similar levels of abstraction.

Remember that the patterns listed here aren't exhaustive. There are plenty of other patterns to experiment with that may help deepen your design, such as *composite*, *chain of responsibility*, and *state*. A pattern-rich model will be much easier to understand than one without.

Still, although from a business functionality standpoint CarServ has been extended substantially, from a technical viewpoint it is still rather naive. Even with patterns, we're still thinking of it as a single big lumpy domain model, and at some point it will get too big to fully comprehend. So in the next chapter, we're going to look at techniques to organize our domain model into smaller chunks. And that too will help deepen our design.

Exercises

Given I only sketched the implementation of the patterns, there are plenty of exercises to tackle in the main text of this chapter. Or if you want, just download the various versions of CarServ, and make sure you are happy with the resultant refactorings.

In the downloads, I've used simple Integers for all monetary amounts. If you want some revision, you could use replace this with the Money value types from the timeandmoney library.

For your own application, the exercise—you guessed it—is to refactor it by applying patterns. Perhaps you could ask a friend to think of some enhancements to your app and then try to implement one of their suggestions by applying one of the patterns listed here.

Finally, consider how you might document pattern instances in your code. In the sidebar on the facing page, there are some suggestions as to how you might do this.

Keeping the Model Maintainable

We human beings are remarkable machines, fantastically adept at higher-order processing such as pattern recognition. Yet remembering more digits than in the average phone number will be beyond the ability of most (me, at least).

Software development is a battle against complexity, and to win that battle, we need to keep the number of things we have to consider at any one time manageable. Your own applications will have tens or hundreds of classes and tens of thousands of lines of code. Heck, even CarServ has a couple dozen classes! Since we can't hope to fully comprehend a domain model made up of lots of little parts, there's only one thing we can do: break it up into larger chunks that can be understood *in their own right.*

Programming languages such as Java provide us with mechanisms to modularize our software: classes and interfaces, packages, JARs. But the question is, which *module*s should we create? This chapter is all about answering that question and chunking up or decoupling the elements within our domain model to keep the number of modules manageable. And in doing so, it will again help us to deepen our design.

In the previous chapter, we substantially extended the functionality of CarServ. Let's kick off this chapter (**chapter11-01**) with a review of its current structure; then we'll look at how to start decoupling it.

in context...

Module

Modules group related concepts together, reducing the number of things we need to think about at the same time.

In Java, *modules* are implemented as packages. Typically this means their subpackages as well, so we can also think of *modules* in their distributed form, as JARs, as Maven modules, or as OSGi bundles.

11.1 Analyzing the Structure of CarServ

In Figure 11.1, on the next page, we can see the domain classes of CarServ, with each of the refactorings from the previous chapters applied. As you can see, the diagram uses the familiar UML notation.[1]

Now there are twenty-one classes (count them!) plus repositories, values, and other supporting services. That's too many to remember, so we *are* going to need to do something before CarServ becomes too complex to handle. One thing we can do—and indeed have been doing—is to put our classes into packages, of which we have six. I've annotated the UML diagram with dotted lines to show where the package boundaries are. But is it an improvement?

In Figure 11.2, on the facing page, we see another visualization of the dependencies between classes and/or packages that might be less familiar, called a *dependency structure matrix* (DSM).[2] The cells in the matrix sum up the dependencies of the classes in the column package upon the classes in the row package. For example, payment has two dependencies on service, while service has seven dependencies on payment.

For domain models where there are no cyclic dependencies between packages, there will be numbers in the bottom-left diagonal only (the tool will reorder the columns and rows to make this so). As we can see,

---

1. Reverse engineered using Omondo's EclipseUML, previously mentioned
2. This visualization was created using Structure101, a commercial product from Headway Software, http://www.headwaysoftware.com.

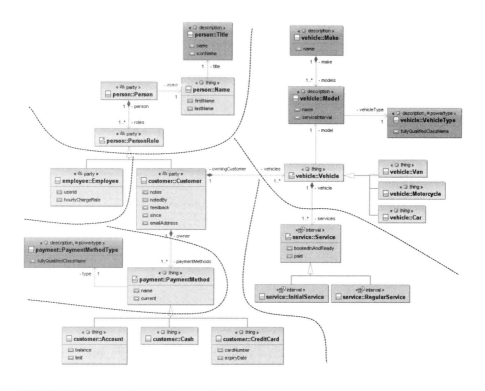

Figure 11.1: CARSERV CLASS DIAGRAM WITH PACKAGE BOUNDARIES

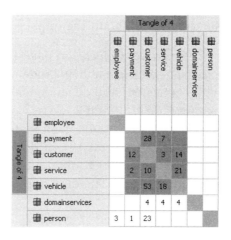

Figure 11.2: THE CARSERV DSM SHOWS CYCLIC DEPENDENCIES.

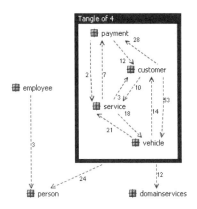

Figure 11.3: CarServ dependency diagram shows cycles.

though, that ain't the case here. That "tangle" indicates that there are four packages involved in a big cyclic dependency.

Why do we care? Well, that tangle means it's not possible for us to think about any one of those packages without having to think about the other three also; they're all interrelated. Any change on any class in those packages could potentially impact any of these other classes. The bigger the tangle, the more difficult the impact analysis.

Back in Section 9.2, *Factoring Out Objects*, on page 148, we used Robert Martin's *single responsibility principle* to help guide us. Most of his guidance relates to coupling, cohesion, and dependencies, at both the class level and the package level. The principle we're violating right now is his *acyclic dependencies principle* (ADP). This states that the dependency structure between packages must be a directed acyclic graph, allowing us to understand the depended-upon packages without reference to those that depend on them. The direction of the dependencies also gives us our layering.

In Figure 11.3, we see the same information as the DSM we saw in Figure 11.2, on the previous page, but this time represented as a dependency diagram. Again, we can see a bidirectional dependency between payment and service. There are seven dependencies from service to payment, but only two in the other direction.

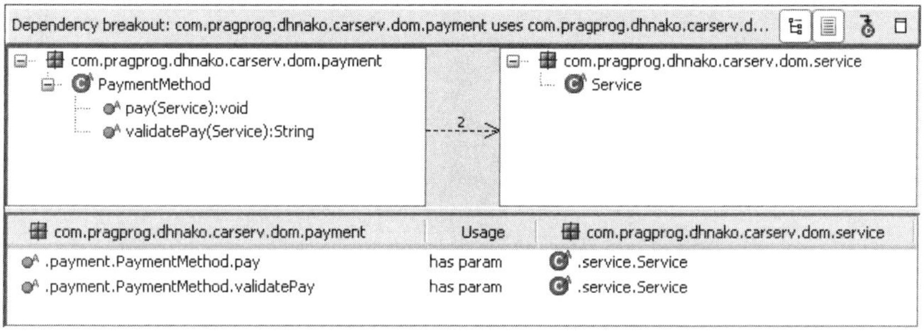

Figure 11.4: The payment package has dependencies on Service.

One way in which we might be able to remove dependencies is just by shifting responsibilities; let's see if we can do precisely that.

11.2 Decoupling by Moving Responsibilities

One of the oft-quoted mantras for good software design is that the modules should be "loosely coupled, highly cohesive." Conversely, if a responsibility is spread out (the module is not highly cohesive), then that will give us higher coupling (that is, more dependencies between modules). Bringing together related responsibilities should reduce dependencies.

We can see this in Figure 11.4, which is the drill-down for how the payment package depends on the service package.[3] The dependencies result from PaymentMethod being responsible for paying Services.

We can see this in the code, too, of course:

chapter11/PaymentMethod-pay.java
```
public abstract void pay(Service service);
public abstract String validatePay(Service service);
```

I suppose in a real system there would be a Javadoc to tell us what PaymentMethods are meant to do with Services, but we'll make do by looking at the actual implementations.

---

3. Again, these screenshots are taken from the analysis provided by Structure101.

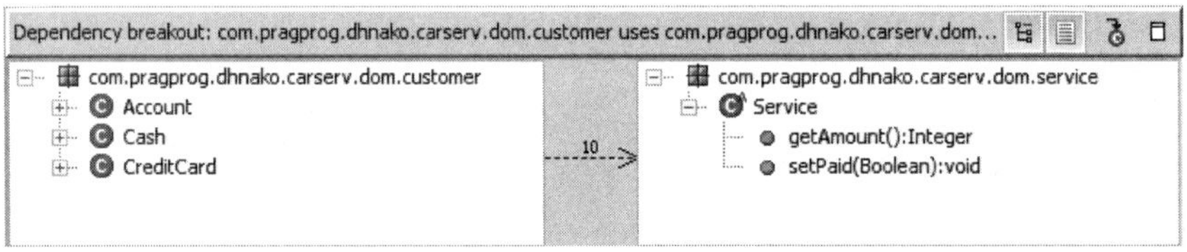

Figure 11.5: THE CUSTOMER PACKAGE HAS DEPENDENCIES ON SERVICE.

For example, the Account implementation is as follows:

`chapter11/Account-pay.java`

```java
@Override
public void pay(Service service) {
    warnUser("Put onto Account");
    setBalance(getBalance() + service.getAmount());
    service.setPaid(true);
}
@Override
public String validatePay(Service service) {
    int available = getLimit().intValue() - getBalance().intValue();
    return service.getAmount() > available?
        "Amount exceeds available credit": null;
}
```

There are two dependencies on Service: to read the amount to pay
(getAmount()) and then to mark the Service as paid (setPaid()). In fact,
all the classes implementing PaymentMethod are in the customer package, so we can use the drill-down, as shown in Figure 11.5, to confirm
these are the only dependencies.

Let's instead change the design so that pay() just accepts an amount
and returns a **boolean** to indicate whether it was paid. If so, then the
Service can mark itself as paid. Account is refactored to this:

`chapter11/Account-pay-refactored.java`

```java
@Override
public boolean pay(Integer amount) {
    warnUser("Put onto Account");
    setBalance(getBalance() + amount);
    return true;
}
@Override
public String validatePay(Integer amount) {
    int available = getLimit().intValue() - getBalance().intValue();
    return amount > available? "Amount exceeds available credit": null;
}
```

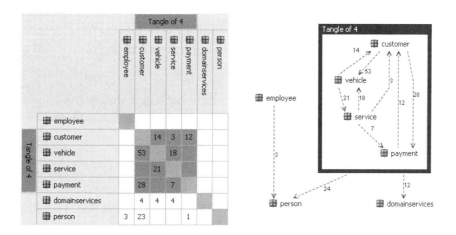

Figure 11.6: PACKAGE DEPENDENCIES AFTER MOVING RESPONSIBILITY

Similarly, Service's payUsing() action becomes the following:

`chapter11/Service-payUsing.java`

```java
public void payUsing(final PaymentMethod paymentMethod) {
    setPaid(paymentMethod.pay(getAmount()));
}
```

In Figure 11.6, we can see the updated dependency diagrams; the dependency from payment to service is gone (**chapter11-02**).

But there is only so much untangling we can do by moving responsibilities. And in fact, one might argue that our new design isn't as good as the previous one, because both objects (Service and PaymentMethod) need to agree to update their respective state, rather than just one object (the PaymentMethod) doing all the work.

To untangle our model further, we're going to have to apply another of Martin's principles, one that lets us modularize the software in pretty much any way we want.

11.3 Decoupling by Introducing Interfaces

The underlying reason that we have all these bidirectional dependencies between our packages is because the classes in our domain model violate the *interface segregation principle* (ISP). This states that a client object should not be dependent on interfaces that it does not use. In other words, the compile-time type that an object uses to reference its collaborators should only expose the behavior that the object will use, and nothing else.

If we consider more carefully exactly how each class uses the functionality of another class, then we'll be able to identify more precisely what these interfaces are. When we do this, two (good) things are going to happen:

- First, if we put those interfaces in the correct package, we'll be able to remove our cyclic dependencies. That is, it'll be possible to understand subsets of the domain model without having to consider the rest of the model.

- Second, we'll find that these interfaces represent some missing domain concepts; our design is going to deepen.

Identifying the roles that different classes play with respect to one another is key to decoupling the design. This is where Coad's yellows come in; it's the distinct lack of yellows in our design that's giving rise to all the coupling. What we want to ask is, "What role does object A play with respect to object B?"

Identifying Payable

Let's start off with the payment/service bidirectional dependency we were looking at in the previous section. We resolved it then by moving responsibilities, but the solution wasn't ideal. Let's rewind and try a different tack (**chapter11-01**).

Looking again at Figure 11.5, on page 198, we see that the only methods called on Service by the PaymentMethod implementations are getAmount() and setPaid(). What we could do is introduce a Payable interface (in the payment package, natch) and make Service implement this interface:

chapter11/Payable.java

```java
public interface Payable {
    public Integer getAmount();
    public void setPaid(final Boolean paid);
}
```

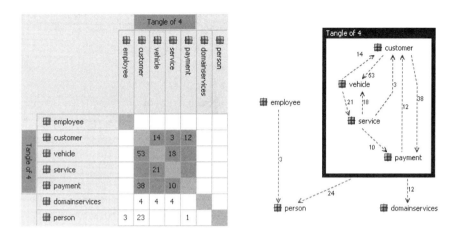

Figure 11.7: PACKAGE DEPENDENCIES AFTER INTRODUCING INTERFACE

The PaymentMethod (and its subclasses) then just uses Payable:

`chapter11/PaymentMethod-pay-refactored.java`

```
public abstract void pay(Payable payable);
public abstract String validatePay(Payable payable);
```

In Figure 11.7, we can see the updated dependencies.

Let's use interface segregation to remove a couple more dependencies.

Identifying PaymentMethodOwner

Looking at Figure 11.7, we can see that the service package has just three dependencies on customer. In Figure 11.8, on the following page, we can see the drill-down on these dependencies.

It looks like all that Service needs is a list of PaymentMethods. We are already committed to service depending on payment (Service is-a Payable), so let's remove the dependency on Customer using a Payment-MethodOwner interface:

1. Create PaymentMethodOwner in the payment package:

   `chapter11/PaymentMethodOwner.java`

   ```
   public interface PaymentMethodOwner {
       public List<PaymentMethod> getPaymentMethods();
   }
   ```
2. Make Customer implement this interface.

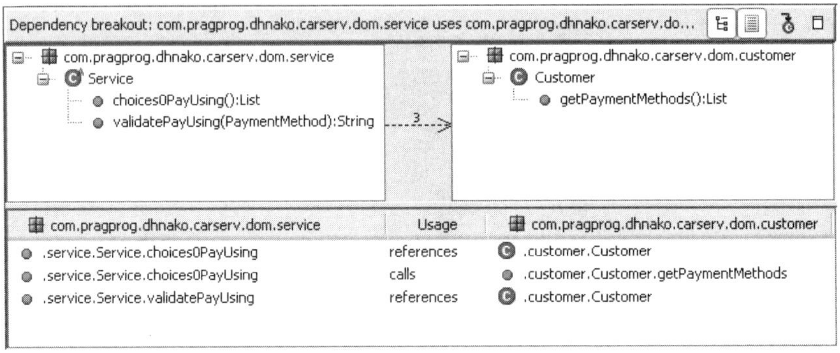

Figure 11.8: SERVICE DEPENDENCIES ON THE CUSTOMER PACKAGE

We now hit a problem, though. Service gets the Customer by asking its Vehicle for it. If instead the Service needs a PaymentMethodOwner, where does it get this from? Well, we've just made the Customer implement PaymentMethodOwner, so the Vehicle could just return its Customer property upcast as a PaymentMethodOwner. However, vehicle doesn't explicitly depend on payment, except transitively by way of customer. Getting rid of one dependency will mean adding another.

Still, we shouldn't be too downhearted, because it has given us some interesting questions to ask our domain experts. After all, just because a Vehicle is owned by a Customer, does it mean that that Customer should pay for all its Services? There's probably more than one car gifted to a newly qualified driver that is maintained by the parents.

For now, let's go with this design (so that the Service *does* gets its PaymentMethodOwner from its Vehicle) and simply make a note that things are a little muddy here. As we continue to decouple, we might be able to reach a deeper insight. Therefore:

1. In Vehicle, introduce a new derived property PaymentMethodOwner (that is, just the *get*ter method), returning the Vehicle's Customer:

```
chapter11/Vehicle-getPaymentMethodOwner.java
@Hidden
public PaymentMethodOwner getPaymentMethodOwner() {
    return getOwningCustomer();
}
```

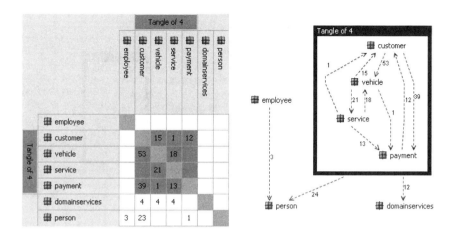

Figure 11.9: UPDATED SERVICE DEPENDENCIES ON THE CUSTOMER
PACKAGE

2. Update Service to use this new property in Vehicle (in the vali-
datePayUsing() and choices0PayUsing() supporting methods).

In Figure 11.9, we can see our progress so far. As we expected, we've
now gained a dependency from vehicle to payment, but we haven't quite
gotten rid of the dependency from service to customer.

Investigating further, that last remaining dependency is because of pay-
mentMethod.getOwner(), which returns a Customer. We originally introduced PaymentMethodOwner to be the owner of a collection of Payment-
Methods, but now (rather obviously in retrospect) this is of course a
bidirectional relationship: PaymentMethod's Owner ought to be a PaymentMethodOwner. Therefore:

1. Make PaymentMethod reference PaymentMethodOwner, adding any
required methods to the interface (Customer already implements
them, of course).

In Figure 11.10, on the following page, we see our final dependencies as
the result of this last refactoring. Wowee! That's a significant improvement.

This is good fun (we'll, I'm enjoying it, anyway). Let's just do one more.

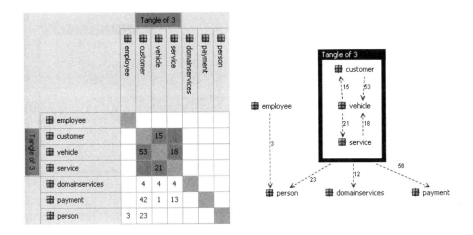

Figure 11.10: SERVICE DEPENDENCIES ON CUSTOMER REMOVED

Identifying VehicleOwner

If you don't have access to the analysis tools I've been using in this chapter, then an approach that works surprisingly well is to simply take the property or collection name and convert it into an interface. We saw this in the previous example with the PaymentMethod's Owner property, and there's another example, too—the Vehicle's OwningCustomer property.

Let's do a similar refactoring and make Customer implement a new VehicleOwner interface. With a bit of luck, the dependency counts will be lower:

1. Create a new VehicleOwner interface in the vehicle package.
2. Factor out methods relating to Vehicle from Customer into VehicleOwner, and make Customer implement this interface.
3. Make Vehicle reference VehicleOwner instead of (owning) Customer; also, rename the property from OwningCustomer to just Owner.

So far, so good, but the code won't quite compile. Remember Vehicle's getPaymentMethodOwner() method that we puzzled over before.

This now reads as follows:

`chapter11/Vehicle-getPaymentMethodOwner-puzzle.java`

```java
@Hidden
public PaymentMethodOwner getPaymentMethodOwner() {
    return getOwner();
}
```

Now we see much more clearly the issue we swept under the carpet a couple of sections ago: who's to say that the vehicle's owner is also the payment method owner? Of course, Customer happens to implement them both, but Vehicle certainly can't assume that.

For now, let's resolve the problem by saying that, yes, the vehicle owner will indeed be paying the bills. The code *is* the model, so let's say it through code:

`chapter11/VehicleOwner.java`

```java
public interface VehicleOwner extends PaymentMethodOwner {
    ...
}
```

This in turn simplifies Customer:

`chapter11/Customer.java`

```java
public class Customer extends PersonRole implements VehicleOwner {
    ...
}
```

And now our code compiles (***chapter11-03***). In Figure 11.11, on the next page, we can see the impact of this new interface on our decoupling efforts.

What's nice about these refactorings is that the interfaces can be introduced with very little risk. As we saw earlier, generally speaking extracting interface does not break existing code. In the one place where it did, it helped us to deepen the design.

Decoupling the model isn't just a game of removing dependencies, though; it also helps make implicit concepts explicit. In our *ubiquitous language*, we can now talk about payment method owners and vehicle owners and talk about the relationship between the two. When all we had was Customer, that was much harder to do. Evans talks about the *conceptual contours* of a domain model; to extend that metaphor, the interfaces we introduce define the hills and valleys that make up the contours.

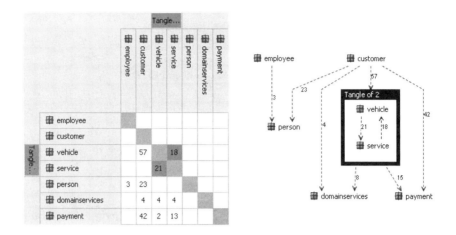

Figure 11.11: VEHICLEOWNER REMOVES FURTHER DEPENDENCIES.

So far in this chapter we've been breaking dependencies in whichever direction has seemed most natural. But what if the dependencies must flow in a certain direction? For example, we might have some existing code that we want to reuse, or indeed we might want to create domain models that could be reused in the future. It's time to take a somewhat more architectural approach and talk about layering.

11.4 Layering Modules

In our CarServ case study, there are still two packages in a bidirectional relationship, vehicle and service. Let's resolve the issue with an architect's hat on.

In Figure 11.12, on the facing page, we see an alternative representation of CarServ's package dependencies, with packages shown in layers. The packages in each layer depend on the layers below; the heavy dotted lines indicate dependencies that violate the layering.

There are three options. In option (A), we take the easiest approach and declare that vehicle and service are so interrelated that we may as well combine them into a single package. In this case, those packages will probably become subpackages of a new parent package. That's easy to do and sometimes the right thing to do, but it's not right for us in this case.

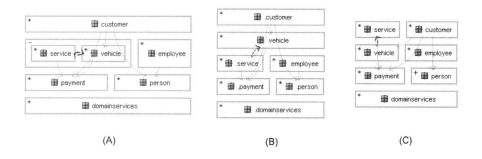

Figure 11.12: CarServ layering options

Options (B) and (C) show two further layerings. In (B), vehicle depends on service, while in (C), service depends on vehicle; in each case, the lower package is the one that has no knowledge with respect to the upper. If we already have (or wanted to develop) a generic work management model, then we could think of Services as work. In this case, (B) might best reflect our architecture, with Vehicles implementing an interface in the service package but service itself being unaware of Vehicles. On the other hand, if we already have a rich asset management model, with Vehicles being one particular type of asset, then (C) is better (with Vehicles unaware that they can be serviced).

Whichever we go with, we should follow another of Martin's principles: the *stable dependencies principle* (SDP). This says that a package should only depend on those packages that are more stable than it is. There's no point trying to reuse code that is forever changing.

If we decide on option (B) and make vehicle depend on service (and remove the dependency from Service to Vehicle), then we should again be able to use the technique of the previous section and decouple by having Service reference a Serviceable interface (instead of referencing Vehicle directly). Instead, though, let's go with the alternative option (C) and make service depend on vehicle; doing so will allow us to explore another technique for decoupling.

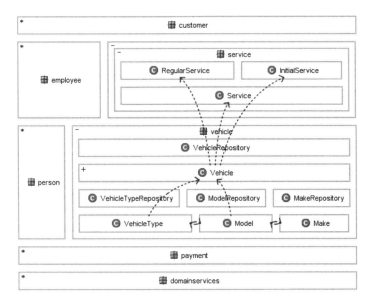

Figure 11.13: VEHICLE DEPENDENCIES ON SERVICE

11.5 Decoupling by Splitting Classes

In Figure 11.13, we can see the dependencies for option (C) at the class level (with some irrelevant classes excluded). As we can see, the main culprit is Vehicle.

Again, the drill-down, as shown in Figure 11.14, on the facing page, gives us the detail; Vehicle holds a collection of Services and is responsible for creating the RegularService and InitialService subtypes.

To get the architectural layering we desire, we are going to have to split Vehicle into two and move all its knowledge about Services into a ServiceableVehicle subclass, which then moves into the service package.

The following are the steps to make this refactoring:

1. Move Vehicle and all of its subclasses from vehicle into service, and rename it to ServiceableVehicle (we'll extract the Vehicle superclass back out in a minute).

2. Similarly, move VehicleRepository, rename it to ServiceableVehicle-Repository (plus its implementations), and update nakedobjects. properties.

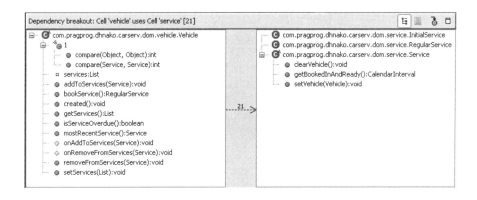

Figure 11.14: DRILL-DOWN OF VEHICLE'S DEPENDENCIES ON SERVICE

3. Now use an IDE to extract Vehicle as a superclass of ServiceableVehicle. Include everything except the Services collection, the book-
Service() action, the PaymentMethodOwner (derived) property, the
created() life-cycle method, the injected CalendarService, and the
mostRecentService() and isServiceOverdue() helpers.

4. Similarly, use an IDE to extract VehicleRepository back out from ServiceableVehicleRepository and again the implementations. Include
everything except the findVehiclesWithoutRecentService() action.

When I used Eclipse to do these refactorings, it left a number of references to ServiceableVehicle rather than Vehicle. So, go through Customer (its Vehicles collection), CustomerTakeOn, Model, VehicleType, and
anything else that references ServiceableVehicle, and use Vehicle if
possible.

There's one further quick refactoring I'd like to do, if you'll indulge me,
and then we'll check our progress.

11.6 Introducing an Application Package

The CustomerTakeOn class doesn't really have anything to do with the
customer domain; instead, it is a *process object* introduced for the purposes of this application. This should be reflected in the package structure, with a new application package. (In fact, there's even an argument
for moving this into a different Maven module/Eclipse project, but we'll
make do with a new package.)

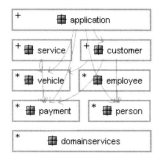

Figure 11.15: THE FINAL ARCHITECTURE HAS NO LAYERING VIOLATIONS.

However, if we just move CustomerTakeOn out into its own application package, we'll end up with a bidirectional dependency because we currently use CustomerRepository to create CustomerTakeOns. So, we should split out CustomerRepository, similar to the way in which we split VehicleRepository.

The other thing that the application package should hold is any concrete classes specific to this application. So, rather than Car, Van, and Motorcycle living in the service package, we could move them instead to the application package. One might also move the PaymentMethod subtypes here too.

Let's make these refactorings:

1. Create the new application package.
2. Move CustomerTakeOn into the application package.
3. Move CustomerRepository into the application package, and rename to CustomerApplicationRepository. Then extract back out the CustomerRepository interface. Do the same with the implementations, and update nakedobjects.properties.

And now (drumroll, maestro) for the moment of truth. In Figure 11.15, we can see the refactored CarServ architecture layers. Or, if you prefer, in Figure 11.16, on the facing page, we can see the DSM and dependency diagram. Look, Ma! No cyclic dependencies!

And of course, we can also view CarServ as a UML class diagram, as shown in Figure 11.17, on the next page. Note all those new interfaces we've added are the yellows ("role" stereotype); I promised we'd get some into the model eventually (*chapter11-04*).

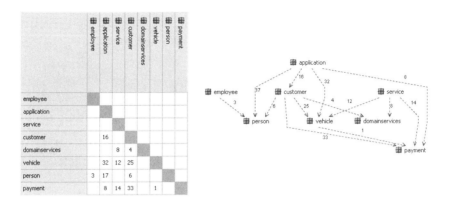

Figure 11.16: THE FINAL DSM SHOWS NO TANGLES.

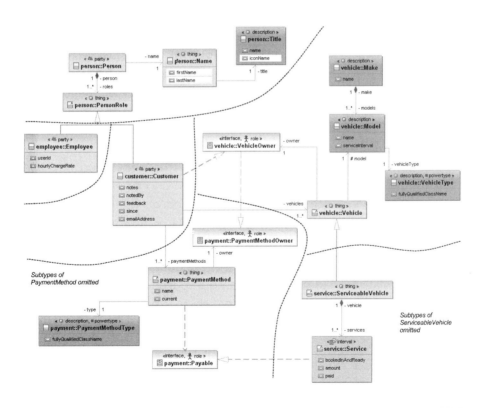

Figure 11.17: THE REFACTORED CARSERV CLASS DIAGRAM HAS ROLES.

It's good to know that by applying some techniques and principles we can decouple pretty much any tangled mess... but it'd be even better not to get into a tangle in the first place! Let's see how.

11.7 An Application Architecture Blueprint

Let's just recap the techniques we've applied in the preceding sections of this chapter:

- Bundle classes with similar responsibilities into packages (see Vehicle, Make, and Model).
- Consider moving responsibilities to split out bidirectional dependencies (see payment and service).
- Use interfaces to decouple relationships (see Vehicle and VehicleOwner).
- Split different responsibilities across super/subclasses, in different packages (see Vehicle and ServiceableVehicle).
- Use an application package as the highest-level package, and put *process object*s there (see CustomerTakeOn).
- Use higher-level packages (if necessary, the application package) for the concrete classes, binding together a set of responsibilities through the interfaces they implement. For example, Customer implements VehicleOwner and PaymentMethodOwner; Van is a ServiceableVehicle.
- Use higher-level packages (if necessary the application package) to hold factory implementations (see ServiceableVehicleRepository). Any factory implementations need to be at the same level (or higher) as the concrete classes that they instantiate.

Another way to think about decoupling is in terms of "slicing" the design. As in Figure 11.15, on page 210, the domain model slices horizontally into layered *subdomains*, with application sitting on top of customer and service, both sitting on top of vehicle, and so on.

As we go down the layers, the *subdomains* are more likely to become abstract. This is Martin's *stable abstractions principle* (SAP). In CarServ, we can indeed see this: customer, near the top, is completely concrete, whereas payment, near the bottom, defines two interfaces and an **abstract** class. Sometimes too there is a base on which everything else rests, an *abstract base*. CarServ doesn't yet have one of its own, though we could perhaps argue that the AbstractDomainObject (from the Naked Objects applib) is in effect performing this role.

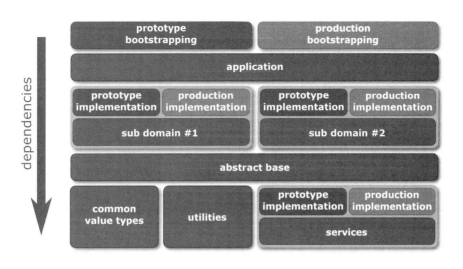

Figure 11.18: AN APPLICATION ARCHITECTURE BLUEPRINT

Our domain model may also slice vertically into a number of *subdomain*s that are peers of each other and have no dependencies. So, again in CarServ, we can see that service and customer are independent *subdomain*s and so are person and payment.

Using these techniques we've decoupled CarServ using a whole bunch of bottom-up refactorings. That's OK, of course; it's just a learning example. But if we were doing this "for real," we should recognize from the outset that we want a decoupled domain model and plan for it accordingly. In Figure 11.18, we can see one way to structure a domain application.

In the diagram, you'll see that I've identified one of these *subdomain*s as being the *core domain*. The *subdomain*s are unlikely to be of equal importance to the business; we should be focusing our efforts on the core—the stuff whose correct design is a make-or-break decision for the business. Although it might sound vaguely irresponsible, we should consciously devote less effort to the *subdomain*s that fall outside this *core domain*. In the case of CarServ, I'd identify the customer and service packages as representing the *core domain*; it's the domain classes in these packages that provide the most value to the business.

Often the supporting *subdomain*s are generic, such as asset management or human resources. In these cases, we may choose to use an

> ### DDD in Context: Core Domains and Generic Subdomains
>
> The *core domain* is the heart of the system, containing the most valuable and specialized concepts. It should consist of a single module or a small number of modules.
>
> The supporting *subdomains* provide additional functionality that is very often generic and whose precise analysis and implementation is not critical to the overall success of the domain application. These should be separated from the *core domain* as different modules. Some *generic subdomains* may be implemented using third-party systems, linked through domain services.

external system to implement the functionality. The classes in these *generic subdomains* may then act as proxies to these external systems and interact using injected domain services (as described in Chapter 8, *Isolating Infrastructure Services*, on page 125).

The blueprint diagram also shows infrastructure/domain services as well as value types and utilities. Some of these may be scoped with the *subdomains*, but it's possible that some (especially infrastructure services such as EmailService) will have enterprise-wide applicability. The utilities package meanwhile is just a place to put all those silly little helper classes such as StringUtils.

You'll notice also that the architecture provides for different implementations of the repositories (scoped to each *subdomain*) and of the services. Thus far, we've only ever used in-memory repository implementations suitable for prototyping. When we get to integrating for production, we'll need to replace them with real implementations that query the database using Hibernate or what have you. But more on that in Chapter 16, *Integrating with the Database*, on page 287.

To summarize:

- Decide what's core and what's not. Spend more time on the *core domain*, and spend less on the supporting *subdomains*.

- For the supporting *subdomains*, determine whether it is generic.

  If so, see whether it can be implemented using existing third-party libraries or by interfacing to an external system. (There's more on this topic in Chapter 17, *Integrating Within the Enterprise*, on page 311, by the way.)

- Decide on the layering of your domains, using the *stable abstractions principle* to guide you.

I reckon that's a good point to bring this chapter to a close.

Coming Up Next

Although there's nothing in domain-driven design that requires your domain models to be implemented using object-oriented paradigms, most DDD models will also be OO. And that certainly is the case if using Naked Objects.

In the past few chapters, we've seen a number of idioms, patterns, principles, and techniques that together have substantially extended the business functionality of CarServ while ensuring it remains maintainable from a technical standpoint. Can I suggest that (if you aren't already familiar with them) they are good ones to master initially? However, once you get beyond them, do start to mine the rich seam of OO literature to help you build better domain models.

In the next and final chapter of the second part of the book, we're going to be looking at a couple of approaches for testing, focusing mostly on scenario testing.

Exercises

You want some exercises? Really? Well, OK, if you insist.

For CarServ, rework the service/vehicle dependency that we resolved in Section 11.5, *Decoupling by Splitting Classes*, on page 208, but instead introduce a Serviceable interface so that vehicle depends on service. And as a further exercise, why not have a go at moving the application package out of the dom project and into its own carserv-app project?

And then, of course, you need to decouple your own application. Unless you've been reading the book backward (!) and thought about all this up front, your application is quite possibly a tangle of bidirectional dependencies, just as CarServ was. See whether you can tease it apart, thinking about the layering as you go.

Scenario Testing

Software applications are among the most complex things that human beings create. A suspension bridge is constructed from thousands of cables and box sections, but at least those components are standardized and the mathematics that say the thing won't fall down have been known for more than hundreds of years.

A software program in contrast will have at least thousands and possibly millions of parts, but with software each of those parts is different. Moreover, there isn't any big calculation that you can perform to ensure that all those variables, loops, if statements, and polymorphic methods interact correctly. . . there just isn't.

Thus far in the book we've been flat-out focused on developing our domain model but paid scant regard as to whether the code we're writing really works as expected. So in this chapter, we're going to redress the balance using two testing techniques that work at different levels of granularity. We'll start off with developer (or unit) tests that work down at the method level. They are easy to write, give us good test coverage, and are great for picking up silly little bugs in our code.

However, developer tests aren't something you could show to a business domain expert to ask, "Does this test establish the behavior we want?" So, we'll spend a larger portion of the chapter writing scenario tests that exercise a bunch of objects involved in a scenario. These second set of tests will be much more accessible to a nontechnical audience. . . to the extent that they could even write them themselves!

Let's kick off this chapter with those developer tests. As usual, we'll be using CarServ to plot our path.

12.1 Writing Developer Tests

We use developer tests to verify the functionality of a single unit of code, which generally means a method. There's no need to instantiate a whole graph of domain objects and wire them together; we simply instantiate the domain object we want to test and verify it behaves as we want.

In "classic" *test-driven development* (TDD), we write the tests first and use them to define the signatures of the methods and the responsibilities of those methods. We can do this with a Naked Objects–developed domain model too; we just must bear in mind the naming conventions of the programming model.

Our Developer Testing Toolkit

The testing toolkit we're going to be use—and already added to the Maven pom.xml files for CarServ (***chapter12-01***)—consists of JUnit 4.*x*, JMock 2.*x*, and Hamcrest 1.*x*.[1] These are all well-respected and established testing toolkits: JUnit is the testing framework proper, JMock provides the ability to write mocks for each of collaborators of the object under test, and Hamcrest is a predicates library that we use to write both mock expectations (that is, interactions that should occur between the object and its collaborators) and test assertions (changes in state of the object under test).[2]

To speed us up, there are some additional templates. Use Windows > Preferences > Java > Editor > Templates, and browse to the $NO_HOME/resources/ide/eclipse/templates directory. Then import junit4-templates.xml and jmock2-templates.xml. The first provides a bunch of templates prefixed with *ju*, and the second provides templates prefixed with *jm*. We're now set to write some tests.

Developer Tests Using Given/When/Then

Let's make this concrete by writing a test for some existing functionality, the Customer's deleteVehicle() action, and its supporting methods.

---

1. JUnit is hosted at http://junit.org, JMock at http://jmock.org, and Hamcrest at http://code.google.com/p/hamcrest/.
2. There is still plenty of innovation going on in testing frameworks. For example, a more recent mocking library is Mockito (hosted at http://mockito.org/), which some prefer over JMock. You should have no difficulty using Mockito with Naked Objects.

chapter12/Customer-deleteVehicle.java

```
public void deleteVehicle( final Vehicle vehicle ) {
    vehicle.delete();
}
public String validateDeleteVehicle( final Vehicle vehicle) {
    return getVehicles().contains(vehicle)?
            null: "Customer does not own this vehicle";
}
public List<Vehicle> choicesODeleteVehicle() {
    return getVehicles();
}
public Vehicle defaultODeleteVehicle() {
    return getVehicles().size() == 1? getVehicles().get(0): null;
}
public String disableDeleteVehicle() {
    return doesntOwnAnyVehicles()? "No vehicles to delete": null;
}
```

To pick up on just three of these methods, let's test (in the order that the framework would call them):

- disableDeleteVehicle(): We can attempt to delete a Vehicle if the Customer owns any, otherwise not.

- validateDeleteVehicle(): It is valid (returns **null**) if the Customer owns the Vehicle; otherwise, it's not valid (non-**null**).

- deleteVehicle(): The Customer should ask the Vehicle (a collaborator) to delete itself.

So, in the carserv-dom project, use File > New > Source Folder to create a new src/test/java directory; this is Maven's standard location for tests. Then let's write our first test for the disableDeleteVehicle() method (use the jubefore, jutest, and juassert templates to save some keystrokes):

chapter12/GivenCustomerWithNoVehiclesTest.java

```
public class GivenCustomerWithNoVehiclesTest {
    private Customer customer;
    @Before
    public void setUp() throws Exception {
        customer = new Customer();
    }
    @Test
    public void whenAttemptToDeleteVehicleThenShouldBeDisabled()
            throws Exception {
        assertThat(customer.disableDeleteVehicle(), is(nullValue()));
    }
}
```

Here I'm using the *given/when/then* style of test writing, where the "given" tells us the state of objects under test, the "when" tells us what happens in the test, and the "then" tells us what the result should be.[3] Translating this to JUnit, the "given" is the test name, and the @BeforesetUp() method (which is run before each of the tests) specifies this initial state. The "when" and the "then" combine to give us the test method name.

Let's write a similar test for the validateDeleteVehicle() method:

```
chapter12/GivenCustomerWithSomeVehiclesTest.java
```
```java
@RunWith(JMock.class)
public class GivenCustomerWithSomeVehiclesTest {
    private Mockery context = new JUnit4Mockery();
    private Vehicle mockOwnedVehicle, mockOtherVehicle;
    private Customer customer;
    @Before
    public void setUp() throws Exception {
        customer = new Customer();
        mockOwnedVehicle = context.mock(Vehicle.class, "owned");
        mockOtherVehicle = context.mock(Vehicle.class, "other");
        customer.getVehicles().add(mockOwnedVehicle);
    }
    @Test
    public void
    whenAttemptToDeleteVehicleNotOwnedByCustomerThenShouldBeInvalid()
            throws Exception {
        assertThat(
            customer.validateDeleteVehicle(mockOtherVehicle),
            is(not(nullValue())));
    }
    @Test
    public void
    whenAttemptToDeleteVehicleOwnedByCustomerThenShouldBeValid()
            throws Exception {
        assertThat(
            customer.validateDeleteVehicle(mockOwnedVehicle),
            is(nullValue()));
    }
}
```

We have this in a new test class because it has a different "given": the method would only ever be called for Customers that have Vehicles. The @BeforesetUp() method again sets up the state of this given.

---

3. Given/when/then was, I believe, first described by Dan North in his blog article, http://dannorth.net/introducing-bdd.

We're also now using JMock to create mock Vehicles; the context field acts as JMock's mock factory. We could have created concrete instances such as Car, I suppose, but written this way, the test emphasizes that the logic being tested applies to any type of Vehicle. Also, because we haven't written any expectations for the mocks, the test implicitly says that we aren't expecting any method calls on Vehicle itself. Note that we're using JMock's test runner (the @RunWith annotation); this is what validates the mocks' expectations for us. Again, if you're typing the previous, use the jmmock, jmcontext, and jmrunwith templates.

To test the last method, deleteVehicle(), we can use the same given, so it's just a new test method in the same class. If Customer interacted with Vehicle through an interface (as many of the domain objects do), then we would mock out that interface. However, in this particular case, Customer actually references the class, Vehicle. Because we want to define expectations on this Vehicle class, we need to change the way we create JMock's context:

`chapter12/GivenCustomerWithSomeVehiclesTest-v2.java`

```java
private Mockery context = new JUnit4Mockery() {{
    setImposteriser(ClassImposteriser.INSTANCE);
}};
```

The test itself is where those expectations appear:

`chapter12/GivenCustomerWithSomeVehiclesTest-v2.java`

```java
@Test
public void
whenDeleteVehicleThenShouldAskVehicleToDeleteItself()
        throws Exception {
    context.checking(new Expectations() {{
        one(mockOwnedVehicle).delete();
    }});
    customer.deleteVehicle(mockOwnedVehicle);
}
```

This says that we expect the method to work by calling the Vehicle object with the specified method. This is really quite a specific assertion about the design: in effect we're explaining the way in which we've distributed responsibilities.

We shouldn't only write developer tests for *entity objects* such as Customer, though.

Other Developer Tests

In addition to testing *entity object*s (**chapter12-02**), we should also write developer tests for the following:

- *Value type*s: In particular, make sure you test equals() and hash-Code() to ensure that they work correctly. Many of them will implement Comparable too, which should also be tested.

- Value semantics providers: As we learned in Chapter 7, *Using Value Types*, on page 109, we need to write implementations of ValueSemanticProviders so that Naked Objects can interact with our *value type*s. These need tests.

- *Specification*s: Earlier, in Chapter 6, *Implementing Business Rules*, on page 91, we learned how to use the @MustSatisfy annotation as a way of declaratively specifying business rules implemented by *specification* objects. These *specification*s are easy to test in isolation.

- Domain object interactions with services: We provide a mock for each injected service and then use an expectation to ensure that the domain object calls the service with the correct arguments.

- *Service* implementations themselves: We should make sure that the "real" services that we inject also work as expected. Note that this includes repositories.

You should find that the JUnit/JMock/Hamcrest toolkit is sufficient for all of these tests.

Is it worth the effort, though? Well, TDD is actually about more than just ensuring that there are no bugs in the code; it also helps us drive out the internal design. In the sidebar on page 155, we noted that a domain object does not need to become bloated and implement all its behavior itself; it may well have inner workings that are not otherwise visible to the end user. We can use TDD to help drive out the design of such helper objects.

Applying TDD also gives us a regression test suite, which in turn allows us to experiment with refactorings without fear of breaking the application. I think of refactorings as just-in-time design, so this is a key enabler to adopting agile development practices. Developer tests also act as documentation to explain the code both back to ourselves and other developers.

This isn't a book on TDD, but there are plenty of good books out there that tackle the topic more thoroughly than I have the space to do. One I would heartily recommend is Michael Feathers' *Working Effectively with Legacy Code* [Fea04]. Please don't be put off by that horrid word *legacy* as I nearly was!

But if you are already "test-obsessed," then as we've seen, there's nothing about a Naked Objects–developed domain model that is incompatible with writing small, tightly focused tests.

Still, looking at these developer tests, we definitely wouldn't want to show them to our average nontechnical domain expert because they are at a level of detail that will make little sense. They also provide very little context (we just instantiate the domain object and set it up however we want), so a domain expert would find them hard to understand for this reason too.

Instead, we need another higher level of testing that will be understandable by domain experts and developers alike, that provides an explicit business context for the test, that can be written in a nontechnical format, and that is expressed in terms of the *ubiquitous language*.

These higher-level tests are scenario tests. Using them, we should, with our domain experts, be able to agree not only on what the model *is* but also on what the model *does*. Let's see how.

12.2 Scenario Testing Using FitNesse

Naked Objects supports scenario testing by integrating with FitNesse, a popular open source testing framework where the tests are written as tables within a wiki.[4] Built upon the earlier Fit framework, FitNesse's objective is to allow nontechnical business users—the domain experts— to specify the requirements of the application in a natural way; the table structure is really there to separate out the nouns from the verbs. The developers on the team (that is, us) then relate these tests to the functionality being tested in the application.

The trick that FitNesse has up its sleeve is that not only can it execute these tests, but it also shows the output of the tests by annotating the cells of the original acceptance tests. Green means pass, red is fail, and yellow is an unexpected error. This creates the feedback loop we want.

---

4. FitNesse's home page is http://fitnesse.org.

Of course, it needn't be just the domain experts who write tests. One of FitNesse's goals is to increase collaboration between the business people and the technical people in the team. Requirements might start out being jotted down at a high level by the business, with only a sketch of what its acceptance tests might look like, perhaps even just as prose. As the implementation progresses, the acceptance tests act as a common ground for the team to flesh out the requirements by formalizing the acceptance tests into tables. Indeed, Rick Mugridge and Ward Cunningham, the originators of Fit and FitNesse, describe Fit tests as a "natural way to help develop the *ubiquitous language*" (see *Fit for Developing Software* [MC05]).

Writing tests in a wiki also makes the test writing very quick. As often as not, a test will fail not because the code is at fault, but because there is an error in the test itself. Avoiding the complete compile/deploy cycle to fix these errors substantially speeds up development.

To allow FitNesse to do its magic, we write what are called *fixtures*. Don't think of these as quite the same thing as the Naked Objects fixtures we met in Chapter 4, *Rapid Prototyping*, on page 63, because they have a somewhat larger responsibility. In common with Naked Objects' own fixtures, FitNesse's fixtures set up initial state prior to a test. But they also drive the application itself, representing the interactions by the end user (or any other actor, for that matter). To distinguish between the two, I'll use the term *table fixtures* to represent FitNesse's fixtures and *programmatic fixtures* to represent the Naked Objects variety.

If we were using FitNesse to test a "conventional" application, then at least some part of the development effort would go into designing the table structure and implementing the table fixtures to drive the underlying application. I have good news! Using Naked Objects, these table fixtures are fully generic, so no additional table fixtures are required. Using CarServ as usual, let's see how.

12.3 Getting Ready to Write Scenario Tests

Naked Objects' support for FitNesse is actually provided by a sister open source project, namely, *Tested Objects*, under the same license as Naked Objects itself.[5] It also bundles FitNesse, so there's no need to install FitNesse first.

---

5. Tested Objects and a number of other sister projects are collectively all referenced from http://www.starobjects.org. The code itself is hosted on SourceForge.

Figure 12.1: THE CARSERV-FITNESSE PROJECT

The Tested Objects sister project provides a Maven archetype that generates a new Maven submodule, which in turn sets up the FitNesse software and contains an initial FitNesse wiki to hold the tests. By default, some sample tests are generated to exercise the demo claims application that we used in Chapter 1, *Getting Started*, on page 3. If you want to try this archetype, see the Tested Objects documentation.

We're going to pick up the story with a version of CarServ that has already had this archetype run (**chapter12-03**) and contains a new subproject called carserv-fitnesse (see Figure 12.1). This project:

- Contains the FitNesse wiki pages; this is the FitNesseRoot directory highlighted in the screenshot

- Runs the FitNesse wiki server from Eclipse (the .launch file)

- Runs our FitNesse tests from a JUnit harness (the InteractionFixtureTest class)

To get us started, I've already done some of the initial legwork for our tests, including removing the example tests that were generated by the archetype for the demo claims application. Let's get FitNesse started, and then we'll walk through what's been done and what's still to do.

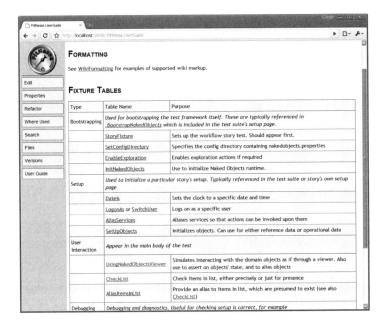

Figure 12.2: TESTED OBJECTS' FITNESSE USER GUIDE

Starting FitNesse

Navigate to the ide/eclipse/launch directory in the fitnesse project, and then right-click Run As to start the fitnesse-wiki-server.launch launch configuration. Point your favorite web browser at http://localhost:9090, and you should see the FitNesse front page.

As the front page tells us, if we want FitNesse to run our tests, then we need to build the CarServ application using mvn clean install in the root (carserv) directory. FitNesse runs our tests by spawning a test runner as a separate Java process, and this test runner needs its classpath configured correctly to pick up both the domain application classes and Naked Objects framework itself. The archetype does this for us by preconfiguring FitNesse to point to a target/dependency directory and using the Maven dependency plug-in to copy over all the JARs.

Note that you'll need to repeat running mvn clean install whenever you make a change to the application code and want to retest through Fit-Nesse. OK, we're now ready to explore the main content.

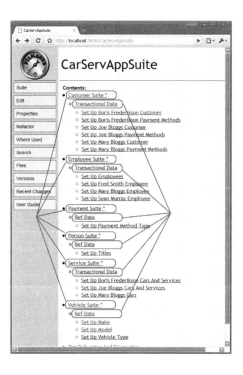

Figure 12.3: *CarServAppSuite* TEST HIERARCHY

The User Guide

From the front page, click through to the *.FitNesse.UserGuide* link (or click the button on the left side). This will take you to the built-in user guide (generated by the Tested Objects archetype), which lists the various types of table fixtures that we can use to write tests.[6] You can see this in Figure 12.2, on the facing page.

Take a look around; when done, return to the *FrontPage* (click the FitNesse logo on the top left).

Exploring the Test Suite Hierarchy

From the front page, click through to the *CarServAppSuite*, as shown in Figure 12.3. This lists a series of test suites, in hierarchical order.

---

6. Note that FitNesse's own user guide has been pruned from this wiki; if you want to learn more about what FitNesse itself can do, see the online user guide at http://fitnesse. org/FitNesse.UserGuide.

CarServAppSuite. VehicleSuite. RefData.

SetUpModel

set up objects	com.pragprog.dhnako.carserv.dom.vehicle.Model			
Name	Vehicle Type	Service Interval	Make	alias as
Focus	carVehicleType	12	fordMake	fordFocusModel
Mustang	carVehicleType	3	fordMake	fordMustangModel
Corolla	carVehicleType	9	toyotaMake	toyotaCorollaModel
Yaris	carVehicleType	18	toyotaMake	toyotaYarisModel
Civic	carVehicleType	12	hondaMake	hondaCivicModel
Ranger	vanVehicleType	9	fordMake	fordRangerModel
Transit	vanVehicleType	6	fordMake	fordTransitModel
Hiace	vanVehicleType	9	toyotaMake	toyotaHiaceModel
Varadero	motorcycleVehicleType	12	hondaMake	hondaVaraderoModel
Shadow	motorcycleVehicleType	12	hondaMake	hondaShadowModel
VFR800	motorcycleVehicleType	12	hondaMake	hondaVFR800Model
Tenere	motorcycleVehicleType	12	yamahaMake	yamahaTenereModel
FZ1 Fazer	motorcycleVehicleType	12	yamahaMake	yamahaFZ1FazerModel

Figure 12.4: *SetUpModel* SETUP PAGE

This is where I've done some work already:

- The *CarServAppSuite* is the main container for all the tests. As we can see, it breaks down into a series of subsuites, broadly corresponding to the main packages of the application.

  These pages are for the most part empty; the tree is generated automatically by FitNesse (using its **!contents** directive).

- Within each subsuite there is a *Ref Data* suite and/or a *Transactional Data* suite, which in turn contain "SetUpXxx" pages for setting up a test scenario. More on these in a moment.

In Chapter 4, *Rapid Prototyping*, on page 63, we learned how to write programmatic fixtures to set up the object, date, and session; using these, we could run a prototype with some representative sample objects. In FitNesse, we need to do the exact same thing; only now it is done using the setup pages mentioned earlier. I've already completed these pages in the download, but rather than take them for granted, we should look at them in more detail.

The SetUp Fixtures

Our FitNesse tests—like our prototypes and for that matter our JUnit tests—need a sample set of objects to work on. Like everything in Fit-Nesse, these are set up using table fixtures.

Why not just use the same programmatic fixtures that we've used thus far? Well, we want to be able to write tests that are completely self-contained and understandable to a (potentially nontechnical) domain expert. And to do that, the domain expert must be able to understand the initial state of the system in order to determine the expected results. Programmatic fixtures aren't really suitable for this task, so instead we put the same information in table fixtures.

For example, in *SetUpModel* (in the *VehicleSuite.RefData* suite), we use the set up object table fixture to set up instances of the Model domain class, as shown in Figure 12.4, on the preceding page. This page and the other two in the same suite correspond broadly to the MakesAnd-ModelsFixture programmatic fixture we've used elsewhere. Notice also the "alias as" column; this gives us a name to reference the objects in the tests themselves.

Similarly, the *SetUpJoeBloggsCustomer* page (in the *CustomerSuite.TransactionalData* suite) sets up (and aliases) a Customer object, equivalent to the JoeBloggsCustomerFixture programmatic fixture, as shown in Figure 12.5, on the following page. You might notice that the transactional objects tend to be set up using the using naked objects viewer for set up table fixture (rather than the set up object fixture); we'll discuss this in Section 12.5, *Hints and Tips*, on page 236.

In addition to the programmatic fixtures for setting up objects, we also have fixtures to set up the date and the current user. These also have setup pages, for example *DateIs9July2008* (which uses the date is table fixture) and *LogonAsFsmith* (which, no surprise, uses the logon as table fixture). You'll see these linked from the front page.

Now that we're acquainted with the test set ups, let's get to it and write some scenario tests.

12.4 Writing Scenario Tests

To illustrate scenario tests, we'll rewrite the tests relating to deleting vehicles, but this time in such a way that the behavior we're establishing can be verified by a nontechnical domain expert.

CarServAppSuite. CustomerSuite. TransactionalData.

SetUpJoeBloggsCustomer

PERSON & CUSTOMER ROLE

using naked objects viewer for set up				
on object	alias as	perform	using member	with arguments
customers	joeBloggsPerson	invoke action	new customer	
joeBloggsPerson	joeBloggsName	get property	name	
joeBloggsName		set property	title	mrTitle
			last name	Bloggs
			first name	Joe
joeBloggsPerson		save		

using naked objects viewer for set up			
on object	alias as	perform	using member
joeBloggsPerson	joeBloggsRoles	get collection	roles

alias items in list	joeBloggsRoles		
title	type		alias as
Mr Joe Bloggs	com.pragprog.dhnako.carserv.dom.customer.Customer		joeBloggsCustomer

Figure 12.5: *SetUpJoeBloggsCustomer* SETUP PAGE

Designing a Test Scenario Hierarchy

We can place test scenarios anywhere, but we'll put them in the appropriate functional subsuite. Since we're testing the functionality of a Customer, we'll use the *CustomerSuite*.

One way to structure the test scenario is as a given/when/then hierarchy: a "given" may have many "whens," and a "when" may have many "thens." So, let's create the hierarchy as follows:

- *GivenCustomersWithNoVehiclesSuite*
  - *TheGiven* (more on this in a moment)
  - *WhenAttemptToDeleteVehicleSuite*
    * *TheWhen* (more on this in a moment)
    * *ThenShouldBeDisabledTest*

The convention I'm using here is to put the actual setup in a sub-page, *TheGiven*. This uses FitNesse's **!include** syntax to bootstrap Naked Objects and set up the data (fixture) for the test. The parent page (*GivenCustomersWithNoVehiclesSuite*) is then free to put any related documentation (FitNesse is a wiki, after all), as well as to list any subpages (the **!contents -R2** keyword). Similarly, the *TheWhen* subpage separates out the actual event that's being tested from its parent page. We'll be exploiting this separation in a minute.

Let's now fill in "the given" itself.

Writing the Given

We'll be able to test this particular scenario if we have Boris Customer with some Cars and Mary Customer with none. Therefore, in the *The-Given* page, use **!include** to include the following:

chapter12/GivenCustomerWithNoVehiclesSuite/TheGiven/content.txt

```
!include -c .BootstrapNakedObjects
!include -c .AliasServices
!include -c .LogonAsFsmith

Ref data
!include -c <CarServAppSuite.VehicleSuite.RefData.SetUpVehicleType
!include -c <CarServAppSuite.VehicleSuite.RefData.SetUpMake
!include -c <CarServAppSuite.VehicleSuite.RefData.SetUpModel
!include -c <CarServAppSuite.PersonSuite.RefData.SetUpTitles

Boris has some Cars...
!include -c <CarServAppSuite.CustomerSuite.TransactionalData.\
            SetUpBorisFrederiksonCustomer
!include -c <CarServAppSuite.ServiceSuite.TransactionalData.\
            SetUpBorisFrederiksonCarsAndServices

Mary has none...
!include -c <CarServAppSuite.CustomerSuite.TransactionalData.\
            SetUpMaryBloggsCustomer
```

I've wrapped some lines to fit the book's margins; you mustn't, though.

Let me explain what's going on:

1. The first two **!include**s start up Naked Objects itself (in a headless mode, with no GUI); the *AliasServices* page (accessible from the front page of the wiki) is broadly analogous to the services entries in the nakedobjects.properties file.

2. The next **!include** specifies who the effective user is for the test. This particular test is not date sensitive, so there is no need to specify the date as well.

3. The next block of **!include**s sets up the necessary reference data objects. In general, we should only include the objects we need; for this method, we aren't setting up any PaymentMethodTypes, for example.

4. The remaining !includes set up the transactional objects we need for the test. Again, we only include those that are required.

It'd be nice to check that this "given" is correct, and indeed we can.

Verifying the Given

Modify the *GivenCustomersWithNoVehiclesSuite* page to read as follows:

```
chapter12/GivenCustomerWithNoVehiclesSuite/content.txt
```

```
!contents -R2 -g -p -f -h
----
!include -c GivenCustomerWithNoVehiclesSuite.TheGiven
!|Run Viewer|
```

This run viewer table fixture will actually start up the DnD viewer at the point of the test, allowing us to inspect the current state of the objects.[7] It's a bit like a breakpoint, but from an end user's perspective.

To try this out, though, we need to do two things. First, remember the instruction on the front page of the wiki? We need to make our application available for Fitnesse to find, so run mvn clean install. Second, we need to temporarily alter the *GivenCustomersWithNoVehiclesSuite* suite page to run as a test page. To do this, update the page's properties (the Properties button on the left side), and check the test box.

OK, now click Test. The DnD viewer should appear with Mary and Boris. Click around and confirm the other setup is as we expect. Once this is working, update the page back to being just a suite.

Being able to debug test fixtures like this is extremely valuable; it's the main reason for separating the *TheGiven* subpage from its parent.

Completing the Test

To complete the test, we need a "when" and a "then." First modify the *TheWhen* page, as shown here and in Figure 12.6, on the facing page:

```
chapter12/GivenCustomerWithNoVehiclesSuite/When/content.txt
```

```
!|using naked objects viewer|
|on object|perform|using member|that it|with arguments|
|mary...Customer|check action|delete vehicle|is disabled|boris...Focus|
```

The using naked objects viewer table fixture interacts with the domain model in the same way that a "real" viewer would. (Note in the code snippet I've abbreviated some of aliases to fit the page margins.)

---

7. At the time of writing the HTML viewer is not supported.

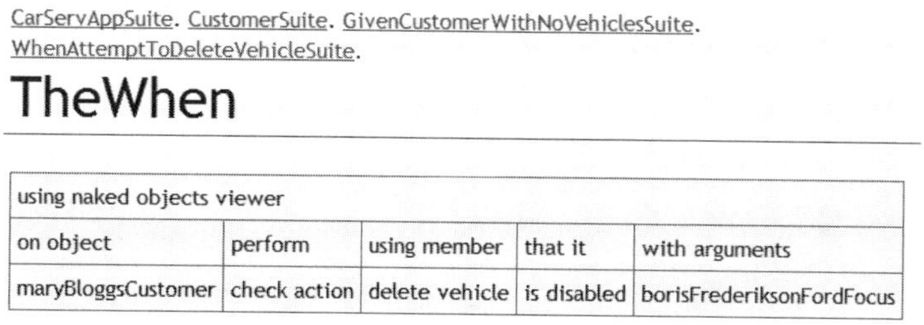

CarServAppSuite. CustomerSuite. GivenCustomerWithNoVehiclesSuite. WhenAttemptToDeleteVehicleSuite.

TheWhen

using naked objects viewer				
on object	perform	using member	that it	with arguments
maryBloggsCustomer	check action	delete vehicle	is disabled	borisFrederiksonFordFocus

Figure 12.6: WHEN ATTEMPTING TO DELETE A VEHICLE. . .

And finally, to the test itself, the "then." In this particular case, there are no post-conditions to check, so we simply include the pages that make up the scenario:

chapter12/GivenCustomerWithNoVehiclesSuite/When/Then/content.txt

```
!include -c <GivenCustomerWithNoVehiclesSuite.TheGiven
!include <WhenAttemptToDeleteVehicleSuite.TheWhen

then...

no change.
```

Note that the *TheWhen*   !include doesn't have a -c flag, meaning it shouldn't be collapsed. It's up to you whether to collapse included pages using -c, but in this case because there aren't any postconditions to assert upon, I think the reader of the test would want to see the "when" in full.

And so, finally. . . running this test should confirm the behavior we want, as shown in Figure 12.7, on the next page.

On the other hand, what if it didn't? After all, here we're just testing code that we know works, but in reality there's every likelihood that the test could fail. If that were the case, then we'd want to use all the power of our IDE to look into the issue. Help is at hand: we can run the test from JUnit too.

Running the Test from JUnit

The Tested Objects archetype also provides another way of running the tests, using a JUnit 4–based test harness called Trinidad.[8] Rather than

---

8. Trinidad was originally hosted at http://code.google.com/p/trinidad but is now part of the main FitNesse distribution. See also http://www.fitnesse.info/trinidad.

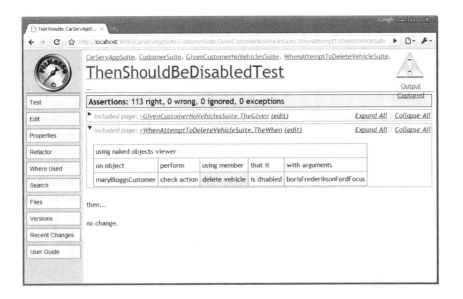

Figure 12.7: ... THEN SHOULD BE DISABLED

have the FitNesse wiki server spawn off our tests, Trinidad parses the wiki pages itself and runs the tests in-process. We can therefore put breakpoints in our domain objects and inspect state or step through the code as necessary.

Open up the generated InteractionFixtureTest class (in src/test/java). Most of this is boilerplate; the only bit that matters is the list of pages to test. Normally we comment out all except the test we're debugging:

chapter12/InteractionFixtureTest.java

```java
@RunWith(Parameterized.class)
public class InteractionFixtureTest {
    @Parameters
    public static Collection<Object[]> data() {
        return Arrays.asList(new Object[][]{
            {"CarServAppSuite.CustomerSuite."+
                "GivenCustomersWithNoVehiclesSuite."+
                    "WhenAttemptToDeleteVehicleSuite."+
                        "ThenShouldBeDisabledTest"},
            ...
        });
    }
    ...
}
```

Try this as an alternative way of running the tests using Eclipse's Run > Run As (or indeed, Debug > Debug As having set a breakpoint).

A further benefit of testing this way is that—because FitNesse isn't actually running the tests anymore—it is no longer necessary to run the mvn clean install command after each code modification.

The Remaining Tests

We set out to write three scenario tests and have completed the first (**chapter12-04**). Let's take a look at the other two. The second scenario checks that we may only delete a Vehicle that is owned by the Customer. Here's a design for this test:

- *GivenCustomersEachWithVehiclesSuite*

    The corresponding *TheGiven* page should include (say) Mary and her Cars and Boris and his Cars.

- *WhenAttemptToDeleteOtherCustomersVehicleSuite*

    The corresponding *TheWhen* should (like the previous test) use the "naked objects with viewer" table to attempt to delete one of Boris' Vehicles for Mary.

- *ThenShouldBeInvalidTest*

    Like the previous test there are no post-conditions, so this page just consists of !includeing the given and the "when."

The check in the "when" should this time, though, check that the argument is invalid (rather than the action being disabled).

Our final test, where we succeed in actually deleting the Vehicle, has the following design:

- *GivenCustomerWithSomeVehiclesSuite*

    The corresponding *TheGiven* page should include (say) Boris and his Cars.

- *WhenDeleteVehicleSuite*

    The *TheWhen* should use the using naked objects viewer table to invoke the action.

- *ThenVehicleShouldBeRemovedFromCollectionTest*

    This time there are some post-conditions; we should check that the Car has been removed from the collection.

You can check whether the Car has been removed using the using naked objects viewer table fixture to check that Boris' vehicles collection no longer contains the reference. Alternatively, you could use the check list table fixture to inspect the actual contents.

There aren't any additional techniques to learn to write these last two tests, so I'm going to leave it to you to complete them. Yes, I thought you'd enjoy that! Actually, though, all the hard work has been done, so you won't find there's much to it.

Before we wrap up the chapter, a few handy pointers.

12.5 Hints and Tips

FitNesse can be a very effective way of developing, but like any tool it needs to be used effectively.

Use !include Pages

The most significant downside of FitNesse (at the time of writing, at least) is the lack of refactoring support. If I change a property name in the Java code, then that will break any test that references it.

The best workaround for this at the moment is to use !include wherever possible to factor out any duplicated setup. That way, following a refactoring, we have a much smaller number of places to manually fix up. The name of the included page should use a declarative style (for example *SetUpJoeBloggsPaymentMethods*) to make it easier to do this impact analysis.

Use Given/When/Then

Try to follow the given/when/then style of structuring tests, and remember the following:

- The "given" will be the largest page of the three, even accounting for the fact that it should consist mostly of !includes.

- The "when" should really consist only of a single action or event. Most of the time this will be using the using naked objects viewer.

- The "then" post-condition should only read and validate the state of the system. If there is more than one post-condition, then have more than one "then" page.

If you prefer to flatten into single pages, that's fine too, so long as you use !include to remove any duplication between them. I do suggest that you keep the *TheGiven* subpage separate, because it makes it easy to test the given using the run viewer table fixture.

Structure Tests Similarly to the Application

In the *CarServAppSuite*, we had separate subsuites for each of the main packages. That makes it easy to locate tests once written.

You might also choose to have a "WorkInProgressSuite" for anything that is being currently being developed, for example in the current iteration. When the iteration is done, move the tests to the correct subsuite. We'll be discussing development practices in Chapter 13, *Developing Domain Applications*, on page 241.

Where Possible, Prefer Tables to Scripting

In the *CarServAppSuite*, you'll see that the reference object pages are set up using the generic set up objects table fixture, while the transactional objects tend to be set up using the using naked objects viewer for set up table fixture.

Of the two, the set up objects approach is probably to be preferred. For one thing, it's easier for the domain expert to review the state of the object prior to the test; and ultimately, scenario tests are all about improving communication.

Another reason for preferring set up objects is that it is possible to generate such pages. For example, one could generate pages for all reference data (or even sample transactional data) from the production database. This will give the domain experts realistic data to work with.

On the other hand, the using naked objects viewer for set up is powerful, because it can invoke actions on the domain object that could perform a whole bunch of work. For some scenarios, it may make more sense to describe a "given" in terms of actions that have previously occurred.

Use Symbolic Links to Support Multiple Environments

FitNesse has support for symbolic links, which—in combination with declared variables—can be used to run the same test suite in different environments. Explaining this is beyond the scope of this book, but it would allow us, for example, to run the same test in both in-memory mode and then against a real database once the integration with the DBMS has been performed (see Chapter 16, *Integrating with the Database*, on page 287). See the web site http://fitnesse.org/FitNesse. UserGuide.SymbolicLinks for more information.

For more on scenario testing and the broader topic of agile acceptance testing, have a look at Gojko Adzic's excellent book *Bridging the Communication Gap* [Adz09].

Coming Up Next

In this chapter, we saw two complementary approaches for testing applications. Developer tests ensure the code is built right; scenario tests ensure that the right code is built.[9]

This chapter concludes Part II of the book. In the final part, we're going to think about how to use Naked Objects in "the real world." We'll talk about approaches for organizing the development process, about using Naked Objects just as a design tool, and about integration with web frameworks and the database, and we'll finish up describing how to deploy our domain application as a web app or client-server.

Exercises

Starting with the developer tests, it's common practice to use code coverage tools such as *Cobertura* to establish how much of the code is being exercised through tests.[10] Write some further tests for CarServ, and verify that the code coverage improves. On your own application too, put together some developer tests, and then steadily improve the test coverage.

For the scenario tests, the first exercise (if you didn't already do this) is to complete the two tests whose design was sketched out in the chapter. Then, use scenario testing to develop a new feature. Rather than simply marking Services as being paid, instead have them save a reference to the PaymentMethod that was used to pay them.

Then likewise, using the Tested Objects archetype (see Tested Objects' documentation), add FitNesse support for your own application. Use the built-in user guide and the CarServ download to guide you.

---

9. I can't take credit for this pithy motto. That goes to Andy Dassing; see http://tech. groups.yahoo.com/group/fitnesse/message/10115.
10. The Maven Cobertura plug-in is at http://mojo.codehaus.org/cobertura-maven-plugin.

Part III

Practices

Chapter 13

Developing Domain Applications

In Part I of this book, we learned the tools to build a basic domain model using Naked Objects, while in Part II we learned some techniques to create a much more sophisticated model using idioms, patterns, and other OO principles, as well as how to test our application.

Part III of the book focuses on practices to develop, integrate, and deploy DDD applications written using Naked Objects. In this chapter, we're going to identify a number of ways to deploy Naked Objects, discuss why you might choose one over another, and see how this impacts exactly what you need to develop in each of these cases. Subsequent chapters in this final part of the book will explore these deployment options in more detail.

We'll continue to use CarServ during Part III, but in a slightly different way than in the previous two parts. Since we are integrating with other technologies, it isn't practical (or relevant) for me to explain all the non–Naked Objects code that we are integrating with. So, from here on, the CarServ downloads are already complete, and I ask you to download them so we can review the code. But if you aren't at your computer as you read the book, then don't worry; all the relevant code snippets are also listed in the book.

In this chapter, we're also going to discuss development practices. Different activities are involved in developing enterprise applications, and to be effective, we need to think about *how* they are done and also *when* they are done. But let's start off the discussion by considering *what* it is exactly we're aiming to develop and integrate.

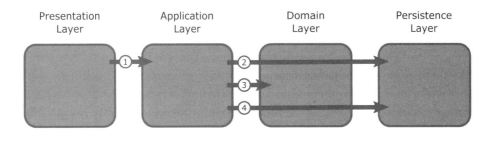

Figure 13.1: INTERACTIONS WITHIN A LAYERED ARCHITECTURE

13.1 The Layered Architecture

Back in Section 1.5, *How Naked Objects Helps with DDD*, on page 16, we briefly discussed how Naked Objects helps DDD by rigorously enforcing the separation between the domain layer and the other layers of the architecture. One of the points that Evans makes is that domain-driven design requires only one particular layer—the domain layer—to exist. Using Naked Objects helps ensure that this domain layer has in it all the business logic that it should.

But what of the other layers? What are their responsibilities? Well:

- The *presentation* layer has the logic for rendering a user interface through which the user can interact with the application.

- The *application* layer has the logic that manages the user's current session- and conversation-level state and possibly controls interactions between those states.

- The *domain* layer (as we know) holds the business logic applicable to all users and all applications, that is, across the entire domain.

- The *persistence* layer (perhaps labeled more generally as an infrastructure layer) is where domain object state and perhaps application logic state is stored.

One of the main purposes of an architecture is to define and ideally constrain how these layers interact. After all, if any object could interact with any other object irrespective of layering, then the architecture wouldn't really be providing much organization. In Figure 13.1, we see the typical interactions between these four layers.

For example, to view an object, follow these steps:

1. The presentation layer asks to read the state of existing objects.

2. The application layer interacts with the persistence layer to retrieve the objects from storage.

3. The application layer reads the state of the retrieved objects and assembles it to be returned to the presentation layer.

If we are modifying an object, then the interactions are similar, but there is an additional step:

1. The presentation layer requests to modify the state of existing objects.

2. The application layer interacts with the persistence layer to retrieve the objects from storage.

3. The application layer modifies state of the object(s); in Naked Objects terms, this means modifying a property/collection or invoking an action.

4. The application layer flushes any changes of state to the persistence layer.

In the diagram, I've shown the application layer interacting directly with the persistence layer. This is simplifying things slightly; using DDD terminology, the application layer would probably call a domain service or repository whose *interface* is part of the domain layer but whose *implementation* is within the persistence layer. The diagram also doesn't show how domain objects can be retrieved from the persistence layer by traversing associations. But the diagram is close enough for our purposes.

Let's now relate this to the various deployment options.

13.2 Deployment Options

Naked Objects provides four ways to deploy our domain applications.

"Pure Pojo" Deployment Option

As we've seen, domain classes written to follow the Naked Objects programming model are basically pojos. There's therefore nothing to stop us from taking our domain model and deploying it with a handcrafted presentation layer, persistence layer, and everything else required. This

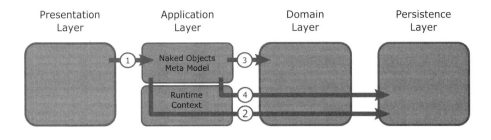

Figure 13.2: INTERACTIONS WITH THE "EMBEDDED METAMODEL" DEPLOYMENT OPTION

is the *pure pojo* deployment option. In effect, we restrict Naked Objects' use solely to the development environment.

We discuss this option in more detail in Chapter 14, *Naked Objects as a Design Tool*, on page 259. But let's move onto our next deployment option where Naked Objects starts working for us in the runtime environment too.

"Embedded Metamodel" Deployment Option

While a *pure pojo* deployment requires custom code for every layer, with an *embedded metamodel* deployment we use the Naked Objects metamodel to enforce the business rules (such as @Disabled or @MaxLength) that are intrinsic to the domain.

In Figure 13.2, we can see a modified version of the previous diagram, this time embedding the metamodel. The interactions between the layers are ultimately the same, but the metamodel does all the interaction with the domain objects on our behalf. We still handcraft the presentation layer and persistence layer, and we provide a *runtime context* to enable the metamodel to interact with our custom persistence layer.

With this option we're still doing a good deal of the work in handling all of the persistence concerns, and in Chapter 15, *Integrating with Web Frameworks*, on page 269, we'll see what this means with a fully worked example. But let's now look at our next deployment option where we leverage a little more of Naked Objects' functionality.

"Custom Presentation" Deployment Option

The next step on from *embedded metamodel* is to allow Naked Objects to handle persistence as well and only write a custom presentation layer. For want of a better name, this is the *custom presentation* deployment option.

Again, there's a full worked example of this option in Chapter 15, *Integrating with Web Frameworks*, on page 269, demonstrating how you can evolve from one option to the next.

Note that asking Naked Objects to do the persistence for us doesn't necessarily mean there is no work to do here. True, the in-memory object store we've used for prototyping requires no configuration. However, in production, we will most likely use a relational database, so Naked Objects' own persistence mechanisms will require some configuration. Indeed, this is the topic of Chapter 16, *Integrating with the Database*, on page 287.

Let's now go on one further step to examine the final deployment option.

"Full Runtime" Deployment Option

With a *full runtime* deployment, we are basically deploying the same application that we've prototyped, but with a properly persistent (rather than in-memory) object store and possibly a different viewer. The full Naked Objects runtime is deployed and takes care of the presentation layer, application layer, and persistence for us automatically. Again, depending on the persistence mechanism used, there may be some integration work, but that is pretty much the only work we need to do.

However, we needn't restrict ourselves to the two viewers we've used thus far. Naked Objects has a number of sister projects that provide other viewers. Some of these viewers offer customization capabilities, blurring the boundaries between this deployment option and the previous one. We're going to look at this option in detail in two chapters, Chapter 17, *Integrating Within the Enterprise*, on page 311 and Chapter 18, *Deploying the Full Runtime*, on page 333.

So, there's more detail on the "how to" for all of these options in the chapters that follow, but we still need to decide why you might choose one option over another.

13.3 Which Option to Choose?

Two key factors will determine which deployment option you select. The first is a good old-fashioned risk/benefit assessment; how much framework code are you happy to deploy into your own production environment? The second relates to the type of user using your application. Let's explore each in turn.

Assessing Risk/Benefit

If you've ever tried to introduce some new technology or framework into your workplace, I suspect you have encountered some pushback. The architects will want to know about its scalability, performance, and reliability; the CIO might want to know about licensing costs; the production support manager will want to know what support options are available; and so on it goes. Realistically, you can expect the same types of questions if you argue to adopt Naked Objects in your organization.

To help make your case, the following table summarizes where framework or custom code is used for each of the options:

Option	Presentation	Application	Domain	Persistence
Pure Pojo	Custom	Custom	Custom	Custom
Embedded Metamodel	Custom	Custom / Framework	Custom	Custom
Custom Presentation	Custom	Framework	Custom	Framework
Full Runtime	Framework	Framework	Custom	Framework

What that means is:

- A *pure pojo* deployment introduces no particular risk because Naked Objects isn't part of the deployment. You are basically using Naked Objects as a design tool in the same way that you might otherwise have used a UML case tool.

- An *embedded metamodel* deployment does include an element of Naked Objects technology in the runtime deployment, so although you get some benefit, you might also equate that with some risk.

- The *custom presentation* layer is further along the scale; now you are relying on the framework to take care of persistence for you.

- And the *full runtime* deployment option of course provides the most bang for your buck, but by the same token some will view it as the riskiest.

Of course, one could argue this the other way: there's at least as much likelihood of a defect in custom written code as there would be in framework code. Even so, most developers I know would rather contend with a bug in their code than a bug in some framework code (even if that framework's code is open source).

How you determine the risk/benefit I'll leave to you and your team, but there's also a second factor that you should take into account.

Matching Deployment Option to User Experience

The other factor to consider is the background and skill level of the user audience. Here's a useful distinction, originally made by Alan Cooper:[1]

- A *sovereign application* is one that its user would use intensively for several hours at a time, and often every day.

    Examples include a word processor for a writer or an IDE for a developer. The UNIX shell is also a good example.

- A *transient application*, on the other hand, is one used for much briefer periods, and often much more occasionally.

    An example might be a time-tracking application. Kiosk applications also fall into this category, as do many websites.

The object-oriented UIs provided by Naked Objects are generic in nature (they work for any domain), but that means they are *not* particularly suitable for transient applications. There are two reasons for this. First, a casual user will not know and does not care for the subtleties or complexity of the domain model; they need to be presented with the minimum necessary to get the task at hand done. A custom presentation layer may bear very little relation to the underlying domain model.

The second reason why Naked Objects' object-oriented interfaces are not suitable for transient applications is that a casual user generally needs explicit guidance in how to actually use the application. Transient applications therefore tend to be more task- or process-oriented, with lots of step-by-step wizards. The next time you fly, consider the

---

1. The original citation was the online article "Your Program's Posture" published on Cooper's website, http://www.cooper.com. However, the article is no longer available.

Using Presentation Models

The presentation layer of most *transient* applications still interacts with the underlying domain model; it just selects which objects, collections, and actions to expose, and often it aggregates information from several objects into a single screen.

Some DDD practitioners go further than this, though, by creating a separate simplified model just for presentation purposes, sometimes called a *presentation model*. This presentation model is then linked back to the domain model.

We should be careful if we do this, though, because it can undermine the idea of a *ubiquitous language*. The presentation model underpinning the presentation layer (which after all is what the business users see) effectively defines one vocabulary, while the classes of domain model within the domain layer define another. It's difficult enough to ensure that a single model is self-consistent; ensuring that these two vocabularies match up can become a major problem.

If you really do believe that you need a simplified presentation model, then of course you can use Naked Objects to develop both the presentation model and the "real" domain model. If deployed in the same physical tier of the system, then the integration between the two may be quite simple: the presentation objects simply call the domain objects, with the real domain objects always hidden from view. Alternatively, though, the presentation model may reside on one tier and the domain model on another, in which case the integration effort to link the two will be substantial.

kiosk application you use to check in at the airport. That is a classic transient application. So, if you are building a transient application, then you probably should choose a deployment option that allows you to write your own presentation layer specific to your domain model.

All that said, *most* internal line-of-business operational systems fall into the sovereign application category. Such users tend to have a good understanding of the domain and need to understand the subtleties of the domain. So, for these applications, the Naked Objects' generic OOUIs are ideal.

Going down the generic OOUI route also leaves the door open to leverage future improvements in Naked Objects viewers. In Chapter 18, *Deploying the Full Runtime*, on page 333, we see some of the newer viewers currently in development, and the existing DnD viewer also has a road map for future improvement. There's also currently a lot of innovation going on in user interface technology in general (think Ajax, Flex, Silverlight, JavaFX, iPhone, Android), any of which could be platforms for new (possibly customizable) viewers.

As mentioned in the introduction, the subsequent chapters in this final part of the book go into the various deployment options in more detail. But irrespective of which deployment option we select, we also need to organize our development efforts. So, let's now turn to consider the development process—how we go about developing our applications.

13.4　Development Activities

You can develop domain applications with Naked Objects using any development process—agile, waterfall, whatever. However, it's worth separating the three activities of *exploration*, *implementation*, and *integration*. Let's start with exploration.

Exploration

During *exploration*, we use exploration stories to actively work with the domain experts in the team, trying ideas and hunting for the domain concepts and their broad responsibilities, in effect identifying the requirements of the application. The domain experts will typically have a number of key business problems to act as their focus, but we're also looking to understand the broader business processes, to understand the actors (human or otherwise) involved in those processes, and to figure out where the system boundary might be. It's quite possible we may solve some business problems by adjusting—outward or inward—the scope of the system.

This sounds like a tall order, but because Naked Objects requires us to write only the domain layer, it's quite feasible for the team to rapidly build working prototypes exercising the main domain concepts. A good way to drive this is with a strong business analyst to guide a workshop with the domain experts, along with a strong developer to act as scribe. It's even feasible to develop the prototype in real time, and it can be quite exhilarating if you do.

Agile Modeling

Scott Ambler describes a similar activity to exploration in his book *Agile Modeling* (Amb02). In Ambler's world, what he is doing is developing fairly classical UML diagrams, with the idea being to do "just barely enough modeling" that implementation can start.

In exploration we're trying to explore just barely enough of the domain that we feel comfortable starting the main implementation work. What's different, though, is that our models of the domain are not UML diagrams but are functional Naked Objects prototypes.

To organize these sessions, we need a fixture to represent the scenario being explored. This can be a programmatic fixture (as described in Chapter 4, *Rapid Prototyping*, on page 63), or alternatively you might use a set of table fixtures (making up a "given," as described in Chapter 12, *Scenario Testing*, on page 217). One advantage of the FitNesse approach is that you can also capture any working notes about the scenario directly in the FitNesse wiki. It also leads very naturally into the next activity (implementation) discussed. However, not every exploration scenario necessarily gets implemented. That's the point really; there will be some dead ends. If using FitNesse from the start, then make sure you clean up any such dead ends; you don't want the wiki to become an unmanaged jungle.

Code written during exploration should *not* have any tests. Tests and test-driven development are an important way of driving out detailed designs, but they aren't appropriate during exploration; we're still doing requirements analysis. To use agile jargon, explorations are spikes.

It's a good idea for the domain experts to take the outputs of the exploration workshops and expose them to a wider audience. After all, although the domain experts are empowered to represent the larger business community, realistically they cannot know every detail and nuance. The domain experts can take the working prototype, complete with a realistic set of fixtures, and demonstrate it to their peers.

Alternatively, the team can use a screen capture tool to provide an animated and annotated walk-through of the prototype.[2] These can be made available on the Web and so reviewed by anyone (including perhaps rank 'n' file members of the user community) without having to deploy any code onto users' desktops.

In terms of practicalities, it's a good idea to perform exploration in a separate code branch, because the quality of the code may well be low, especially if doing live coding in workshops. We'll look more at this in Section 13.5, *Configuration Management*, on the following page.

Let's now move onto the next of our three activities, implementation.

Implementation

Following on from exploration is *implementation*, where we more formally specify the requirements by confirming implementation stories and writing scenario tests (the topic of Chapter 12, *Scenario Testing*, on page 217) for those stories. The domain experts must decide on the priority of the user stories, and the developers in the team provide the estimates.

Whereas exploration code has no tests and uses a relatively broad brush, implementation is where much of the effort in identifying subtle business rules goes. We use scenario tests to verify these are implemented correctly. If using table fixtures during exploration, you will already have a "given" to represent your scenario; this will probably represent the happy case (that is, when the system performs something useful). During implementation you should flesh out this "given" by considering different "whens" and documenting more of the postconditions (in the "thens"). But you should spend even more time identifying alternative "givens" to represent the error scenarios (the sad cases) as well as the happy case.

As we implement, we should be looking to apply the techniques in Part II of the book; why invent the wheel when there are already idioms and patterns to draw upon? And as we've seen, ensuring that the model remains decoupled not only keeps it manageable, but it may also draw out new concepts relating to the roles between the domain classes.

---

2. A good open source tool for creating animated demos is Wink (http://www.debugmode. com/wink); another is CamStudio (http://www.camstudio.org). There are also some very good commercial tools.

It is *possible* to perform implementation on the same code branch as exploration, but it's risky. Remember that exploration code is written without tests, and it's easy to lose track of what code has formal tests and what does not. It's much better to start a new branch and discard the exploration code as a spike. If you use the same code branch, then don't do too much exploration, and find a way by which you can switch off any untested code so it doesn't accidentally get released. For example, you can annotate actions with @Exploration so that they won't be available in production.

Let's now discuss the final of the three activities, integration.

Integration

The deliverable from implementation is a tested domain model that supports the user stories identified. The *integration* activity that follows uses implementation stories where the focus is to bind this tested domain model into the other layers of the application for a particular deployment environment.

As discussed in Section 13.2, *Deployment Options*, on page 243, Naked Objects supports a number of different deployment options allowing us to mix and match framework code with custom code for each of the layers of our application. The deployment option chosen directly impacts the amount of work to be done during integration.

The output of the integration activity is a version of the application that can be run end to end in a production-like environment. This is usually the point where system testing (automated or manual) kicks in.

Integration may be performed in the same branch as implementation, or the implemented code may be promoted into a different branch where it is integrated.

In fact, let's pull together the various suggestions on branching and put them into context with the rest of the codebase.

13.5 Configuration Management

No matter what your development process is, you need a decent configuration management mechanism to control your code. Not only should your source code control system do the usual things such as file versioning, but it should also support robust branching and merging of

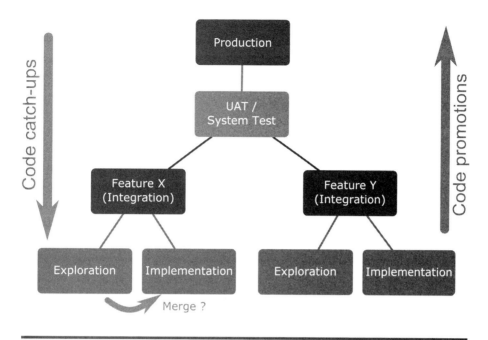

Figure 13.3: SUGGESTED BRANCHING STRATEGY

code. The ability for small teams to develop in parallel is especially important if you are using agile development practices.

In Figure 13.3, we see a suggested branching strategy for exploration, implementation, and integration. At the top we have the code currently running in production. Below this is a branch for user acceptance testing (UAT) and for system testing; this is the code being made ready for the next production release. I've bundled UAT and system testing together, but you might of course have several testing environments (UAT, performance load testing, system test, and so on).

Underneath this we have a number of parallel developments, which I've called *features*. Each has its own branch. The scope of these and their duration will depend on your development process. They may last for many months or even years, in which case *project* is probably a better name. Or they may last just a few weeks; they could even be down to an individual story. Whichever—they need to be substantial enough to justify the effort of the keeping the branches in sync.

For a given feature/project/story, we have an exploration branch and an implementation branch. Initial work is done in the exploration; once prototypes start popping out, we can start over in the implementation branch. Optionally, we might do merges from exploration to implementation. Once implementation is done and the acceptance tests are passing, the code can be promoted up to the parent feature branch. This is where integration can be performed.

Let's also note the close relationship between branching and continuous integration. With *continuous integration*, we use an automated server to monitor the code branch. Whenever a code change is made (which includes code catch-ups), then the server notices the change, checks out the latest version of the code, compiles the code, and reruns our tests. This keeps all the code *within* a branch consistent, providing early visibility of any problems.

The diagram shown is just a suggestion, and there are several possible variations to it.[3] You might decide not to have separate branches for exploration and implementation; just be sure to understand the risk here in mixing nontested code with tested code. You might also want to perform integration in the same place as implementation. That would probably mean just having an exploration branch and performing implementation in the parent feature branch.

You might also have an intermediary development branch between UAT/system test and the feature branches. This would be a good place for production defects to be fixed and minor enhancements to be implemented. Or, this bug fix branch might be a peer of the feature branches. The rule of thumb with branching is, only do so if you need to isolate and decouple different pieces of work.

Of course, while we are working on our feature, other teams will be working on their features, and production defects will be getting fixed. It's important to never let branches get too far out of sync with each other, so every so often (every week, say) child branches should do a *code catch-up*, that is, merge any changes from their parent down. Conversely, any completed work should be *promoted* (merged back to its parent). We should always do a catch-up before a promotion, though, and rerun any regression tests to minimize the chance of breaking code in the parent once we promote.

---

3. A very useful white paper on branching strategies is available from Microsoft at http://www.codeplex.com/BranchingGuidance. Although it targets its (rather good) Team Foundation Server product, much of its advice is generally applicable.

in context...

Continuous Integration

Continuous integration (CI) means continually verifying that the current codebase is sound.

In practical terms, this usually means running a CI server that continually monitors the source code repository for a particular branch. If there is more than one branch, then there is more CI "job" setup.

The CI job compiles the latest version of the code and runs all regression tests whenever a change is detected. Most CI servers also come with monitors to alert team members working on that branch if the tests fail.

Configuration management is hardly the most glamorous of subjects, but its importance cannot be underestimated. Indeed, robust configuration management combined with *continuous integration* is pretty much a prerequisite if you want to use agile development practices. There's an overhead in keeping all those plates spinning, of course, but it more than pays for itself in terms of being able to ship our regular releases month after month.

We'll finish off this chapter with a suggestion as to how you might work more effectively.

13.6 Working Effectively

Your overarching development process will influence the amount of time between the three activities of exploration, implementation, and integration.

If you are a waterfall shop, then these activities naturally correspond to project phases: exploration will happen in an exploration phase lasting several months, followed by an implementation phase again of several months, followed by an integration phase again of, well, whatever.

If you are an agile shop, then the activities of exploration, implementation, and integration are performed user story by user story, each activity done on a just-in-time basis. You may well be used to counting

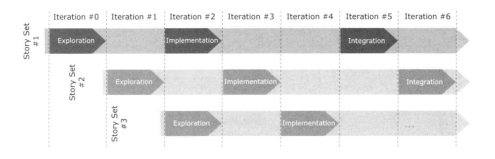

Figure 13.4: CONSCIOUSLY DEFER WORK.

the user story as "done" only once all the activities are complete (if fully integrated). However, this changes under Naked Objects. Instead, you must separate your original user stories into exploration stories, implementation stories, and integration stories. Typically the exploration will happen in iteration n; the implementation will happen in iteration $n+2$, and the integration will happen in iteration $n+4$ or $n+5$. This is illustrated in Figure 13.4.

What we are doing by introducing these gaps is consciously deferring work that might never need to be done. The gap between exploration and implementation is needed to allow for feedback "from the field"; something missed by the domain expert could invalidate any implementation stories. Similarly, a gap is also needed between implementation and integration to allow the team to deepen their design as further stories are implemented. Any integration work done prematurely as the domain model is still stabilizing would only need to be redone. This also means that deployment options that require more integration work should have a longer gap, but in any event it shouldn't be less than two to three iterations if using agile development practices.

Coming Up Next

In this chapter, we talked about the various ways to deploy a domain application developed using Naked Objects, identified the main activities that make up the development process, saw how to use configuration management to manage these activities, and discussed how we can prevent rework by consciously deciding when to decide.

Deciding When to Decide

If I own a "buy" option to purchase a stock for $100 and the price goes up to $110, that option still lets me buy for the original cheaper price. I can then immediately sell the stock and take my profit. So, that buy option itself has a worth based on the length of time it is valid and the volatility of the underlying stock. If the stock doesn't go up, then of course I don't exercise the option. I still had to buy the option in the first place, so I am down on the deal. The wonderful world of derivatives!

Chris Matts and Olav Maasen use the term *real options* to apply similar thinking to software development.* If I defer implementation or integration work, then I am in effect buying the option to change my mind. If I do change my mind, then I've exercised the option by saving more downstream rework. But if I don't change my mind (that is, the analysis was spot-on first time), then overall the cost of development will be more because it would have been more efficient to just do the exploration, integration, and implementation all in one go.

The gap between the steps is therefore a function of how much uncertainty there is in the requirements and how much work you would incur to redo the later steps.

* For more details, see http://www.infoq.com/articles/real-options-enhance-agility.

The remaining chapters in Part III go into more detail on the deployment options. We start with the *pure pojo* option where we use Naked Objects solely in the development environment as a design tool.

Exercises

Consider the most recent enterprise application that you worked on. Was it a sovereign application or a transient application? If it was a sovereign application, what accommodation did it make for being used by users who have a deep understanding of the domain? How much of the user interface might be considered generic, and how much was specific to the domain?

It's good practice to have a continuous integration (CI) environment running on your code branch, and certainly you should by the time you get into implementing user stories. Luckily, if using Maven (which we are), it's very easy to do this using the open source Hudson continuous integration server.[4]

Therefore, check in your code to a supported source code repository (Subversion is a good bet), and then have a go at setting up Hudson.[5] Plenty of blogs show how to do it, so with a following wind, it might only take five minutes.

---

4. Hudson is downloadable from http://hudson.dev.java.net.
5. Subversion is downloadable from http://subversion.tigris.org.

Chapter 14

Naked Objects as a Design Tool

Here's the scenario for this chapter: you like using Naked Objects in the development environment, and you're happy that the domain models you're producing are better than you might otherwise have developed. Even so, you're not ready or able to use Naked Objects as part of the runtime environment. This is the *pure pojo* deployment option introduced in the previous chapter.

We're going to spend most of this short chapter seeing how to decouple our domain model from the framework completely and identifying what custom code you'll need to write to do the work that the framework would otherwise do. But we'll start off by considering how this deployment option impacts the development process.

14.1 Using Naked Objects Only in Development

Even if you're "only" going to use Naked Objects for development, you still have a choice:

- You could use Naked Objects for just initial exploration and prototyping but then once implementation starts switch to a different technology.

- Alternatively, you might want to continue using Naked Objects to develop the domain layer even while you use other technologies to implement the other layers of the application.

The first option might be suitable if your organization tends to outsource development. You can use Naked Objects to help you explore the domain and to scope the system and thus write the system's spec. The resultant prototype could even be part of this spec. The outsourced development team could implement the application using whichever technology was most suited.

The second option is more suitable for applications that are built incrementally and are likely to have multiple releases (so probably developed in-house). Because the domain layer remains "compatible" with Naked Objects, you can continue to explore and prototype new features even after the application has been shipped. Naked Objects also helps define the boundaries between the layers, preventing business logic from seeping out of the domain model. But that could be viewed as a negative too; your developers might have difficulty in switching between two different mind-sets for the different layers of the application.

You should also think about how the application will be tested. If you want to adopt the testing approach described in Chapter 12, *Scenario Testing*, on page 217, then you would need to use the second option. But if you already have a substantial investment in automated testing using other technologies, then this probably isn't the deciding factor.

Whichever option you choose, it's going to be important that your domain model is decoupled from the Naked Objects runtime. So, let's see what that means.

14.2 Decoupling from the Framework

While the Naked Objects' Maven archetype generated five different projects for us, the only project that will be used in the runtime environment is the dom project that contains our domain model.

You'll see from the Maven pom.xml for this project that its only dependency in our domain project is on the Naked Objects applib, which is very deliberately separate from the rest of the framework. In fact, the purpose of the applib is to distill down all the semantics and general services that an enterprise application might need (irrespective of whether the application is deployed using Naked Objects).

If we look further into the applib, most of our dependencies relate to the use of annotations (such as @RegEx or @Named) and most likely the convenience superclasses (such as AbstractDomainObject). As we'll see shortly, there's also an implicit—if not explicit—dependency on the DomainObjectContainer interface.

We'll tackle the superclasses and the container in the sections that follow, but for now let's start with the issue of annotations.

Annotations

One way to think of our annotations is as a specification:

- Annotations that capture declarative business rules (such as @RegEx or @MaxLength) in effect specify the behavior of the application layer and persistence layer ("make sure any value you provide for this property or parameter meets this regular expression and is no longer than this length").

- Annotations that provide rendering hints (such as @MemberOrder or @Named) act as a specification for the presentation layer ("make sure that this property comes before this one, and has this label").

Alternatively, you could take the view that it's not enough to just specify these rules in the domain layer; their implementation should be in the domain layer too. In that case, you have two options:

- First, you could replace the declarative business rules with imperative business rules, using the supporting methods. OK, you still need to ensure that the application layer calls these imperative rules, but the implementation is in the domain layer.

- Or, you could write your own code that processes the annotations in the same way that Naked Objects does itself. One option is to write some aspects using AspectJ; alternatively, you might consider using APT.[1,2]

Let's now turn our attention to those convenience superclasses.

Not Using the Convenience Superclasses

Although throughout we've been subclassing from the convenience superclasses (such as AbstractDomainObject) in the applib, this has been *just* for convenience. If you have a reason for your classes to subclass from some other superclass, you can. By the way, this applies to all the deployment options, not just the *pure pojo* deployment option.

If you take a look at the source code of these classes, you'll see that all they really do for us is provide a *set*ter so that a DomainObjectContainer can be injected and then provide convenience methods that delegate to that container.

---

1. http://www.eclipse.org/aspectj/
2. http://java.sun.com/j2se/1.5.0/docs/guide/apt/GettingStarted.html

For example, the persist() method is as follows:

`chapter14/AbstractContainedObject-persist.java`

```
protected void persist(final Object transientDomainObject) {
    getContainer().persist(transientDomainObject);
}
```

It's therefore trivial to inline this functionality within your own classes and remove the superclass or replace it with a superclass of your own.

Of course, what we haven't done yet is remove the dependency on DomainObjectContainer, which is now explicit, whereas previously it was implicit. So, let's discuss that next.

Implementing DomainObjectContainer

As we learned earlier in Chapter 8, *Isolating Infrastructure Services*, on page 125, most domain objects applications use the DomainObjectContainer one way or another, including generic searches for objects, persisting objects, instantiating new objects, raising warning messages, and obtaining the security context.

While you could rip out the dependency on this interface from your classes, you'd end up replacing it with something very similar. In any case, DomainObjectContainer is an interface, so my suggestion is to leave this dependency as is and just provide your own implementation. At the end of the day, it's just another domain service that your domain object depends upon.

One method that is in the DomainObjectContainer that might puzzle you is newTransientInstance(). Why not simply instantiate the class using its constructor? We'll answer that in the next section.

Injecting Dependencies

Again, as we learned in Chapter 8, *Isolating Infrastructure Services*, on page 125, Naked Objects uses dependency injection to inject both domain and infrastructure services into domain objects that need them. In CarServ, we've injected an EmailService and a CalendarService, for example, but in fact Naked Objects will inject any of the services registered in nakedobjects.properties.

If we're not using the Naked Objects runtime, then we need to do this dependency injection ourselves. There are two cases to consider: injecting into already persisted objects that are being pulled back from the persistence layer and injecting into newly instantiated objects.

Dealing with the first of these isn't too difficult to implement if using an object-relational mapping (ORM) framework, because most provide APIs to allow this. For example, Hibernate has a LoadEventListener interface:

chapter14/InjectServicesLoadEventListener.java

```java
public class InjectServicesLoadEventListener
        implements LoadEventListener {
    public void onLoad(
            final LoadEvent event,
            final LoadEventListener.LoadType loadType)
            throws HibernateException {
        Object domainObject = event.getResult();
        // ... inject services into domainObject ...
    }
}
```

The second is also easy enough, thanks to the newTransientInstance() method. Our implementation of the DomainObjectContainer could be as simple as this:

chapter14/DomainObjectContainerImpl-newTransientInstance.java

```java
public <T> T newTransientInstance(final Class<T> ofClass) {
    try {
        T domainObject = ofClass.newInstance();
        // ... inject services into domainObject ...
        return domainObject;
    } catch (InstantiationException e) {
        throw new RuntimeException(e);
    } catch (IllegalAccessException e) {
        throw new RuntimeException(e);
    }
}
```

These are not the only implementation options available to you. For example, if you use the Spring Framework, then you can achieve the same effect using its @Configurable annotation.[3]

By the way, If you really don't like that newTransientInstance() method, you could replace it with an AspectJ aspect associated with a constructor join point. And if you are using Spring, then you'll find AspectJ is already part of its runtime.

The previous takes care of the compile-time dependencies, but there's a more subtle dependency that we also must understand.

---

3. Spring Framework is hosted at http://www.springsource.com. For usage of @Configurable, see http://www.gridshore.nl/2009/01/27/injecting-domain-objects-with-spring/.

14.3 Implementing the Programming Model Interaction Protocol

We spent a good chunk of Part I of the book learning the set of conventions that make up a Naked Objects domain model, that is, its programming model. This programming model in effect defines a protocol for the interaction between the application layer and the domain layer so that the domain objects' business rules are honored.

With the other deployment options, we don't need to worry too much about this protocol because one way or another there is framework code in the application layer that implements it. But with the *pure pojo* deployment option, we are writing all the layers ourselves and so we do need to ensure our application layer interacts with the domain layer in the same way that the Naked Objects framework would.

We can visualize this protocol as a sequence diagram, as shown in Figure 14.1, on the facing page.

So:

1. When the user goes to use a Customer object, the presentation layer (UI) requests from the application layer a list of those properties (and collections and actions) that are visible, and for each asks whether they are enabled or disabled.

2. Then, for an enabled property (such as the Customer's lastName), the presentation layer requests to set a new value. The application layer again checks that the property is visible and usable. Assuming that it is, it then also checks whether the proposed new value is valid. If that passes, then the property is set.

Adding and removing from collections works in the same way, as does invoking actions.

In general, the application layer should check whether the class member is visible; if so, whether it is usable; and finally (if being modified) if the new value is valid. Or as we summarized in Chapter 6, *Implementing Business Rules*, on page 91: Can you see it? Can you use it? Can you do it?

Ultimately then, decoupling our domain model from the framework boils down to providing to a DomainObjectContainer implementation, implementing dependency injection into domain objects, and ensuring that the application layer interacts with the domain model "in the right way."

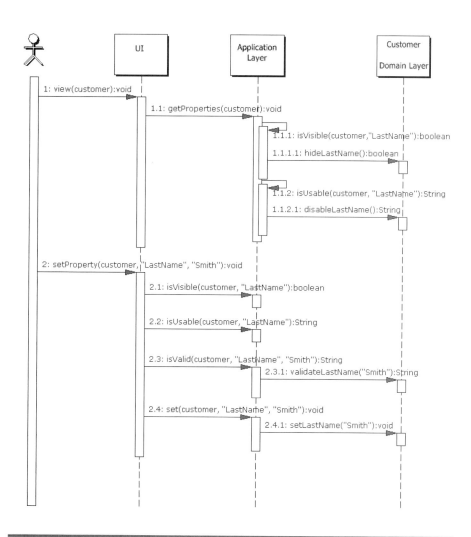

Figure 14.1: NAKED OBJECTS' INTERACTIONS WITH DOMAIN OBJECTS

To finish off this chapter, there's one more thing to explore: how to go about changing the conventions of the Naked Objects programming model itself.

14.4 Changing the Programming Model

To hide a property, we can either use the @Hidden annotation or write a hideXxx() supporting method that returns **true**. These are just a couple of the conventions that make up the Naked Objects programming model.

These conventions have been refined over a number of years, so I don't suggest you change them arbitrarily. On the other hand, if you want your code to coexist with some other (less flexible!) framework, you might have good reason to do so.

The programming model is defined by a set of FacetFactorys, each of which is responsible for identifying and handling a particular element of the programming model. For example, here's how we pick up the @MemberOrder annotation:

`chapter14/MemberOrderAnnotationFacetFactory.java`

```java
public class MemberOrderAnnotationFacetFactory
        extends AnnotationBasedFacetFactoryAbstract {
    public MemberOrderAnnotationFacetFactory() {
        super(
            NakedObjectFeatureType.PROPERTIES_COLLECTIONS_AND_ACTIONS);
    }
    @Override
    public boolean process(
            final Class<?> cls,
            final Method method, final MethodRemover methodRemover,
            final FacetHolder holder) {
        Class<MemberOrder> annotationClass = MemberOrder.class;
        final MemberOrder annotation =
            getAnnotation(method, annotationClass);
        return FacetUtil.addFacet(create(annotation, holder));
    }
    private MemberOrderFacet create(
            final MemberOrder annotation, final FacetHolder holder) {
        return annotation == null ? null :
            new MemberOrderFacetAnnotation(
                    annotation.name(), annotation.sequence(), holder);
    }
}
```

The viewers then look for these Facets in the metamodel to render the domain object.

It's too large a topic for us to go into detail, but using the naked-objects.properties file, you can easily remove existing facets or add your own:

chapter14/nakedobjects-FacetIncludes.properties

```
nakedobjects.reflector.facets.include=\
        com.mycompany.nakedobjects.facets.MyFacetFactory
```

Or, alternatively you could subclass Naked Objects' own Programming-ModelFacetsJava5 class (which lists all the FacetFactorys) and define your very own programming model:

chapter14/nakedobjects-ProgModel.properties

```
nakedobjects.reflector.facets=\
        com.mycompany.nakedobjects.facets.MyProgrammingModel
```

And that's it for this chapter.

Coming Up Next

In this chapter, we focused on the *pure pojo* deployment option. We discussed two different approaches for Naked Objects in your development process and also learned how to decouple our domain model from both compile-time and more subtle runtime dependencies on the Naked Objects framework.

In the next chapter, we're going to look at two more of our deployment options, the *embedded metamodel* option and *custom presentation* option.

Exercises

Thinking about the organization or client you work for, which of the two approaches to using Naked Objects might fit best? Would you just use Naked Objects to bootstrap a new project, or might you be able to continue following the conventions of a (possibly customized) Naked Objects programming model once initial exploration is complete?

Why don't you also try customizing the standard programming model? Can you can find the FacetFactory that looks for the hideXxx() supporting methods and write a new one that uses an "invisible" suffix instead?

(Indeed, if you are working on a non-English-speaking project, you might want to change all the suffixes or annotations to your preferred language.) Register your new FacetFactory in nakedobjects.properties, and remove the original one.

And if you want to explore further in terms of implementing your own business rules and annotations, then the InteractionAdvisorFacet is a good place to begin your investigations.

Integrating with Web Frameworks

There sometimes seems to be as many Java web frameworks out there as there are Java developers. Well, perhaps not quite that many, but looking around I found 58 catalogued on a single website alone![1] So, there's a good chance you've spent at least some of your time as a developer using one of these frameworks.

In this chapter, we're going to see how to integrate our domain model using one such web framework and, in so doing, provide worked examples of the *embedded metamodel* deployment option (whereby both presentation and persistence is handled using custom code) and also the *custom presentation* deployment option (where just the presentation layer is custom coded).

The framework we'll use is Apache *Wicket*, which I've chosen because it's easy to learn and has an architecture that targets the layers we want to write ourselves.[2] But the techniques we cover here equally apply to other mainstream web frameworks (such as Struts, JSF, Spring MVC, Tapestry, and even GWT).

We're not going to spend lots of time learning how Wicket works; if you like what you see and are interested in learning more, then the definitive book is *Wicket in Action* [DH08]. But, we will look at how Wicket can use the facilities that Naked Objects provides.

We'll start off with the *embedded metamodel* deployment option.

---

1. http://java-source.net/open-source/web-frameworks
2. http://wicket.apache.org

> **Fast Track to a Customized Web App**
>
> In this chapter, I've chosen Wicket to demonstrate that we can integrate with an existing third-party web framework. But if you have no particular prejudice as to which framework to use, then the shortest route to a customized web application is probably Scimpi.*
>
> You could think of Scimpi as a "preintegrated" web framework for Naked Objects (it is in fact a next-generation viewer). We discuss it in a little more detail in Chapter 18, *Deploying the Full Runtime*, on page 333.
>
> _____
>
> *. Scimpi is hosted at http://scimpi.org, licensed under Apache Software License v2. The project lead for Scimpi is Robert Matthews (the project lead for Naked Objects itself).

15.1 Deploying an Embedded Metamodel

We don't want to get distracted by lots of code relating to the specifics of the Wicket APIs, so (as I explained in the introduction of Chapter 13, *Developing Domain Applications*, on page 241) in this chapter we start off with a version of CarServ (**chapter15-01**[3]) that has already had the changes made to it.

Running the Application

First things first. Let's run the application. You can either:

- Use Run > Run Configurations and then create a "Maven Build" launch configuration with a base directory of carserv-wicket and a goal of jetty:run. When we run this launch configuration, Maven will launch a Jetty web server for us. Then navigate to http://localhost:8080/carserv-wicket.

- Or, somewhat quicker, you can navigate to the Start class under src/test/java and simply run it as a Java application. This "test class" launches its own instance of Jetty. The URL to navigate to is simply http://localhost:8080.

_____

3. Based on chapter12-03; also includes a solution to the Chapter 12 exercise for Services to hold a reference to the PaymentMethod by which they were paid.

Figure 15.1: CARSERV RUNNING ON WICKET

In Figure 15.1, we can see the application once it's running. Initially the page shows just the panel on the left side listing all the Customers. If you click the "vehicles" link for Joe Bloggs, then you'll see his list of vehicles. Similarly, click the "edit" link, and you'll see some of the details that you can then modify.

As you can see, this little application doesn't expose the vast majority of the functionality in the domain model, but it's sufficient for our purposes. Play around to familiarize yourself, and then let's move on to look at the code.

The Application Class

In Wicket the application object acts as a shared top-level container for all the components and resources that make up the application. As such, it's an ideal place to hold the Naked Objects metamodel.

We start off by subclassing Wicket's WebApplication class:

```
chapter15/NakedObjectsApplication-MetaModel.java

public class NakedObjectsApplication extends WebApplication {
    private final NakedObjectsMetaModel nakedObjectsMetaModel;
    ...
    public NakedObjectsApplication() {
        ...
        nakedObjectsMetaModel = new NakedObjectsMetaModel(
                embeddedContext,
                CustomerApplicationRepositoryInMemory.class,
                ServiceableVehicleRepositoryInMemory.class,
                EmployeeRepositoryInMemory.class,
                VehicleTypeRepositoryInMemory.class,
                ModelRepositoryInMemory.class,
                MakeRepositoryInMemory.class,
                PaymentMethodTypeRepositoryInMemory.class,
                EmailServiceDemo.class,
                CalendarServiceDemo.class);
        nakedObjectsMetaModel.init();
        ...
    }
    ...
}
```

You'll probably recognize most of the (varargs) arguments passed to the NakedObjectsMetaModel constructor; these are the services that we've previously seen in the nakedobjects.properties file. Naked Objects uses the services to discover the classes that make up the metamodel.

The first argument, embeddedContext, is new, though. This is an implementation of EmbeddedContext, an adapter interface that acts as the runtime context shown in Figure 13.2, on page 244. Our implementation is called EmbeddedContextWicket. Some of its implementation is very straightforward, for example, instantiating a new object:

```
chapter15/EmbeddedContextWicket.java

public Object instantiate(Class<?> type) {
    try {
        return type.newInstance();
    } catch (InstantiationException ex) {
        throw new RuntimeException(ex);
    } catch (IllegalAccessException ex) {
        throw new RuntimeException(ex);
    }
}
```

Some of the calls delegate to the web framework's APIs, for example, raising messages:

chapter15/EmbeddedContextWicket.java

```java
public void informUser(String message) {
    Session.get().info(message);
}
```

And many of the remainder delegate to some persistence store:

chapter15/EmbeddedContextWicket.java

```java
public void makePersistent(Object object) {
    getObjectStore().persist(object);
}
```

The implementation of the persistence store is up to you (that's one of the points of this deployment option). I've implemented an ObjectStore, which—as might be apparent if you look at its code—is similar to Naked Objects' own in-memory object store. But you could use JPA or JDBC or any other persistence technology.

One bit of EmbeddedContextWicket that is a little tricky is its getPersistenceState() method:

chapter15/EmbeddedContextWicket-getPersistenceState.java

```java
public PersistenceState getPersistenceState(Object object) {
    if (getObjectStore().isPersistent(object)) {
        return PersistenceState.PERSISTENT;
    }
    NakedObjectSpecification spec =
        getSpecificationLoader().loadSpecification(object.getClass());
    if (!spec.containsFacet(ValueFacet.class)) {
        return PersistenceState.TRANSIENT;
    } else {
        return PersistenceState.STANDALONE;
    }
}
```

If you recall Chapter 6, *Implementing Business Rules*, on page 91, you'll remember we can write business rules such as @Hidden(When.UNTIL_PERSISTED). To enforce these rules, the metamodel needs to know if a given domain object is persistent or not, something our object store tells us.

However, this applies only to *entity objects*. *Value objects* are considered "stand alone"; after all, it doesn't make sense to talk about the persistence of the number 5. The spec variable (of type NakedObjectSpecification) in the previous code is a reference into Naked Objects' metamodel;

it's broadly analogous to java.lang.Class. Using this, we can tell whether the object is an *entity* or a *value* by checking for the presence of the ValueFacet facet. This basically corresponds to the @Value annotation that we learned about in Chapter 7, *Using Value Types*, on page 109.

Going back to NakedObjectsApplication, you'll see there's a method called getHomePage(). This is part of Wicket's API, and it determines which page to render initially. Let's look at this now.

The Home Page

If you're browsing the code, you might already have noticed that Wicket pages come in pairs: an HTML page and a corresponding Java class. Wicket uses the HTML page to render the page and dynamically replaces content using code from the Java class.

In the application class, the home page is specified as Index.class, and so Wicket initially renders Index.html. The *<div>* element with wicket:id= *customerList* is replaced using this code from the Index class:

```
chapter15/Index-customerList.java
PageableListView customerList =
    new PageableListView(
            "customerList",
            getCustomerRepository().allCustomers(), 5) {
        ...
        protected void populateItem(ListItem item) {
            Customer customer = (Customer) item.getModelObject();
            String customerName =
                customer.getPerson().getName().title();
            item.add(
                new Label("name", customerName));
            item.add(
                new ReplaceLink<Customer>("showVehiclesLink", ... ));
            item.add(
                new ReplaceLink<Customer>("editCustomerLink", ... ));
        }
        ...
    };
add(customerList);
```

This calls the CustomerRepository to retrieve all the Customers; these are then rendered in the left-hand panel.

When we click the "vehicles" link, a vehicles panel appears on the right side. Let's look at how this works in a little more detail.

Customer Vehicle Panel

Drilling into the code in the Index class a little deeper, the "vehicles" link corresponds to the following:

chapter15/Index-showVehiclesLink.java

```java
item.add(new ReplaceLink<Customer>(
            "showVehiclesLink", item.getModel()){
    ...
    protected Panel getReplacementPanel(
            String id, Customer selected) {
        return new CustomerVehiclesPanel(id, selected);
    }
});
```

Here ReplaceLink is a little helper class subclassing Wicket's own Link class that replaces an empty panel on the right side with the CustomerVehiclePanel.

Like pages, panels also come in pairs, an HTML file and a corresponding Java class, with dynamic content being generated similarly.

Because the vehicle panel is read-only, there's not much else to talk about, so let's now move onto the more interesting edit customer panel.

Edit Customer Panel

So far in our Wicket application, we've simply displayed information. When it comes to editing the Customer, though, there are some business rules that we want to enforce. The *embedded metamodel* works by allowing our presentation code to request a *view object* for each underlying domain object. This view object is just a proxy or decorator; in the same way that mocking libraries work, it is the same type as the underlying object, and our presentation code can use it in the same way as the original domain object.

Well, not quite. What the view object also does is to enforce the business rules of the domain object, in the way as described in Section 14.3, *Programming Model Interaction Protocol*, on page 264. If a property is hidden and we attempt to read it, it will throw a HiddenException (a subclass of RuntimeException). If a collection is disabled and we attempt to add to it, it will throw a DisabledException. If an action argument is invalid and we attempt to invoke the action, it will throw an InvalidException.

More generally, the view object checks visibility, then usability, and finally validity. If all three checks are OK, it will delegate to the underlying object and return the value. Otherwise, it throws an exception.

> ## Persisting Objects using the Interface
>
> View objects have a further trick up their sleeve; they also implement the ViewObject interface. The ViewObject interface has a save() method. This is the programmatic equivalent of hitting the save button in the DnD or HTML viewer.
>
> We can therefore downcast the view object to ViewObject and invoke this save() method. If the underlying domain object is transient and is in a valid state, then it will be persisted; otherwise, an InvalidException will be thrown.

Moreover, the view object also restricts the methods we may invoke to *getters* and *setters* for properties, the *getter*, the addTo() and removeFrom() methods for collections, any **public** method representing an action, the title() method, and the defaultNXxx() or choicesNXxx() supporting methods for properties and action parameters.

Invoking the supporting methods that implement business rules (such as hideXxx(), disableXxx(), or validateXxx()) will throw an UnsupportedOperationException. The view object also restricts which methods can be invoked on collections obtained from a *getter*; any methods that mutate its state (such as add() or removeAll()) will similarly throw an exception.

Let's see how this is put together in the Wicket application. Similar to the CustomerVehiclesPanel we saw previously, the EditCustomerPanel appears on the right side (replaces the empty panel) when we click the "edit" link for a Customer. In EditCustomerPanel, we have the following code:

chapter15/EditCustomerPanel-addForm.java

```java
private void addForm(final Customer customer) {
    EditCustomerForm form =
        new EditCustomerFormUsingViewObjects(
            "editCustomerForm", getContainer(), customer);
    add(form);
    ...
}
```

where EditCustomerFormUsingViewObjects inherits from EditCustomerForm, which in turn subclasses Wicket's own Form class. The job of EditCustomerForm is to set up the form components; the interesting code is in subclass. In its constructor, it is passed a Naked Objects HeadlessViewer; this is actually just an implementation of DomainObjectContainer that also acts as a factory for view objects:

chapter15/EditCustomerFormUsingViewObjects-constructor.java

```
EditCustomerFormUsingViewObjects(
        String id, HeadlessViewer headlessViewer, Customer customer) {
    super(id, headlessViewer.view(customer));
}
```

As we can see, the first thing that the constructor does is to wrap the provided Customer domain object in a view object using HeadlessViewer's view() method. With this done, we can then apply the business rules. For example:

chapter15/EditCustomerFormUsingViewObjects-configureEmailFieldRules.java

```
protected void configureEmailFieldRules(LabelAndFormComponent lafc) {
    try {
        String emailAddress = getCustomer().getEmailAddress();
        getCustomer().setEmailAddress(emailAddress);
    } catch (HiddenException ex) {
        lafc.setVisible(false);
    } catch (DisabledException ex) {
        lafc.setEnabled(false);
    }
}
```

At first glance, this code seems to do nothing; it reads the value of emailAddress and then sets it back. However, that call to getCustomer() is in fact returning the view object. When we read the emailAddress property using the *get*ter, the view object checks to see that the property is visible; if not, an exception is thrown, and so we in our code we hide the field. Similarly, when we write the value back using the *set*ter, the view object checks whether the emailAddress property is usable; again, an exception is thrown if not, and we disable the field.

The previous shows how visibility and usability rules are applied, but what of validity such as the maximum length of the notes property?

> ### Using the Headless Viewer in Domain Objects
>
> It's possible to use view objects in our own domain classes. This is sometimes useful if we want to interact with other objects as if through a Naked Objects viewer.
>
> To use this feature, set the nakedobjects.persistor.domain-object-container property in the nakedobjects.properties file; the generated Maven archetype has (commented out) the value to use. You also need to include the org.nakedobjects.plugins : headless-viewer Maven module in your commandline project's pom.xml. If you need to use the ViewObject interface, then your domain project's pom.xml will also need to reference the org.nakedobjects.plugins : headless-applib module.

Here we need to gently persuade Wicket to play nicely by overriding the inherited process() method and dealing with any InvalidException:

chapter15/EditCustomerFormUsingViewObjects-process.java

```java
public boolean process() {
    try {
        return super.process();
    } catch (WicketRuntimeException ex) {
        Throwable cause = ex.getCause();
        if (cause instanceof InvalidException) {
            error(cause.getMessage());
            return false;
        } else {
            throw ex;
        }
    }
}
```

Let's see this in action. Looking at the Customer class, we can see the following:

- The feedback property should be visible only for valuable Customers (those with two or more Vehicles).
- The notes property is disabled for Customers with no Vehicles.
- The notes property has a maximum length of 255 characters.

Navigate to the MaryBloggsCarFixture and comment out the call to createCar(), and for JoeBloggsCarFixture comment out the lines that give him a second Car. That will give us Mary with no Cars, Joe with one Car, and Boris with three. Now run the application and click "edit" for each of Mary, Joe, and Boris. For Mary and Joe, you shouldn't be able

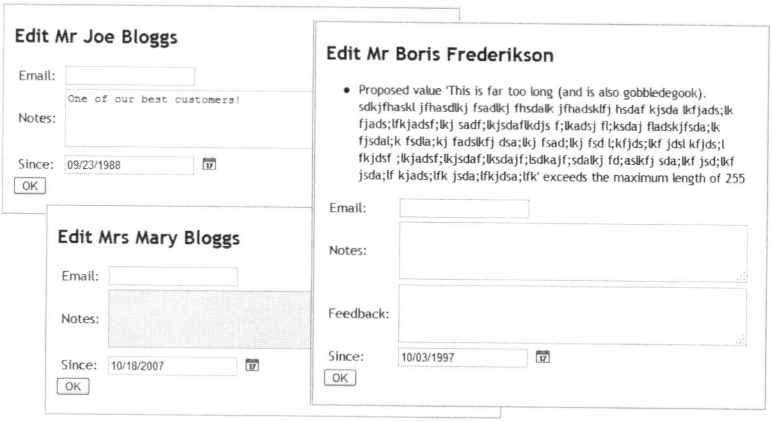

Figure 15.2: CARSERV BUSINESS RULES IN WICKET

to view the feedback property, and for Mary only the notes property should be disabled. For Boris, both feedback and notes should be visible and usable. Finally, for either Joe or Boris, attempt to update the notes property to a string longer than 255 characters; the change should be rejected. All this is shown in Figure 15.2.

If we look at the validation message, it isn't clear whether it is the notes or feedback property that is invalid. That's because we only handle the InvalidException at the form level (that overridden process() method). Let's see how to improve on this.

Validating Individual Properties

Like many frameworks, Wicket allows us to install validators at the field level. This will give us the more specific error messages that we're after.

If you have downloaded the code, then you might have noticed that there is another subclass of EditCustomerForm, namely, EditCustomerFormUsingViewObjectsExtended. This overrides configureNotesFieldRules():

chapter15/EditCustomerFormUsingViewObjectsExtended-configureNotesFieldRules.java

```
@Override
protected void configureNotesFieldRules(
        final LabelAndFormComponent lafc) {
    super.configureNotesFieldRules(lafc);
    installMaxLengthValidator(
            Customer.class, lafc.getFormComponent());
}
```

```
private void installMaxLengthValidator(
        final Class<?> domainClass, final FormComponent field) {
    NakedObjectAssociation association =
        getAssociation(domainClass, field);
    MaxLengthFacet maxLengthFacet =
        association.getFacet(MaxLengthFacet.class);
    if (maxLengthFacet != null) {
        field.add(StringValidator.maximumLength(
                    maxLengthFacet.value()));
    }
}
```

What this code is doing is reaching into the Naked Objects metamodel and looking for a specific facet that represents the @MaxLength annotation. If found, it then installs a corresponding Wicket validator.

To see this in action, go back to the EditCustomerPanel, and modify its addForm() method to use this extended version of EditCustomerForm:

chapter15/EditCustomerPanel-addForm-Extended.java

```
private void addForm(final Customer customer) {
    EditCustomerForm form =
        new EditCustomerFormUsingViewObjectsExtended(
            "editCustomerForm", getContainer(), customer);
    add(form);
    ...
}
```

When you run the application, you should see that the error message has changed; it is being generated by Wicket rather than Naked Objects. I'm not sure this new version is necessarily an improvement, though. To me, it violates the DRY principle because we have to remember to install a Wicket validator for each and every Naked Objects facet that represents as a validity rule. In practice, I would stay with the original version.

The HeadlessViewer is only one way of interacting with the Naked Objects metamodel. We can also reach deeper into the metamodel and, for example, be able to determine which property is invalid. It's time now to move onto the last deployment option for this chapter, the *custom presentation* option, where Naked Objects does the persistence (so there is no longer any EmbeddedContext to implement). We'll also see how to use the alternative way of exploiting the metamodel.

15.2 Integrating Layers with the Custom Presentation Option

For the custom presentation deployment option, we again have a new version of CarServ (***chapter15-02***). So, once more, download and follow along (but if you're not at your computer, all the relevant code is in the text).

Running the Application

You can run this new version of CarServ in the same way as the last version. The only difference is that if using mvn jetty:run, then the URL to navigate to changes is http://localhost:8080/carserv-wicket2.

The first thing you'll notice when you browse to the web app is a sign-on page; this version also integrates Wicket's security with Naked Objects' own authentication mechanism. We'll look at how this works in a moment, but for now sign on with a username of *sven* and a password of *pass*. You should then arrive at the same home page as previously, except that we can also see (in a footer) the username we have logged in as. Browse around; you should see the application is pretty much the same.

It's time once again to look at the code.

The Application Class

As before, we use a subclass of WebApplication to bootstrap Naked Objects, in the NakedObjectsApplication class. However, this time we're bootstrapping all the Naked Objects runtime, not just the metamodel:

chapter15/NakedObjectsApplication-constructor.java

```
ConfigurationBuilderDefault configurationBuilder =
    new ConfigurationBuilderDefault();
configurationBuilder.add(SystemConstants.NOSPLASH_KEY, ""+true);

NakedObjectsSystemBootstrapper systemBootstrapper =
    new NakedObjectsSystemBootstrapper(configurationBuilder, getClass());

system = systemBootstrapper.bootSystem(DeploymentType.EXPLORATION);
```

The NakedObjectsSystem object *is* the Naked Objects runtime; the bootstrapper class reads the configuration to determine which components make up the runtime. Once instantiated, the components are made available to us using **static** methods in NakedObjectsContext. They have different scopes, but one that has global scope is the AuthenticationManager. Let's see how we integrate with this.

Authentication

In this version of CarServ, the NakedObjectsApplication class actually subclasses Wicket's AuthenticatedWebApplication (rather than plain WebApplication as previously). We override getSignInPage() to indicate which HTML/Java class pair to use to render a sign-in page.

There's nothing to see in the sign-in page itself. Instead, the AuthenticatedWebApplication has another hook method that we override, namely, getWebSessionClass(). Here we return a custom subclass, NakedObjectsAuthenticatedWebSession. The integration code is in its authenticate() method:

chapter15/NakedObjectsAuthenticatedWebSession-authenticate.java

```java
import org.apache.wicket.authentication.AuthenticatedWebSession;
import org.nakedobjects.metamodel.authentication.AuthenticationSession;
import org.nakedobjects.runtime.authentication.AuthenticationManager;
...
public class NakedObjectsAuthenticatedWebSession
        extends AuthenticatedWebSession {
    ...
    private AuthenticationSession authenticationSession;
    public boolean authenticate(
            final String username, final String password) {
        AuthenticationRequestPassword authenticationRequest =
            new AuthenticationRequestPassword(username, password);
        authenticationSession =
            getAuthenticationManager().authenticate(
                    authenticationRequest);
        return authenticationSession != null;
    }
    private static AuthenticationManager getAuthenticationManager() {
        return NakedObjectsContext.getAuthenticationManager();
    }
    ...
}
```

We subclass Wicket's AuthenticatedWebSession to store a Naked Objects' AuthenticationSession. And as you can see, getAuthenticationManager() uses the NakedObjectsContext to obtain the Naked Objects' bootstrapped AuthenticationManager.

Since we haven't said otherwise, we're using Naked Objects' default implementation of AuthenticationManager. This is discussed in more detail in Section 18.2, *Securing the Application*, on page 342, but for now all we need to know is that it reads usernames and passwords from the config/passwords file. The format is as follows:

```
user1:password1:roleA|roleB|roleC
user2:password2:roleA|roleD|roleF
```

Look at this file, and you'll see each of *our* users is in the USER role:

chapter15/passwords

```
sven:pass:USER
dick:pass:USER
bob:pass:USER
joe:pass:USER
```

We use this to secure the Index page:

chapter15/Index.java

```
@AuthorizeInstantiation("USER")
public class Index extends NakedObjectsWebPage { ... }
```

This takes care of Wicket's view of authentication, but we also need to propagate the current user principal into the Naked Objects runtime. We do this by overriding yet another hook method in NakedObjectsApplication, namely, newRequestCycle(). Here we return our own NakedObjectsWebRequestCycle that does the necessary:

chapter15/NakedObjectsWebRequestCycle.java

```
public class NakedObjectsWebRequestCycle extends WebRequestCycle {
    ...
    protected void onBeginRequest() {
        super.onBeginRequest();
        NakedObjectsAuthenticatedWebSession wicketSession =
            NakedObjectsAuthenticatedWebSession.get();
        if (wicketSession == null) {
            return;
        }
        AuthenticationSession nakedObjectsSession =
            wicketSession.getAuthenticationSession();
        if (nakedObjectsSession == null) {
            return;
        }
        NakedObjectsContext.openSession(nakedObjectsSession);
        getTransactionManager().startTransaction();
    }
    ...
    protected void onEndRequest() {
        if (NakedObjectsContext.inSession()) {
            NakedObjectTransaction transaction =
                getTransactionManager().getTransaction();
            if (transaction != null) {
                getTransactionManager().endTransaction();
            }

            NakedObjectsContext.closeSession();
        }
        super.onEndRequest();
    }
    ...
}
```

This is analogous to Hibernate's *open session in view* pattern. It provides us with a persistence context for the domain objects we are using.[4] We also start a transaction, with one transaction per session. Let's now move on to see how we implement business rules using the full Naked Objects runtime.

Implementing Business Rules

As before, EditCustomerForm is the class that sets up the form widgets. This time, though, most of the heavy lifting is done by a helper class that I've called NakedObjectsPropertyAdapter, a descendant of LabelAnd-FormComponent from the previous version of CarServ. The bit we care about is the configureRules() method:

```
chapter15/NakedObjectsPropertyAdapter-configureRules.java
```

```
private void configureRules() {
    setVisible(visibilityConsent().isAllowed());
    setEnabled(usabilityConsent().isAllowed());
    final class NakedObjectsPropertyValidator
            extends AbstractValidator {
        ...
        protected void onValidate(IValidatable validatable) {
            Object proposedValue = validatable.getValue();
            Consent validityConsent = validityConsent(proposedValue);
            if (validityConsent.isVetoed()) {
                String reason = validityConsent.getReason();
                reasonBuf.setLength(0); // clear
                this.reasonBuf.append(reason);
                error(validatable);
            }
        }
    };
    getFormComponent().add(new NakedObjectsPropertyValidator());
}
```

This method does three things. First, it configures visibility using the visibilityConsent() helper method:

```
chapter15/NakedObjectsPropertyAdapter-visibilityConsent.java
```

```
private Consent visibilityConsent() {
    return getAssociation().isVisible(
            getAuthenticationSession(), getModelAdapter());
}
private NakedObjectAssociation getAssociation() {
    NakedObjectSpecification noSpec =
        getSpecificationLoader().loadSpecification(getModelClass());
    return noSpec.getAssociation(getFormComponent().getId());
}
```

---

4. See http://www.hibernate.org/43.html for more on the *open session in view* pattern.

> ## Large-Scale Widgets
>
> The NakedObjectsPropertyAdapter class wraps up a single property of an object, but it would be easy enough to write a NakedObjectsForm that wraps up *all* the properties of a given domain object. This could do a lot of the donkey work but allow you to break out into custom presentation code as you'd like.
>
> Indeed, this is exactly the objective of the *MetaWidget* open source project.* This is unrelated to Naked Objects, but it provides a series of components built from various metamodel sources. In principle, the Naked Objects metamodel could act as a back end for MetaWidget's various front ends.
>
> _____
> *.   http://www.metawidget.org.

Second, it similarly sets up usability using the usabilityConsent() helper:

chapter15/NakedObjectsPropertyAdapter-usabilityConsent.java

```java
private Consent usabilityConsent() {
    return getAssociation().isUsable(
            getAuthenticationSession(), getModelAdapter());
}
```

And lastly, it installs a Wicket validator for each field using the validityConsent() helper:

chapter15/NakedObjectsPropertyAdapter-validityConsent.java

```java
private Consent validityConsent(final Object proposedValue) {
    return getOneToOneAssociation().isAssociationValid(
            getModelAdapter(), adapterFor(proposedValue));
}
```

It's this last piece that's significant. Whereas in the previous version installing Wicket validators was fragile because it violated the DRY principle (see Section 15.1, *Validating Individual Properties*, on page 279), we now can support all Naked Objects validation rules generically. Have metamodel, will use!

To see this in action, try entering more than 255 characters for Boris' notes property; it should be rejected, and moreover you should see that the invalid field is highlighted.

And that's as far as we're going to take this example.

Coming Up Next

In this chapter, we saw firsthand how to put a custom user interface to an existing domain model. We used two different approaches: the *embedded metamodel* deployment option (that lets us also provide our own custom persistence layer) and the *custom presentation* option (where persistence is taken care of by the Naked Objects framework). We also saw two different ways of using the metamodel, either through the headless viewer or using the Naked Objects metamodel API directly.

In this chapter, we were looking mostly at the layers "in front" of the domain model. In the next, though, we'll look in more detail at the persistence layer that sits "behind" the domain model. We'll start looking at the XML object store provided by Naked Objects itself, but we'll spend most of our time configuring the JPA object store provided by one of Naked Objects' sister projects, allowing us to store our domain objects in a relational database.

Exercises

Have a go at enhancing the NakedObjectsWebRequestCycle (in the **chapter15-02** version of CarServ) to support the info() and warn() methods provided by DomainObjectContainer. When called, these messages ultimately end up in a transaction-scoped component called the MessageBroker. In the onEndRequest() method, you can therefore retrieve the MessageBroker and copy over any messages and warnings into the NakedObjectsAuthenticatedWebSession. These will appear wherever a Wicket feedback panel exists (for example, on the EditCustomerForm).

You also have the statutory exercise to do: put a custom front end onto your own application. You might want to start with one of the versions of CarServ and adapt it as need be. If you don't know Wicket, you might want to explore using Scimpi.

Integrating with the Database

These days it's fairly common to build systems by initially mocking out the persistence layer and focusing on the domain layer and other layers. As we've seen, Naked Objects supports this with the in-memory object store that we've been using throughout.

But there comes a point when the rubber hits the road. We are going to need to persist our domain objects in some sort of persistence store; after all, the data we create today needs to be there tomorrow. For the vast majority of enterprises, and for us too, this means storing our objects as data in a relational database. That will allow the business users to use the data in other ways, such as slicing and dicing it using dedicated reporting or business intelligence tools. And from an operational perspective, our DBAs will be able to manage (performance tune, back up, and archive) our domain objects using standard tools, just as in any other enterprise application.

The Naked Objects framework defines an ObjectStore interface so that alternative implementations can be switched in; the in-memory object store we've been using to date is one such implementation. It's beyond the scope of this book (and a reasonably large undertaking) to see how to implement this API, but it is certainly possible, and I expect that further implementations will follow in the future.

In this chapter, we're going to see how to configure two existing object store implementations (also called *persistor*s in Naked Objects parlance). We're going to warm up with Naked Objects' own XML object store, and then we'll move onto an RDBMS-based object store. Let's start with the XML implementation.

16.1 Configuring XML Persistence

The XML object store stores the state of domain objects in a series of XML files, one file per object. There's no need for us to define the schema of these XML files; their format is internal to the persistor and reflects the Naked Objects metamodel.

To use the XML object store, we need to do just two things: tell it how to persist our value types, and tell the framework to use the object store. As with the other downloads in Part III of this book, all the required modifications have already been made in CarServ (***chapter16-01***). Download it to verify the changes, but all the important code snippets are also in the text that follows.

Updating Value Types

You might remember from Chapter 7, *Using Value Types*, on page 109 that using value types may require additional configuration in order to persist them. In CarServ we have two value types, RegistrationNumber and CalendarInterval. Each of these has a ValueSemanticsProvider that provides parsability by returning a Parser implementation. This is sufficient for the viewers.

However, the XML object store also requires the semantics providers to supply EncoderDecoders, which in effect serialize the value's state. The implementations of these is simple enough; for example, RegistrationNumberValueSemanticsProvider is as follows:

```
chapter16/RegistrationNumberValueSemanticsProvider.java

@Override
public EncoderDecoder<RegistrationNumber> getEncoderDecoder() {
    return new EncoderDecoder<RegistrationNumber>() {

        public RegistrationNumber fromEncodedString(
                                        String encodedString) {
            return new RegistrationNumber(encodedString);
        }

        public String toEncodedString(RegistrationNumber toEncode) {
            return toEncode.getValue();
        }};
}
```

The semantics provider for CalendarInterval is similarly straightforward.

All we now need to do is run the application correctly.

```
  \|/   Joe Asks...
  °z°
   ~      How Is the –persistor Flag Interpreted?
```

Naked Objects uses the xml value of the --persistor command-line option to look up an implementation listed in the installer-registry.properties file, which is a resource within the Naked Objects runtime-4.0.0.jar file.

This is just a convenient shortcut; instead of xml, we could also have provided the fully qualified class name of the persistor's installer implementation.

Running the Application

To run the application, we specify the object store either using a command-line flag or using the nakedobjects.properties configuration file.

Open the exploration#viewer_dnd#persistor_xml or exploration#viewer_html# persistor_xml launch configurations; you'll see that both have the --persistor command-line flag as an argument, specifying the value xml. For example:

```
--viewer dnd --persistor xml
```

Run the application and make a change to one of the Customers; then shut down the application. When you next relaunch the application, the change should still be there.

Alternatively, we can specify the persistor in nakedobjects.properties:

chapter16/nakedobjects-xml.properties

```
nakedobjects.persistor=xml
```

Give this a go too; remember to run up the application without using the --persistor flag.

If we look in the commandline project, there should be a new xml/objects subdirectory. The first time we run our application, this subdirectory doesn't exist, so the framework installs the same fixtures we've been using to seed the in-memory object store. On subsequent runs, the fixtures are ignored because the object store is already initialized (the subdirectory isn't empty).

So, that's the XML object store. As we've seen, it's very easy to use, it required no changes to our domain model code, and it required minimal changes to supporting code. It's also resilient to schema change (properties can be added or removed from domain objects without losing data). You'll find it useful for setting up demos to your domain experts, and you could use it as an alternative to writing fixtures by hand (just zip up the xml/objects directory).

However, the XML object store isn't really suitable for anything other than very basic single-user applications. For that we need an object store that persists to a relational database.

16.2 Mapping Entities Using JPA Annotations

Although Naked Objects does have its own Hibernate object store, in this book we use a newer object store implementation provided by the *JPA Objects* sister project.[1] Integration primarily consists of annotating our domain classes with the *Java Persistence API* (JPA) annotations; it can then create a relational database schema and persist our objects to that schema. Under the covers, it too uses the industry-standard Hibernate as the JPA implementation.

Like the Tested Objects sister project we used in Chapter 12, *Scenario Testing*, on page 217, JPA Objects also provides a Maven archetype that does most of the scaffolding and provides annotated versions of the demo claims application that we used in Chapter 1, *Getting Started*, on page 3. If you want to try this archetype, refer to the JPA Objects documentation.

Instead, we'll use a version of CarServ where all the required modifications have already been made (***chapter16-02***). You can therefore just download it and verify the following changes identified here. Again, if you're not at your computer, all the relevant code is in the text.

Before we get into the detail, I should do some expectation management. Configuring ORMs such as Hibernate can be complex, and there are 900+ page books (such as the bible for Hibernate, Bauer and King's *Java Persistence with Hibernate* [BK06]) devoted to the topic. What follows is packed with useful information (of course!), but if you've never done this before, then you might also want to do a little prereading.

---

1. JPA Objects is signposted from http://starobjects.org.

That said, JPA Objects tries to set some best practice in order to reduce the complexity of the mappings. So, you shouldn't need to be an out-and-out expert in Hibernate to use JPA Objects.

OK, let's get to it. Remember that these changes have already been done in the download; all we're doing here is inspecting the changes.

Declaring Entities Using @Entity and @Embeddable

First up we need to declare which domain classes in the model are (JPA) entities. If you look through the code, you should see that most of the domain classes are annotated with @Entity, **abstract** superclasses, and concrete subclasses. For example, Customer is as follows:

chapter16/Customer-Entity.java
```
@Entity
public class Customer ... { ... }
```

However, we don't annotate the repositories or any interfaces. We also don't need to annotate the CustomerTakeOn *process object* because it is not persisted. And we don't annotate value types either.

Also not annotated with @Entity is Name. JPA allows us to embed entities within other entities so that they are persisted in the same database table as their containing entity. Because Name is aggregated, we annotate it as @Embedded:

chapter16/Name-Embeddable.java
```
@Embeddable
public class Name ... { ... }
```

The full list of entities that are annotated, along with the other annotations we'll be looking at shortly, is summarized in Section 16.2, *Annotation Summary*, on page 295.

Next on our list is a mechanism to distinguish different types within the domain.

Distinguishing Concrete Types Using @DiscriminatorValue

When we have inheritance hierarchies in our domain model, JPA allows us to optionally use the @DiscriminatorValue annotation to discriminate between the different concrete subclasses. These are held in "type" columns.

JPA Objects makes this a *mandatory* requirement for *every* concrete class, whether it is part of an inheritance hierarchy or not. These discriminators should be strings, three or perhaps four characters in length; for example, Employee is as follows:

chapter16/Employee-DiscriminatorValue.java

```
@Entity
@DiscriminatorValue("EMP")
public class Employee ... { ... }
```

Again, Section 16.2, *Annotation Summary*, on page 295 summarizes which classes have been annotated.

While the JPA object store needs this information internally, as we'll see in Section 16.4, *Mapping Relationships*, on page 298, it's also necessary to select a discriminator when mapping relationships to interfaces. It's therefore good practice to have these aliases defined; after all, any class could implement an interface. If you keep them short (no more than four characters), they also act as handy type identifiers; team members will use them as aliases in SQL queries, for example.

Next we need a way to distinguish different *instances* of entities.

Identifying Entities Using @Id

The JPA specification offers a number of ways to uniquely identify entities, but at the time of this writing, JPA Objects currently requires that *every* entity has a numeric surrogate key. The Hibernate team strongly recommends this practice anyway.

Therefore, every (nonembedded) entity has defined in it—or inherits from its superclass—an Id property. The form of this is as follows:

chapter16/Id-property.java

```
private Long id;
@Hidden
@Optional
@Id
@GeneratedValue(strategy=GenerationType.AUTO)
public Long getId() {
    return id;
}
public void setId(Long id) {
    this.id = id;
}
```

The name of the property doesn't need to be Id, but it does need to be annotated with @Id. It's also important to use a numeric wrapper class (such as java.lang.Long) and to annotate the class using the (Naked Objects) @Optional annotation; this enables Hibernate to manage the persistence life cycle. We also use @GeneratedValue annotation so that the JPA object store will automatically assign unique values for us. In the usual way, the (Naked Objects) @Hidden annotation hides the property in the user interface (if not hidden, then it should be @Disabled).

Closely related to identifying objects is versioning them.

Versioning Entities Using @Version

We use the JPA @Version attribute to enforce optimistic locking, annotated on a Version property. This is needed on transactional entities, but we don't need it for any immutable reference entities. The form of this property is as follows:

`chapter16/Version-property.java`

```java
private Long version;
@Hidden
@Optional
@Version
public Long getVersion() {
    return version;
}
public void setVersion(Long version) {
    this.version = version;
}
```

As for the Id property, the name of the property doesn't matter. Any of the types supported by @Version can be used (**int**, Integer, **short**, Short, **long**, Long, or java.sql.Timestamp).

We've already touched on inheritance hierarchies with the @DiscriminatorValue annotation, but there's more to say on this topic. Namely...

Inheritance Hierarchies Using @Inheritance

JPA lets us map inheritance hierarchies using one of three strategies:

- The SINGLE_TABLE inheritance type maps the entire hierarchy to a single table. This table has a column for each of the properties of all the subtypes; each of these columns for the "rolled-up" properties is nullable.

This inheritance type is simple to implement and generally performs well, but from a DBA's viewpoint, a single table can get rather unwieldy to manage/archive. A single table could also be a possible point of contention within the development process with lots of user stories potentially requiring its modification.

- The JOINED inheritance type has one table for the superclass and one table for each subclass.

  Retrieving data in this inheritance type is likely to perform less well than the SINGLE_TABLE strategy, because it requires outer joins to each of the subclass tables. Updates will also probably perform worse. The DBA is also likely to find it easier to manage, though, and there should be less contention in the development process.

- The TABLE_PER_CLASS inheritance type has one table per concrete class, but unlike the JOINED strategy has no table for the superclass. Instead, the properties of the superclass are "rolled down" into each subclass's table.

  This strategy is possibly the most efficient for updates. Retrieving data for a single subclass will also be efficient, but a polymorphic query finding all instances for a superclass will require a SQL **UNION**, which could well be less effective than the other two inheritance strategies. Another disadvantage is that generating unique IDs cannot use an identity column, which is the preferred approach (where supported) for some RDBMS. On the other hand, this strategy is probably the easiest for DBAs to manage, with the least contention in the development process.

We use @Inheritance to specify the mapping strategy, annotating the superclass. In CarServ, there are four inheritance hierarchies: PaymentMethod, PersonRole, Vehicle, and Service.

For example, I selected the SINGLE_TABLE strategy for the PaymentMethod hierarchy since the subclasses don't have much additional state. The strategies that I chose to use are summarized in Section 16.2, *Annotation Summary*, on the facing page. For your own applications, you should give serious thought as to which strategy to use for each inheritance hierarchy.

In addition to the @Inheritance annotation, we also specify the @DiscriminatorColumn annotation, which goes hand in hand with the @DiscriminatorValue annotation we saw earlier. This is where we specify the discriminator column's name, type (a String), and length (3 or 4).

For example, PaymentMethod is as follows:

chapter16/PaymentMethod-Inheritance.java

```
@Entity
@Inheritance(strategy=InheritanceType.SINGLE_TABLE)
@DiscriminatorColumn(
    name="payment_method_type",
    discriminatorType=DiscriminatorType.STRING, length=3)
public abstract class PaymentMethod ... { ... }
```

Ignoring Nonpersisted Properties

Throughout the domain classes there are a handful of derived properties or methods that we need JPA/Hibernate to ignore. We do this by annotating them with the @Transient annotation. For example, the Customer class has an isValuableCustomer() helper method:

chapter16/Customer-isValuableCustomer.java

```
@Transient
private boolean isValuableCustomer() {
    return getVehicles().size() >= 2;
}
```

Note we need to do this even though the method has **private** visibility. The other examples are in Service (its getPaid() method) and in ServiceableVehicle (its getPaymentMethodOwner() and isServiceOverdue() methods).

Annotation Summary

In the preceding sections we've seen a half dozen or so annotations. The following table summarizes which annotations are applied to which CarServ entities.

All of the classes tend to fall into one of four main categories:

- Abstract transactional superclasses, annotated with @Inheritance and also @Version (such as PaymentMethod, PersonRole, and Vehicle)
- Concrete transactional classes that do have a (possibly inherited) @Version property (such as Account, Person, and Car)
- Concrete reference classes, with no @Version property either inherited or declared (for example PaymentMethodType, Title, and Make)

- Embedded classes that are annotated with @Embeddable (for example Name).

Class	Embedding	@DiscriminatorValue	@Inheritance	Id	Version
PaymentMethodType	@Entity	PMT		@Id	
PaymentMethod	@Entity		SINGLE_TABLE	@Id	@Version
Account	@Entity	ACC			
Cash	@Entity	CSH			
CreditCard	@Entity	CCD			
Person	@Entity	PRS		@Id	@Version
Name	@Embeddable				
PersonRole	@Entity		JOINED	@Id	@Version
Customer	@Entity	CUS			
Employee	@Entity	EMP			
Title	@Entity	TTL		@Id	
Make	@Entity	MAK		@Id	
Model	@Entity	MDL		@Id	
VehicleType	@Entity	VTP		@Id	
Vehicle	@Entity		SINGLE_TABLE	@Id	@Version
ServiceableVehicle	@Entity				
Car	@Entity	CAR			
Motorcycle	@Entity	MCY			
Van	@Entity	VAN			
Service	@Entity		SINGLE_TABLE	@Id	@Version
InitialService	@Entity	ISV			
RegularService	@Entity	RSV			

Let's now turn our attention to value types.

16.3 Mapping Value Objects Using JPA Annotations

In CarServ we have two value types, RegistrationNumber and CalendarInterval. As discussed already in this chapter, we need to write implementations of Naked Objects' ValueSemanticProvider so that Naked Objects can parse and display these types. Hibernate also requires adapters so that it can persist (what it calls) *user types* to the database.

Defining Hibernate User Types

Hibernate's adapters are implementations of org.hibernate.usertype.UserType or org.hibernate.usertype.CompositeUserType. The former is used for values that are basically a single scalar value, such as RegistrationNumber. The latter is used for value types such as CalendarInterval that are made up of several underlying values.

In JPA Objects' applib there are a couple of convenience superclasses to help us write these adapters, namely, ImmutableUserType and Immutable-CompositeUserType. For example, here is the implementation for Registra-tionNumber:

`chapter16/RegistrationNumberType.java`

```java
public class RegistrationNumberType extends ImmutableUserType {
    public Class<RegistrationNumber> returnedClass() {
        return RegistrationNumber.class;
    }
    public Object nullSafeGet(
            final ResultSet rs,
            final String[] names,
            final Object owner) throws SQLException {
        final String value = rs.getString(names[0]);
        return rs.wasNull() ? null : new RegistrationNumber(value);
    }
    public void nullSafeSet(
            final PreparedStatement st,
            final Object value,
            final int index) throws SQLException {
        if (value == null) {
            st.setNull(index, Hibernate.STRING.sqlType());
        } else {
            RegistrationNumber regNum = (RegistrationNumber) value;
            st.setString(index, regNum.getValue());
        }
    }
    public int[] sqlTypes() {
        return new int[] { Hibernate.STRING.sqlType() };
    }
}
```

The user type for CalendarInterval is a little more involved (it persists to a date column and an integer column to represent the interval duration), though most of its complexity has to do with getting values in and out of CalendarInterval itself rather than the database!

Now we have some Hibernate UserTypes, so we need to wire them into the domain model.

Annotating the Domain Classes

For each domain class that has user-defined value types (in CarServ, this is Service and Vehicle), we must add two (Hibernate-specific) annotations.

The first is on the class itself and defines the type and an alias for the type. For this we use @TypeDefs/@TypeDef annotations. For example, on the Service class, we have the following:

`chapter16/Service-TypeDefs.java`

```
@TypeDefs({
    @TypeDef(name="calint", typeClass=CalendarIntervalType.class)
    })
public abstract class Service ... { ... }
```

The second is on the property, using the @Type annotation and the @Columns/@Column annotations. So, the Service's bookedInAndReady property is annotated thusly:

`chapter16/Service-Type.java`

```
@Type(type="calint")
@Columns(columns={
    @Column(name="bookedInAndReady_dt"),
    @Column(name="bookedInAndReady_duration")
})
public CalendarInterval getBookedInAndReady() {
    return bookedInAndReady;
}
```

And that's values taken care of. Now we have to tell the object store how the classes relate to each other.

16.4 Mapping Relationships

In Java we associate objects using references or collections of references. If we want a relationship to be bidirectional, then we need to have a reference in both directions. In a relational database, though, we associate instances of different tables together through the values of their respective primary and foreign keys. It's as easy to traverse foreign key relationships in one direction as another.

The point of this little preamble is that relationships in Java-land and in RDBMS-land are quite different in nature, and it's important to map our relationships the correct way. Let's go through each of the relationships in CarServ in turn.

Embedded Relationships

You'll recall that we annotated Name as @Embeddable rather than an @Entity. This now allows us to map the one-to-one relationship from Person to Name using the @Embedded annotation.

chapter16/Person-name.java

```
@Embedded
public Name getName() { ... }
```

The Name object will then be stored inline (in the same table) as the Person object. That's really all there is to embedded relationships. So, let's move onto something slightly more complex.

Unidirectional Many-to-One Relationships

A unidirectional many-to-one (or indeed one-to-one) relationship is where there's the most similarity between Java and an RDBMS. In the former, we have a simple reference; in the latter, we have a foreign key.

In CarServ, we have plenty of examples of this relationship. For example, the relationship from Vehicle to Model is mapped using an @ManyToOne annotation:

chapter16/Vehicle-model.java

```
@ManyToOne(fetch=FetchType.EAGER)
public Model getModel() { ... }
```

For the record, the other examples in CarServ are Name to Title, Service to PaymentMethod, PaymentMethod to PaymentMethodType, and Model to VehicleType.

One decision we do have to make is whether the relationship should be loaded lazily or eagerly. Associations to reference data objects (such as Model and Make) can probably be eagerly loaded, because (if we have enabled second-level caching in Hibernate) these objects are probably already in cache. Other associations should probably be lazily loaded, however. Our next relationship type follows on naturally by making the relationship bidirectional.

Bidirectional One-to-Many Relationships

When we have a bidirectional one-to-many relationship in the code, then we have two references: a collection on the one side and a back reference on the other. As already noted, though, in an RDBMS, this relationship requires only a foreign key.

We therefore map a bidirectional relationship with both an @OneToMany annotation on the collection side and an @ManyToOne annotation for the back reference. But for the @OneToMany annotation, we use a mappedBy attribute that says, in effect, that the relationship can be navigated using the foreign key introduced by the @ManyToOne annotation.

Again, there are plenty of examples in CarServ. For example, a Service-ableVehicle can have many Services. In ServiceableVehicle, we have the following:

```
@OneToMany(mappedBy="vehicle", cascade=CascadeType.ALL)
public List<Service> getServices() { ... }
```

while in the Service class we have this:

```
@ManyToOne(fetch=FetchType.LAZY)
public ServiceableVehicle getVehicle() { ... }
```

Note the mappedBy attribute already mentioned. The other attribute to note is cascade, for the @OneToMany annotation. Among other things this ensures *persistence-by-reachability*: any still-to-be-persisted Services attached to a (persisted) ServiceableVehicle will be automatically saved to the database.

There are two other such relationships in CarServ: Person to PersonRole and Make to Model.

Let's take a look now at one-to-many relationships where the relationship isn't bidirectional.

Unidirectional One-to-Many Relationships

We map a unidirectional one-to-many relationship using the @OneToMany annotation. However, because there is no back reference, we omit the mappedBy attribute.

For example, in CarServ, there is one-to-many relationship from Customer to Vehicle:

```
@OneToMany(fetch=FetchType.LAZY)
public List<Vehicle> getVehicles() { ... }
```

So far, so unremarkable. What is noteworthy, though, is that because there is no back reference, there is therefore no foreign key in the table for Vehicle. Instead, we will get a new association table, Customer_Vehicle, to hold the (customer_id, vehicle_id) tuples.

One type of relationship we don't have in CarServ is a many-to-many relationship. If present, these can be mapped using an @ManyToMany annotation, and they also give rise to association tables.

So, one way to understand the association table introduced by an @OneToMany is to think of it as a degenerate case of the more general @ManyToMany mapping. For the record (as well as Customer to Vehicles), there is one other unidirectional one-to-many relationship in CarServ, namely, Customer to PaymentMethod. And the *reason* that both of these relationships are unidirectional is because the back reference is to an *interface*: VehicleOwner and PaymentMethodOwner, respectively.

Surely mapping to an interface rather than a class doesn't make much difference, does it? Er, yes, it does, so let's see how.

Unidirectional Many-to-One Relationships Using Interfaces

One of the most obvious mismatches between relational databases and object orientation is the former's lack of support for polymorphism.

As we've seen, we can adequately map class inheritance hierarchies such as Vehicle or PaymentMethod. Things get rather muddier when we consider interface inheritance, such as a Customer implementing VehicleOwner. Recall that the reason we added the VehicleOwner abstraction in Chapter 11, *Keeping the Model Maintainable*, on page 193 was (as the chapter title said) to keep the model maintainable by decoupling. This allows us to polymorphically substitute other implementors of VehicleOwner. But these other implementations need not be in the Customer class hierarchy.

What we need is a means to reference any arbitrary object. At the time of writing, this isn't supported by the JPA specification, but we can still accomplish what we want using Hibernate's own @Any annotation, along with @Column, @AnyMetaDef, @MetaValue, and @JoinColumn.

So, we map the Vehicle to VehicleOwner relationship as follows:

```
chapter16/Vehicle-owner.java
@Any(metaColumn=@Column(name="owner_type", length=3),
     fetch=FetchType.LAZY)
@AnyMetaDef(
    idType="long",
    metaType="string",
    metaValues={
        @MetaValue(targetEntity=Customer.class, value="CUS")
    }
)
@JoinColumn(name="owner_id")
public VehicleOwner getOwner() { ... }
```

This, admittedly, is not the prettiest set of annotations you ever saw, but here's what it does: first, in the Vehicle table, the @Any annotation will create the owner_type column, and the @JoinColumn will create the owner_id column. As specified by the @AnyMetaDef annotation, the owner_type will store the identifier to represent the referenced class, namely, CUS for Customer. The owner_id will store the id of the referenced Customer. If we had other implementations of VehicleOwner, then they would be listed as additional @MetaValues.

A couple of points. First, although strictly the CUS identifier does not need to be the same as the @DiscriminatorValue annotation we added earlier, it'd be pretty silly not to keep them in sync. Second, mapping using @Any requires that any implementing class is identified by a single Long property. This is the primary reason why JPA Objects only supports @Id properties and not any of the more esoteric ways of identifying objects.

There is one further @Any mapping in CarServ, from PaymentMethod to PaymentMethodOwner (coincidentally also implemented by Customer). Although we don't have any examples in CarServ, it is also possible to map to collections of interfaces using @ManyToAny.

We now have all the classes mapped over, but there is still the matter of the repository implementations.

16.5 Porting over Repositories

Repositories were one of the first things we covered in Chapter 2, *Identifying the Domain Concepts*, on page 23, and we've been pretty much letting them get on with their job ever since. However, although the existing implementations will work against the JPA object store, they won't perform well in a production environment; we must port them over.

The AbstractFactoryAndRepository convenience superclass provides the three main methods to search for objects: allMatches(), firstMatch(), and uniqueMatch(). Each of these has the same four overloads. For example, the overloaded versions of allMatches() are as follows:

- allMatches(final Class<T> ofType, final Filter<T> filter)
- allMatches(final Class<T> ofType, final String title)
- allMatches(final Class<T> ofType, final T pattern)
- allMatches(final Query<T> query)

Joe Asks...

Don't the Annotations for Interface Relationships Create Dependencies Between Classes?

Hmmm, I was hoping you wouldn't ask that! Yes, because we must list the concrete implementations of classes when mapping an interface relationship, we do in effect re-create a bidirectional dependency between the modules, in part undoing the good work of Chapter 11, *Keeping the Model Maintainable*, on page 193.

There are some solutions to this. The first is simple—don't worry about it, and if using a tool to visualize dependencies, then use its filtering mechanisms if it has them to ignore dependencies arising only from annotations.

An alternative is to push the troublesome annotations into subclasses, all the way into the application package if necessary (see Section 11.7, *An Application Architecture Blueprint*, on page 212). Such subclasses effectively provide a binding between the application's modules.

A third alternative (though not supported by JPA Objects at the time of writing) is to remove the annotations and instead use XML to configure the relationships.

All object store implementations are expected to support the first three of these (so the simple stuff is always supported), but not necessarily efficiently. In CarServ, we've exclusively used the first of these overloads (passing in a Filter<T>), so it should still work, but for the JPA object store, the database query will retrieve all instances of the class, and then the instances will be filtered in Java code. Instead, we want the RDBMS to do the filtering for us and only return the matching instances.

To accomplish this, we should use the last of the overloads and pass in a Query<T> object. The implementation of a Query<T> is dependent on the object store, and some, like the in-memory object store and the XML object store, don't support it at all. For the JPA object store, though, it is supported and equates to the queries defined using the JPA @NamedQuery annotation. The implementation we use is a convenience one provided in the Naked Objects applib, namely, QueryDefault.

For example, let's look at EmployeeRepository's me() action. First we annotate the returned entity (Employee) with the @NamedQuery:

```
@NamedQueries({
    @NamedQuery(
        name="findEmployeeByUserId",
        query="from Employee where userIdName=:userId"),
})
@Entity
public class Employee { ... }
```

Then, in EmployeeRepositoryJpa, we instantiate a QueryDefault object (specifying the query name and a vararg list of parameter name/argument pairs) and pass it into allMatches():

```
public Employee me() {
    final String currentUserId = getContainer().getUser().getName();
    return firstMatch(
            QueryDefault.create(
                Employee.class,
                "findEmployeeByUserId",
                "userId", currentUserId));
}
```

It'd perhaps seem more logical to have the @NamedQuery definitions on the repository rather than on the returned entity, but that doesn't work because Hibernate knows only about the entities, not the repositories.

The CustomerRepositoryJpa's implementation for finding Customers by name is similar. First, here's the @NamedQuery, annotated on Customer:

```
@NamedQueries({
    @NamedQuery(
        name="findCustomersByName",
        query="from Customer " +
            "where person.name.firstName=:firstName " +
              "and person.name.lastName=:lastName")
})
@Entity
public class Customer { ... }
```

Note the use of the *JPA Query Language* (JPA QL) to walk the graph to the Customer's Person's Name.

Next, here's the action method:

```
chapter16/CustomerRepositoryJpa-findByName.java

public List<Customer> findByName(
        final String lastName,
        final String firstName) {
    return allMatches(
            QueryDefault.create(
                    Customer.class,
                    "findCustomersByName",
                    "firstName", firstName,
                    "lastName", lastName));
}
```

The rest of the repository methods are similar.

There's one final modification that's also been made to the repositories. If you look in CustomerApplicationRepositoryJpa, you'll see a set of do-nothing actions like this one:

```
chapter16/CustomerApplicationRepositoryJpa-registerEntity.java

@Hidden
public void registerEntity(Cash cash) {}
```

The JPA object store works by walking the graph of classes and interfaces from the registered repositories outward. All classes that are found are then mapped with Hibernate. For any classes that wouldn't otherwise be discoverable—usually subclasses—we use these dummy hidden actions to ensure that all classes get mapped.

That completes our run-through of the steps taken to integrate CarServ using the JPA object store. All we need to do now is set up a database, and then we should be able to run our application end to end.

16.6 Deploying and Running the Application

Before we can run the application, we need a database.

Creating the Database

If you already have a database set up, know its JDBC URL, and have a JDBC driver for it, then by all means use that. Otherwise, though, we need to install a database server. There are a number of very good open source relational databases around, and the one I've chosen to use is PostgreSQL.[2] It's cross-platform, is easy to set up, has Java JDBC

---

database drivers, and comes with a nice GUI administration tool so we can see what's going on.

So, go to the PostgreSQL website, and download the prebuilt binary install (I selected PostgreSQL 8.3.7) for your operating system. Do the install, remembering the password for the *postgres* superuser.

Once installed, run the *PgAdmin III* GUI admin tool. The RDBMS server should already be running; right-click Connect, and provide the password for the *postgres* administrator.

We could leave it at that, but it's bad practice to use superuser accounts and built-in databases. So, let's create our own login and databases:

1. On the top-level PostgreSQL server node, right-click and select New Object > New Login Role.

2. In the resultant dialog box, enter a role name of *carserv* and a password of *carserv* also. Hit OK.

3. Right-click the Databases node (under the server node), and select New Database.

4. In the resultant dialog box, enter the name *carserv_db*, and specify the owner as *carserv*.

Double-check that everything is set up correctly by logging out and reconnecting as the new *carserv* login.

Next we need to configure Naked Objects to use this database.

Configure Naked Objects

To run the application, we need to update various configuration files in CarServ, which mostly boils down to updating the classpaths and switching in the new repository implementations.

These steps are spelled out in full in the JPA Objects documentation, so refer there for the details. In our CarServ download, though, the necessary changes have already been done:

1. The nakedobjects.properties configuration file has been updated to reference the JPA implementations in carserv-jpa-service.

2. It has also been updated to disable the bytecode providers.

   Internally Naked Objects uses bytecode enhancement to support lazy loading of object graphs so that it can detect when an object is modified. When using Hibernate, however, we can (indeed must) switch this off. We do this by updating the *nakedobjects.reflector. class-substitutor* and *nakedobjects.persistor.object-factory* property keys.

3. It has also been updated to specify the JPA reflector and persistor.

   The *persistor* property key simply indicates we want to use the JPA object store. The *reflector* key meanwhile specifies JPA Objects' extensions to the Naked Objects programming model, thereby allowing Naked Objects to pick up and interpret the JPA annotations.

4. The various project pom.xml files have been updated correctly for versions and dependencies.

5. The hibernate.cfg.xml file (in the carserv-jpa-service project, under src/main/resources) references the PostgreSQL database called carserv_db and is accessed with a login of carserv and a password of carserv.

   We'll set this up in the next section. Or, if you're using a different database, then update the hibernate.cfg.xml configuration file to point to your database.

Next, we need to build the database schema.

Exporting the Schema

Neither the in-memory object store nor the XML object store required us to define the structure of the data being persisted. For JPA Objects, however, we do need to explicitly define the database schema using create table SQL commands and such.

JPA Objects provides a couple of command-line tools to help us, and one of them is the SchemaManager. So, locate the dba - SchemaManager - create only launch configuration and then Run. Inspect your database using the *PgAdmin III* GUI admin tool (or equivalent, if using your own database). We should end up with a database schema, as shown in Figure 16.1, on the next page.[3]

---

3. If you are using PostgreSQL and wondering how I generated the diagram, actually I cheated. This is taken using Microsoft SQL Server Management Studio, freely available for Windows SQL Server Express product. Microsoft SQL Server is another excellent product, but, of course, it isn't open source and runs only on Windows.

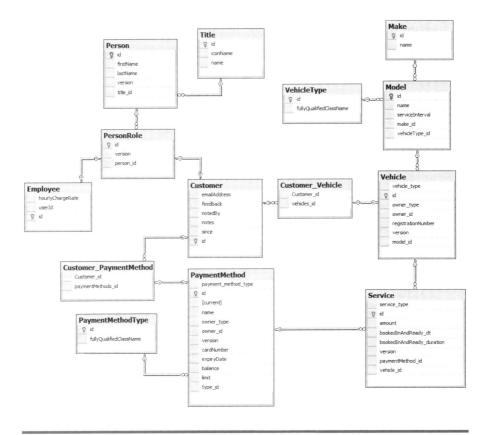

Figure 16.1: CarServ database schema

That's our database schema defined, but a database with no data would be no use! As ever, we use fixtures to populate the object store.

Installing Fixtures

The XML object store figures out on the fly whether any data has been loaded and installs fixtures only when first run. The JPA object store, however, takes a rather more conservative approach: it never loads fixtures at all. After all, we don't want to accidentally trash a production database by loading test data into it.

If we *do* want to load fixtures, for a system test, say, then we use another of JPA Objects' command-line tools, namely, FixtureManager. So, locate the dba - Fixture Manager launch configuration, and run. Rows representing the domain objects should be inserted into the database.

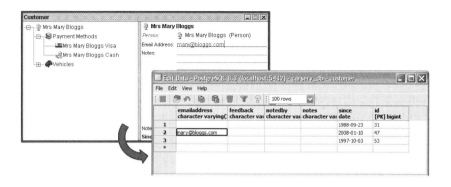

Figure 16.2: CARSERV DATABASE BEING UPDATED

Running the Application

Finally, it's time to run the application, using the exploration#viewer_dnd or exploration#viewer_html launch configurations. Try various actions and edits, and verify the database is updated, as shown in Figure 16.2. In the Console view in Eclipse, you should also be able to see Hibernate submitting SQL (**SELECT**s, **INSERT**s, **UPDATE**s, and so on).

We've now seen all the steps it takes to integrate a domain model into a relational database. It's good to know that pretty much any domain model we come up with can be integrated, but it's also clear that it does take some effort.

As discussed earlier in Chapter 13, *Developing Domain Applications*, on page 241, this is a good demonstration of why we defer the integration as late as possible. If we did all this integration work at the same time as the implementation work, then (being human) we would naturally tend to resist any requests to change the model (not wanting to go through the integration phase again).

That said, once the implementation of a particular user story is stabilizing, we should do its integration (typically lagging an iteration or two). We shouldn't—as we have done here—leave it to one big piece of work at the end.

Coming Up Next

In the previous chapter, we integrated forward to the presentation layer, and in this chapter we integrated backward to the persistence layer. In particular, we saw in detail how to use JPA annotations to map domain objects to a relational database and saw how to rewrite repository implementations to effectively retrieve the objects stored there.

The next chapter is the last of our integration chapters, where we're going to integrate—er—sideways. That is, we're going to look at integrating with other systems using messaging and web services.

Exercises

Of the four inheritance hierarchies in CarServ, we mapped three to SINGLE_TABLE and one to JOINED. Experiment by changing these inheritance types, and check what is generated when you export the schema.

And then, well, I hardly need say, do I? Get to it—map your own domain model to a relational database using JPA Objects.

Integrating Within the Enterprise

Applications don't live in isolation within an organization. Businesses are organized into different operational units (purchasing, marketing, and so on), and each tends to have its own systems to support it.

Even if we wanted to, it's not feasible to build a single system to take care of all operational and reporting requirements of an entire enterprise. There would be too many stakeholders, for one thing. In any case, some operational units have very good *commercial off-the-shelf* (COTS) systems (general ledger and payroll, for example), so why reinvent the wheel? We should concentrate our efforts on supporting those domains that *distinguish* our business from our competitors.

What that means is we need ways to link our domain application into the wider IT landscape. In the case of CarServ, we might want to send messages to a separate invoicing application once a service is complete. Or, we might want to expose information about customers so that a marketing application can do a mail-shot.

In this, the last of our integration chapters, we're going to see how other systems in our organization can call into a domain application using a web service, and we'll learn how our application can interact with other systems asynchronously using Apache Camel, part of Apache's suite of open source *enterprise service bus* (ESB) products.[1] Although this isn't a book about enterprise architecture, we'll also look at some of the considerations for using one interaction mode over another.

Now, the existing DDD literature has quite a lot to say about integrating systems, so we would be remiss not to review it.

---

1. http://camel.apache.org

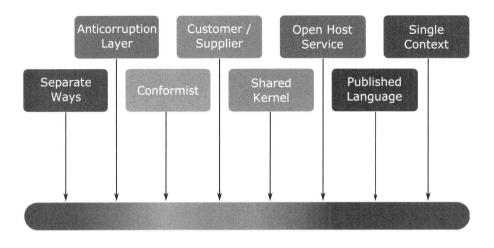

Figure 17.1: Bounded context patterns form a spectrum.

17.1 Bounded Context Patterns

Using DDD terminology, our application and each of these external systems we integrate with is a *bounded context*. Every *bounded context* contains a single domain model, but the idea of a *bounded context* is to make explicit the relationship between one system and another.

As well as coining the term *bounded context*, in his book Eric Evans has a whole catalog of ways in which systems can interact with each other. As shown in Figure 17.1, they form a spectrum of cooperation:

- In the *separate ways* pattern, the two systems don't interact directly at all (other than through nonautomated means).

- In the *anticorruption layer* pattern, one system uses the API of another but protects itself against changes in that API through its own thin translation layer. This is good practice for writing infrastructure services, too, by the way.

- In the *conformist* pattern, one system conforms to the API of another but does not wrap it. In effect, we adopt the domain model of the other system (for the parts of the other system whose functionality we need). For example, if interfacing to a COTS system (which are often strategic investments costing millions and which have a large API that would be too expensive to wrap), we might choose to do this.

in context...
Bounded Context

Every model has a context in which it applies, usually corresponding to the wider organizational structure of the business.

An explicit boundary to the model keeps it focused on the problems it was designed to solve.

- In the *customer/supplier* pattern, the downstream system consumes information from an upstream system. We make the downstream system a stakeholder of that upstream system so that it is possible to change the upstream system and properly impact the downstream system.

- In the *shared kernel* pattern, both systems use a common codebase or database schema and interact through that.

- In the *open host* pattern, one system defines a simple, coherent protocol that exposes its functionality in a standardized way; other systems are free to use that functionality as required.

- In the *published language* pattern, the systems interact using a separately defined language, defined either in-house or possibly by an industry standards organization.

- In the *single context* pattern, we combine two systems into a single codebase and use *continuous integration* (as discussed in Chapter 13, *Developing Domain Applications*, on page 241) to ensure that the codebase stays consistent.

So, if an external system provides a library that exposes its domain concepts directly to us, then we are being *conformist*, and the external systems' domain concepts will become part of our domain's too. If we choose to wrap that library, we are using an *anticorruption layer*, which gives us more control of our domain, but then we also have to maintain that layer of software. Going the other way, if we can work with that external system and influence that library, then we have a *customer/supplier* relationship.

Many systems not only have an online application but also have a reporting subsystem and a batch subsystem. We could think of these subsystems as separate *bounded contexts*, mapped through a *shared kernel*: the common database schema. Or, if we used views and **INSTEAD OF** triggers for the online application, then we in effect isolate the online application from the database schema in another example of an *anti-corruption layer*.

We can think of web services (especially in their RESTful flavor that we'll see shortly) as examples of the *open host service* pattern. Although the format of the data provided is defined and owned by the implementing system, the web service itself is available for any other system to call.

Meanwhile, messaging buses and their big brothers, ESBs, are one way of implementing the *published language* pattern. With an ESB, we define a set of standardized message types; this is our *published language*. The ESB takes responsibility for routing these messages from one system to another, if necessary translating both network protocols and message formats as required.

It's worth taking the time to decide which pattern to adopt when integrating systems; using the wrong pattern (consciously or unconsciously) can be an exercise in frustration. If your organization already has a well-managed ESB, then that may well be the way to go, but as ever with these things, one shouldn't adopt an architectural pattern blindly.

Enough preamble; it's time to get our fingers dirty.

17.2   Exposing a RESTful Web Service for Other Systems

Suppose we want to let other systems access the functionality in our application, following the *open host service* pattern. One way to do this is using a web service.

Web services have been around for a while now, of course, but we should be clear that the web services we'll be exposing are the newer RESTful style rather than the original SOAP style.

SOAP vs. REST

We can distinguish two main styles of web services:

- The first is a *remote procedure call* (RPC) style, effectively exposing a single function, most typically using *SOAP*. A typical example of a SOAP-style web service is one to look up a stock price.[2]

---

2.   There are lots of examples of web services at http://xmethods.net.

- The second more recent style is the *REpresentational State Transfer*, or REST, style of web service. REST web services are in many ways modeled after websites, exposing a system's functionality as a set of *resources* (in the same way that a website exposes a set of pages). REST also exploits the HTTP protocol so that these resources can be manipulated.

With an RPC-based service, the primary concept is that of a function. This doesn't map easily onto a DDD approach because it's not clear which object the function being invoked belongs to (it ends up being a facade to the system). In REST, though, the primary concept is a resource, which maps naturally to the idea of a domain object or a domain service (repository).

Naked Objects' own support for REST is provided by *Restful Objects*, another sister project. This provides an out-of-the-box RESTful web service for our domain objects; all that's needed is to add the RESTful viewer onto the classpath.[3]

The latest download of CarServ (***chapter17-01***) has had this change made (see the Restful Objects documentation for details). The download also has a new project, carserv-restful; more on this in a minute.

Running the CarServ Web Service

Using Run > Run Configurations, find the exploration#viewer_restful launch configuration, and run it. This will start up a Jetty web server on port 8080.

Now what? Well, the point of this web service is so that systems in other *bounded context*s can interact with our system, CarServ. We have an example client application to play in the role of the "other" system.

Calling a RESTful Web Service from a Java Client

In the carserv-restful project, there is a small Java class, FindCustomer. This inherits from a convenience superclass provided in Restful Objects' own applib, which gives us the ability to submit RESTful web service calls. We'll look at its code in a moment.

To try it, though, locate the FindCustomer -n Joe Bloggs launch configuration, and run it. In the console, you should see three different XML

---

3. Restful Objects and a number of other sister projects are collectively all referenced from http://www.starobjects.org. The code itself is hosted on SourceForge.

documents being printed, the last of these being the details about the Joe Bloggs Customer:

```
chapter17/FindCustomer-output.xml
<?xml version="1.0" encoding="UTF-8"?>
<html xml:base="">
    <head>
        <title>Mr Joe Bloggs</title>
        ...
    </head>
    <body id="body">
        <div>
            ... lots more here...
        </div>
    </body>
</html>
```

What FindCustomer (in its findCustomer() method) does is make a succession of calls to the RESTful web service:

1. First we obtain the domain services available, using the get() method inherited from the convenience superclass.

    ```
    chapter17/FindCustomer.java
    Document customersDoc = get(
        combine(getHostUri(),"/services"));
    prettyPrint(customersDoc);
    ```

    The URL that we hit, http://localhost:8080/services, is a REST resource, specifically one that represents the list of domain services (that is, repositories) available to us. That inherited get() method does an HTTP GET to this URL.

    We parse the response using XPath to obtain the resource representing the *Customers* service:

    ```
    chapter17/FindCustomer.java
    String customersServicePath = getAttributeValueElseException(
            customersDoc,
            "//a[@class='nof-service'][text()='Customers']/@href",
            "Unable to find 'Customers' service");
    ```

    This somewhat complex XPath expression gives us the string */object/OID:1*. OIDs are unique *object identifiers* that Naked Objects automatically assigns to all objects and services; this one identifies the *Customers* service. We'll see why the XPath is quite as complex as it is in the next section, by the way.

2. Next, we invoke the findByName() action by using the inherited post() method against http://localhost:8080/object/OID:1/action/find-ByName(java.lang.String,java.lang.String):

```
chapter17/FindCustomer.java
Document customerFindByNameDoc = post(
    combine(
        getHostUri(), customersServicePath,
        "/action/findByName(java.lang.String,java.lang.String)"),
        "arg0", lastName,
        "arg1", firstName);
prettyPrint(customerFindByNameDoc);
```

This URL is a resource to represent the invocation of an action on a particular object instance (the CustomerRepository, in fact), and the post() method performs an HTTP POST. We can use the same technique to invoke an action on any object. Again, we parse the output using XPath:

```
chapter17/FindCustomer.java
String customerPath = getAttributeValueElseException(
        customerFindByNameDoc,
        "//a[@class='nof-action-result']/@href",
        "No Customer found");
```

The string we get (something like "*/object/OID:29*") is the OID of the matching Customer.

3. Finally, we perform a get() on http://localhost:8080/object/OID:29 to retrieve the resource representing the Customer's itself:

```
chapter17/FindCustomer.java
Document customerDoc = get(
        combine(getHostUri(), customerPath));
prettyPrint(customerDoc);
```

Most of us are very familiar with the HTTP GET and POST methods; these are the ones supported by web browsers. However, REST also specifies the use of the less well-known PUT and DELETE methods. The following table shows how these four methods map onto domain objects.

HTTP Method	Object	Property	Collection	Action
GET	Current state of properties	—	Retrieve contents of collection	—
PUT	Persist object	Sets property	Adds object to collection	—
DELETE	Delete persisted object	Clears property	Removes object from collection	—
POST	—	—	—	Invoke

Locate the ObjectResource interface in Restful Objects' applib. This interface isn't actually used by our FindCustomer client, but the javax.rs annotations indicate the format of these method calls. For example, the modifyProperty() method has the following annotations:

```
chapter17/ObjectResource.java
@PUT
@Path("/{oid}/property/{propertyId}")
@Produces( { "application/xhtml+xml", "text/html" })
public String modifyProperty(
        @PathParam("oid") final String oidStr,
        @PathParam("propertyId") final String propertyId,
        @QueryParam("proposedValue") final String proposedValue);
```

This tells us we can perform an HTTP PUT to a URL such as http://localhost:8080/OID:123/property/lastName, with a parameter holding the new proposed value. This should modify the lastName property of the object with OID of *OID:123*.

So, we've now seen how to call a RESTful web service from an application. What we've not yet discussed is the data format of the representations themselves. That brings us to. . .

Using a RESTful Web Service from a Web Browser

As we saw from the FindCustomer application, when we invoke a RESTful web service, *Restful Objects* generates XML that we can parse and process.

REST doesn't mandate the format of this XML. In fact, it doesn't even mandate that we return XML at all. Indeed, many RESTful web services return JavaScript Object Notation (JSON) instead, while others use bespoke XML defined using XML Schema.

However, REST does say that it should be possible to navigate from one resource to another. So, *Restful Objects* follows the advice found in Richardson and Ruby's excellent book, *RESTful Web Services* [RR07], in that it returns XML, but more precisely XHTML, using CSS styles to define a *microlanguage* within the XHTML. The complex XPath expressions we saw in FindCustomer rely on this microlanguage to extract the information that they require.

The big payback comes from the fact that we can actually browse our RESTful web service using a web browser.[4]

To see this in action, point your browser at the web service (http://localhost:8080). As shown in Figure 17.2, on the following page, you should be able to navigate around, inspect objects, and invoke actions on those objects.

If you dig into these pages, you'll see that they also embed a little JavaScript so that we can perform HTTP PUTs and DELETEs. That's because at the time of writing, web browsers do not provide this capability (it's planned for HTML 5).

Now we've seen how to expose our domain model's functionality as web services, let's flip it over to consider how to use an external system's web service.

Calling Web Services from Our Domain Model

We've already seen (in Chapter 8, *Isolating Infrastructure Services*, on page 125) how our domain model can call external infrastructure services. We can use exactly the same approach to call an external web service. The only real difference is that instead of calling some infrastructure API (such as sending email), we'd be calling a business-focused API (such as checking a customer's credit rating). Otherwise, though, there's not much else to say.

The trouble with using web service calls like this (whether calling or being called) is that it creates a coupling between the systems involved. Since the call is synchronous, if the called system is unavailable for any reason, then the calling system fails. Also—since we are applying the *open host* pattern—the calling system must be prepared to use the protocol of the called system (the format of the URLs and the need to parse the resultant XHTML).

---

4. At the time of writing, only Firefox 3.0.*x* support has been tested.

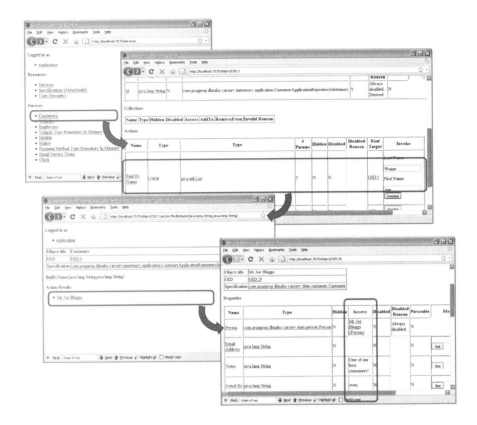

Figure 17.2: RESTFUL OBJECTS SERVES UP XHTML PAGES.

We can address both of these problems using asynchronous messaging and introducing a *published language*. And as mentioned in this chapter's introduction, we can achieve both of these objectives using an ESB.

17.3 Integrating Using an Enterprise Service Bus

Before we wade into the detail, it might be a good idea to quickly review what an ESB is. Then we can get our fingers dirty again integrating our domain application.

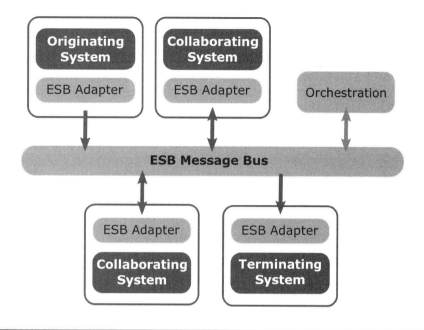

Figure 17.3: A TYPICAL ESB ARCHITECTURE

ESB 101

An ESB works by linking all the systems that need to interact to a common service (or message) bus. In Figure 17.3, we see the key elements of a typical ESB deployment.

The *ESB message bus* typically runs on the network somewhere; under the covers there is usually a lower-level messaging system (for example, implementing JMS).

Each system interacts with the message bus through an *ESB adapter*, responsible for converting network protocols and transforming messages into one of the standard message types used by a given business process. These standard message types are understood by (the adapter of) every system on the ESB and are sometimes called the *enterprise message model* or *normalized message*s. In other words, the *published language*.

In addition, the ESB can provide *orchestration*, meaning that it will route a series of messages representing a single business process between all systems involved in that process. The orchestration implementation can vary from relatively simple mappings through to full-blown execution engines supporting *Business Process Execution Language* (BPEL). In effect, we take the business process implicit in the interaction of two (or more) systems and externalize it.

For example, in CarServ, the business process of performing a Service on a Car is also going to require us to invoice the Customer and to replenish any parts that might have been used in that Service. So, when the customer comes to pick up their car, the CarServ application could send a message to the ESB with the details of the completed service. The orchestration module would route this message to a separate invoicing system, which would then send out the invoice to the customer. At the same time, the message would be sent to the parts management system to order replacement parts from the manufacturer.

We're going to be using Apache Camel to represent our ESB. Camel isn't an ESB in itself; instead, it allows us to write adapters to an ESB. Camel's adapters are made up of *routes*, which define how to receive and process messages. In the context we're going to use Camel, a route describes how to read a message from the ESB and/or how to publish a message to the ESB. In effect, Camel is the bit of an ESB that our code "touches." The ESB implementation (the bit that lives on the network) could be anything; for Camel, an obvious choice would be Apache's ServiceMix.[5]

If you haven't encountered ESBs before, then please don't conclude that this short introduction covers everything there is to say! A good resource for further study of enterprise integration in general (and that forms the basis of Camel's concept of routes) is Gregor Hohpe and Bobby Wolfe's *Enterprise Integration Patterns* [HW04]. But here we have enough context to carry on.

Calling Our Domain Application from an ESB

ESBs are quite capable of calling web services, so one option for calling our domain application from an ESB would be to write an ESB adapter that calls the RESTful web service we used in Section 17.2, *Exposing a RESTful Web Service for Other Systems*, on page 314.

However, that would give us two separate Java applications to manage: the Naked Objects application acting as a server and the ESB adapter acting as a client. An alternative approach is to embed Naked Objects

---

5. Apache ServiceMix is an open source ESB hosted at http://servicemix.apache.org. To integrate ServiceMix and Camel, see http://servicemix.apache.org/servicemix-camel.html.

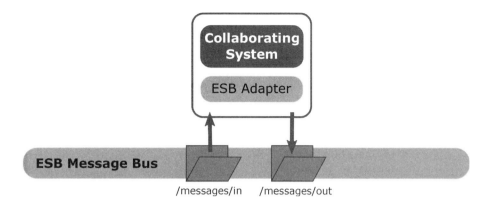

Figure 17.4: THE EXAMPLE ADAPTER USES DIRECTORIES AS A SIMPLIFIED ESB.

and our domain model into some custom ESB adapter code, similar to the way we embedded Naked Objects into Wicket in Chapter 15, *Integrating with Web Frameworks*, on page 269. That way, we'll just have a single application to run and won't need to parse any XML either.

To motivate this section, let's consider the use case of looking up Customer email addresses from CarServ; it's a bit contrived perhaps, but it'll do. In the next download of CarServ (**chapter17-02**), there's an implementation of such an ESB adapter, using Apache Camel. Again, if you're not at your computer, all the relevant code snippets are listed in the following pages.

To keep the demo small, the adapter just processes messages retrieved from a directory and writes out updated messages to another directory, as shown in Figure 17.4.

The adapter itself lives in the new carserv-camel-inout project. To run the demo, copy the files from src/testdata into the messages/in directory. While you're at it, take a look at one of the messages:

chapter17/message1-in.xml
```
<?xml version="1.0" encoding="UTF-8" standalone="yes"?>
<customerMessage>
    <firstName>Joe</firstName>
    <lastName>Bloggs</lastName>
</customerMessage>
```

"In real life," such messages would be much more complex, but this simple one will do for us. Now run the CamelEsbAdapter launch configuration. You should see the files in messages/in disappear and new files appear in messages/out, populated with the email address:

chapter17/message1-out.xml

```xml
<?xml version="1.0" encoding="UTF-8" standalone="yes"?>
<customerMessage>
    <firstName>Joe</firstName>
    <lastName>Bloggs</lastName>
    <email>joe@bloggs.com</email>
</customerMessage>
```

It's time to look at the code. In CamelEsbAdapter's bootstrapCamel() method, we have the following route that tells Camel how to process the messages:

chapter17/CamelEsbAdapter-LookUpEmailRoute.java

```java
private final class LookUpEmailRoute extends RouteBuilder {
    @Override
    public void configure() throws Exception {
        String packageName =
            CustomerMessage.class.getPackage().getName();
        JaxbDataFormat jaxb = new JaxbDataFormat(packageName);
        from("file:messages/in")
            .setOutHeader("nakedObjectsSession")
                .constant(currentAuthenticationSession())
            .convertBodyTo(String.class)
            .unmarshal(jaxb)
            .process(new LookUpEmailProcessor())
            .marshal(jaxb)
            .to("file:messages/out");
    }
}
```

Let's untangle that long chain of method calls:

1. The from() method—inherited from RouteBuilder—tells Camel where to pick up messages from (the messages/in directory).

2. The setOutHeader() attaches credentials for the LookupEmailProcessor later in the chain.

3. The convertBodyTo() and unmarshal() methods convert the XML into a corresponding Java object.

4. The process() method delegates to the LookupEmailProcessor (more on this in a moment).

5. The marshal() and to() methods convert the output into XML and dump to the messages/out output directory.

It's a pretty standard technique using JAXB or similar to convert the XML messages (the *published language*, remember) to and from corresponding Java objects, and it means the processing can just work with regular objects rather than fiddling around with XML.[6] You'll find tools to generate such Java classes from XML schema definitions, so there's no need to violate the DRY principle.

The LookUpEmailProcessor is where the actual work is done:

chapter17/LookUpEmailProcessor.java

```
public class LookUpEmailProcessor
        extends AbstractNakedObjectsProcessor {
    public void doProcess(Exchange exchange) {
        Message message = exchange.getIn();
        CustomerMessage customerMessage =
            (CustomerMessage) message.getBody();

        NakedObject customerRepositoryAdapter =
            getService("customers");
        CustomerRepository customerRepository =
            (CustomerRepository)customerRepositoryAdapter.getObject();

        List<Customer> customers = customerRepository.findByName(
            customerMessage.getFirstName(),
            customerMessage.getLastName());

        Customer customer = first(customers);
        if (customer != null) {
            customerMessage.setEmail(customer.getEmailAddress());
        }
        message.setBody(customerMessage);
        exchange.setOut(message);
    }
    private <T> T first(List<T> list) {
        return list.size() > 0? list.get(0): null;
    }
}
```

We first look up the CustomerRepository (the *customers* service) and then use information from the inbound CustomerMessage to invoke the findByName() action. Finally, we update the same CustomerMessage and set it as the outbound message.

---

6. JAXB is part of Java 6. The reference implementation is hosted at https://jaxb.dev.java.net/.

Eliminating Overnight Batch Jobs

It has been a good many years since mainframes ruled the roost, but many systems still have a sizable suite of overnight batch jobs.

When the batch functionality is also in domain objects, it violate the DRY principle. And since the batch and the domain model tend to be implemented with different technologies, it is difficult to verify they are consistent.

So long as the throughput requirements are low to moderate, having an ESB offers an alternate architecture. Rather than batching up lots of work to do overnight, we can perform this processing continually throughout the online day using the functionality of the domain model.

There are multiple advantages to this: we keep to the DRY principle, resulting in a system that is easier to maintain and modify; if we have no batch, then we can make the system available to users for longer, perhaps even 24/7; the information gets processed more quickly (there was a time not so long ago when it would take a week for a check to clear); and finally we can explore, prototype, and implement the business functionality exclusively through the domain model.

Note that this implementation bypassess any business rules that might be encoded in the domain model. If we wanted our ESB to honor those rules (and I imagine that we would), then we could interact with the domain model either using the headless viewer approach or through the Naked Objects metamodel. We used these same techniques when integrating with Wicket; refer to Chapter 15, *Integrating with Web Frameworks*, on page 269 if need be.

We could make several other improvements to this code. For a start, the ESB message bus and adapter should probably interact using a JMS queue rather than directories.[7] The adapter should also be able to cope with various types of messages by routing each to its own specific

---

7. I'm simplifying here. *Java Business Integration* (JBI) is the Java standard for ESBs, so our Camel adapter would probably use JBI *endpoint*s to interact; under the covers this would still probably map to a JMS queue, though. See http://camel.apache.org/jbi.html for more details.

processor. And we would need to use a proper authentication scheme (Naked Objects supports pluggable authentication, as we'll see in Chapter 18, *Deploying the Full Runtime*, on page 333).

This adapter integrates our domain application when it is being called *from* the ESB. But we haven't yet seen how our application might send *to* the ESB. Well, as you might have guessed, sending to an ESB means writing a service that uses Camel to publish messages onto the bus for us. Since we'd like these messages to be XML, the main design decision we have to make is where to do the conversion from the domain objects into XML. One option is to simply pass domain objects to Camel and let it do all the work in a custom processor. But an alternative is to let the Naked Objects framework do some of the XML marshaling for us.

It's time for a quick digression.

Generating XML Snapshots

Thanks to its metamodel, Naked Objects has the ability to generate an XML snapshot for any domain object (along with the corresponding XML schema definition). We can put this to good use in a variety of integration scenarios, as we'll soon see.

Download CarServ (***chapter17-03***), and run the application using the DnD viewer. Retrieve a Customer; it should have a takeSnapshot() action (as a submenu). Invoke this action, and as Figure 17.5, on the following page shows, a web browser should be launched displaying the XML.

The action we've invoked is not actually on the Customer class; instead, it is a contributed action from the new SnapshotService (see Section 9.5, *Contributing Actions from Services*, on page 158 for a refresher on contributed actions):

chapter17/SnapshotService.java

```
@Named("Snapshots")
public interface SnapShotService {
    public void takeSnapshot(Snapshottable snapshottableObject)
        throws ApplicationException;
    public void takeSnapshotXsd(Snapshottable snapshottableObject)
        throws ApplicationException;
}
```

We get the action appearing for the Customer class because that class implements Snapshottable (in the applib). Because Snapshottable is a marker interface, there is no code we need to write to make any class be snapshottable; we just implement the interface.

Figure 17.5: CUSTOMER OBJECTS CAN BE SNAPSHOTTED.

If you look at Customer, you'll see it actually implements a subinterface, SnapshottableWithInclusions. This *does* specify an additional method to return a list of XPath-like expressions to include in the snapshot. In the case of Customer, it returns the string *person/name*. What that means is for Naked Objects to not only include details of the Customer but also the object referenced by the Customer's person property (a Person) and in turn the object referenced by the Person's name property (a Name). You can see this in the screenshot.

The snapshotting magic is done by the XmlSnapshot class in the Naked Objects framework, which is wrapped by the SnapshotServiceImpl service:

chapter17/SnapshotServiceImpl.java

```java
public void takeSnapshot(Snapshottable snapshottable)
        throws ApplicationException {
    try {
        XmlSnapshot xmlSnapshot = createSnapshot(snapshottable);
        viewSnapshot(xmlSnapshot.getXmlDocument());
    } catch(Exception ex) {
        throw new ApplicationException(ex);
    }
}
```

```
public void takeSnapshotXsd(Snapshottable snapshottable)
        throws ApplicationException {
    try {
        XmlSnapshot xmlSnapshot = createSnapshot(snapshottable);
        viewSnapshot(xmlSnapshot.getXsdDocument());
    } catch(Exception ex) {
        throw new ApplicationException(ex);
    }
}


private XmlSnapshot createSnapshot(Snapshottable snapshottable) {
    return XmlSnapshot.create(snapshottable).build();
}
```

End of digression. Let's see how we can use this snapshotting capability with ESBs.

Calling the ESB from our Domain Application

Suppose a Customer pays for a Service using the payUsing() action. What we'd like to do is publish (a normalized version of) the updated Service onto the bus, specifying the PaymentMethod details.

Here's the design, then: we'll inject a MessagePublisher infrastructure service into the Service domain object. When the Service is paid, it calls the MessagePublisher, which snapshots the calling Service to obtain the XML. Based on the type of message, the MessagePublisher applies XSLT to normalize the message. For demo purposes, we'll just dump the normalized messages into a directory.

We have another version of CarServ to download (***chapter17-04***) with the changes already made, so let's try it:

1. Run the exploration#viewer_dnd launch configuration, and navigate to a Customer with a CreditCard payment method.

2. Navigate to one of the Customer's (unpaid) Services.

3. Ensure there is a nonzero amount; then use the payUsing() action, and select the Customer's CreditCard. Hit OK.

Now look at the messages/service/creditcard directory in the carserv-com-mandline project; there should be a file there capturing the details of the updated Service; look inside, and you'll see it is XML.

Let's trace the code. The Service's payUsing() action calls to our Pay-mentMethod, which calls back to the Service (as a Payable)'s markAsPaid()

method. This in turn calls modifyPaymentMethod(). The hook for this, onModifyPaymentMethod(), is where the MessagePublisher is called:

chapter17/Service-onModifyPaymentMethod.java

```java
protected void onModifyPaymentMethod(PaymentMethod paymentMethod) {
    try {
        messagePublisher.publish(this);
    } catch (Exception ex) {
        throw new ApplicationException(
                "Failed to publish Service object onto ESB", ex);
    }
}
```

The implementation of MessagePublisher is MessagePublisherImpl in the carserv-camel-out project. The bit that matters is the setting up of the Camel route:

chapter17/MessageBrokerImpl-ServiceMessageRoute.java

```java
private final class ServiceMessageRoute extends RouteBuilder {
    @Override
    public void configure() throws Exception {
        from("direct:in")
        .choice()
        .when().xpath(
                "/app:RegularService/app:paymentMethod/app:CreditCard",
                regularServiceNamespaces())
            .to("xslt:RegularServiceToServiceMessage.xslt")
            .to("file:messages/service/creditcard")
        .otherwise()
            .convertBodyTo(String.class)
            .to("file:messages/unknown");
    }
}
```

This accepts the XML snapshot, uses XPath to check that the payment is indeed for a credit card, and then applies some XSLT to normalize the message. If the payment is not for a credit card, then it just writes the file out.

The only thing that's missing is the XSLT. The structure of the resultant XML is defined by ServiceMessage.xsd, which also lives in the carserv-camel-out project in src/main/resources, This schema belongs to our enterprise message model, defining the set of normalized messages that are permitted to be sent across the bus. To translate between the input XML snapshot and the desired XML standard message, we use XSLT, which admittedly isn't everyone's cup of tea. However, since we have a schema for both input and output, we can use a graphical mapping

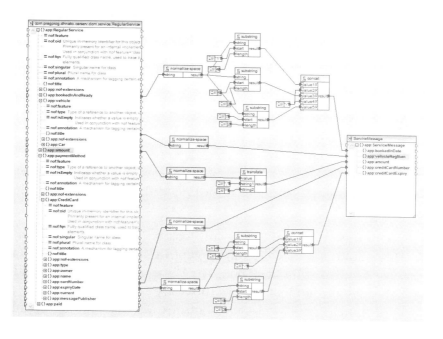

Figure 17.6: MESSAGES CAN BE NORMALIZED USING XSLT.

tool.[8] In Figure 17.6, we can see a screenshot of such a tool (don't strain your eyes trying to read it; my point is that we can wire together XML schemas with simple drag and drop).

Going back to Camel, I think its Java-fluent API is rather elegant. But if you prefer to represent routes using other notations, Camel also supports XML configuration using Spring and an intriguing Scala DSL.

Coming Up Next

In this chapter, we saw how to open up our domain model so that it can be accessed synchronously through a RESTful interface and either synchronously or asynchronously using an ESB. We also saw how the Naked Objects framework is able to provide XML snapshots of any object (and learned a bit about Apache Camel along the way).

The next chapter is our last. We're going to be wrapping up the book by reviewing the different ways to deploy Naked Objects applications,

---

8. The (commercial) tool shown in Altova MapForce, http://altova.com.

taking in authentication and authorization. We'll also review a major deployment of Naked Objects and look into the future for other initiatives that will help make your domain-driven applications that much easier to develop.

Exercises

Here's a nice, easy one to start; currently only Customer and Service are Snapshottable. Add this capability to other classes too. Also explore SnapshottableWithInclusions. You might want to add this to your own domain application too.

Building on this, you could write an AuditService, integrating into an ESB. This would use snapshotting to capture the current state of any object before and/or after an action. The MessagePublisher code would be a good start; you could just remove the XSLT processing and leave the snapshots in their "raw" form. Snapshots are also useful when creating communications. A technology to explore here is FDF, used for filling in PDF forms.

We learned earlier that Restful Objects serves up XHTML, meaning we can navigate around using a web browser. OK, so it works, but it ain't pretty. However, most web browsers provide the ability to perform XSLT transforms on the client side. So, an interesting (but big) exercise would be to write some stylesheets to provide your very own web interface to your Naked Objects application. If applying XSLT on the client side sounds a little kooky, then alternatively you could apply it in a servlet filter.

Deploying the Full Runtime

It's all very well being able to develop wonderful domain applications, but eventually our application needs to leave the IDE and enter the big wide world. In this chapter, we'll see how to package up our domain application for deployment in a variety of modes, with authentication and authorization fully enabled. We'll also see how to implement custom security mechanisms to integrate with any existing infrastructure you might have.

We're also going to briefly review some of the sister projects available since these offer alternative deployment options. At the time of writing, some of these are prerelease, but they offer an idea as to what will become available.

And finally, we going to wrap up the book by reviewing a major deployment of Naked Objects and considering once again the strengths and synergies of DDD and Naked Objects. Before that, though, there's work to do.

18.1 Deploying the Application

There are four typical/common options to deploying our domain application into a production environment:

- Single-user: A rich-client application running the DnD viewer, stand-alone against a local single-user database
- Web app: The HTML viewer running within a JEE web application
- Client-server: A rich-client application running the DnD viewer, connecting to a remote stand-alone server using sockets
- Client-server: A rich-client application running the DnD viewer, connecting to a remote web application server (that is, using HTTP)

Our focus here is on *how* Naked Objects is running (that is, as a client or as a server), rather than which viewer is running. Some of the sister projects provide alternative viewers, but for the purpose of this discussion, we'll stick with the DnD and HTML viewers that ship with Naked Objects.

In each of the various deployment permutations, we specify what Naked Objects calls the *deployment type*. The table below summarizes these, along with the default authentication policy and object store of each:

Deployment Type	Authentication	Object Store
Exploration	LogonFixture if available; or else a special *exploration* user	In-memory
Prototype	LogonFixture if available; or else must log on	In-memory
Single-user	Must log on	XML
Client	Must log on; authenticated by server	N/A
server-prototype	Client must provide valid user ID	In-memory
Server	Client must provide valid user ID	XML

We've already seen the object store being overridden (in Chapter 16, *Integrating with the Database*, on page 287); we'll see the authentication mechanism changed in Section 18.2, *Securing the Application*, on page 342.

For command-line deployments, the deployment type is specified using the --type flag. In a web application, there is of course no opportunity to specify a --type flag, so instead we use a *<context-param>* in the web.xml file. For example:

```
chapter18/web.xml

<web-app>
  ...
  <context-param>
    <param-name>deploymentType</param-name>
    <param-value>SERVER-PROTOTYPE</param-value>
  </context-param>
  ...
</web-app>
```

With that preamble over with, let's start by deploying our application for use in stand-alone mode by a single user.

Single-User Deployment

Suppose we've written ourselves a rinky-dink application for personal use to be used with the DnD viewer. It will probably be using the XML object store, or we could use the JPA object store configured to reference a JDBC database running in-process mode.[1] We'd hardly want to boot up an IDE to run the app; instead, we want to start it from a batch file or JAR file.

We can use Maven to do this packaging for us, and in fact the Naked Objects Maven archetype that we ran way back when already included the necessary configuration and supporting files for us.

So, download the latest version of CarServ (**chapter18-01**), which has been configured to be deployed as a single-user application. We will use the Apache Derby database here, so it has the following changes:

- The pom.xmls have been updated to reference the Derby JARs.

- The hibernate.cfg.xml specifies an embedded Derby database:

chapter18/single-user/hibernate.cfg.xml

```
<hibernate-configuration>
  <session-factory>
    ...
    <property name="connection.driver_class">
        org.apache.derby.jdbc.EmbeddedDriver
    </property>
    <property name="connection.username">sa</property>
    <property name="connection.password"></property>
    <property name="connection.url">
        jdbc:derby:carservDB;create=true
    </property>
    <property name="dialect">
        org.hibernate.dialect.DerbyDialect
    </property>
    ...
  </session-factory>
</hibernate-configuration>
```

---

1. For example, see http://db.apache.org/derby/papers/DerbyTut/embedded_intro.html for Apache Derby or http://hsqldb.org/doc/guide/ch01.html#N101A8 for HSQLDB.

Figure 18.1: RUNNING AS A CLIENT REQUIRES LOGGING IN.

- The SchemaManager and FixtureManager tools that we used in Chapter 16, *Integrating with the Database*, on page 287 have been run to create an initial "seed" database.

- The resultant database has been copied to src/main/db in the commandline project. The descriptor.xml file, which specifies what to package up (in src/main/assembly), has then been updated to include this database.

- The nakedobjects.bat and nakedobjects.sh batch files that will be used as the startup (in src/main/assembly/scripts) specify single-user mode:

chapter18/single-user/nakedobjects.bat

```
set DEPLOYMENT_FLAGS=--type single-user --viewer dnd
```

To package up the application, we just need to run mvn clean package in the root project. If we now look in the commandline/target directory; there should be a ZIP file that contains our code, dependencies, and the seed database.

Let's test this deployment. Copy this ZIP file to a new directory, and unzip. You should then be able to start CarServ using nakedobjects.bat or nakedobjects.sh.

Because the application is no longer running in exploration or prototype mode, we'll be prompted with a login dialog box, as shown in Figure 18.1. As we've done in previous chapters, we can log in using a username of *sven* and a password of *pass*.

If you don't want to have to log in, you can add the --user and --password flags to the nakedobjects.bat/nakedobjects.sh batch file.

Let's now move onto a slightly more involved scenario, that of the web app deployment.

Web App Deployment

Thus far, we've been running the HTML viewer in an embedded web server, but for deployment what we want is a standard WAR file. Again, we can get Maven to do the heavy lifting.

When we first ran our Maven archetype for CarServ back in Chapter 2, *Identifying the Domain Concepts*, on page 23, you might remember there was a carserv-webapp project created. We've been ignoring it so far, but now it's time to put it to use. This webapp project contains a web.xml file that is preconfigured to run the HTML viewer. If you look inside the web.xml file, you'll see it sets up the following:

- The NakedObjectsWebAppBootstrapper servlet context listener, which bootstraps Naked Objects

- The LogonServlet, ControllerServlet, and ResourceServlet servlets

  The first of these displays the initial login, the controller manages the application state, and the resource servlet serves up any static content such as CSS files and images.

- The NakedObjectsSessionFilter filter, which sets up a Naked Objects session if the user is authenticated, or redirects to the LogonServlet otherwise

- The StaticContentFilter filter, which decorates any static content with the HTTP headers so that they are cached by the browser

The idea is that you can add other servlets or filters in here as need be, and indeed we'll be doing this when we look at client-server remoting shortly.

For now, though, we need to adjust for the fact that Naked Objects is going to boot from the webapp project instead of the commandline project. So, the contents of the commandline project's config directory need copying into the webapp project's equivalent src/main/webapp/WEB-INF directory. The viewer_html.properties (which holds configuration settings specific to the HTML viewer) should be renamed web.properties (its equivalent name when running as a web app). Finally, the commandline project's static web content (in src/main/webapp)—namely, the CSS files and the images—needs copying to the webapp project's src/main/webapp directory.

Download the next version of CarServ (**chapter18-02**) where these changes have been made. Like the previous version, this one also uses an embedded database, although this time configured with a connection pool (in its hibernate.cfg.xml) to support multiple concurrent users. It'd be easy enough to switch this to a regular client-server (instead of embedded) JDBC connection if you wanted.

The packaging process is again the same: run mvn clean package in the root project. This time, there should be a WAR file in the webapp project's target directory.

Unlike the previous deployment, this time we haven't bundled up the database in the packaging. Instead, the database is specified using an absolute path name for the database, namely, /tmp/carservDB. As we'll see in just a moment, there are several ways we can run our web app, so an absolute directory saves us trying to figure out where the "current" directory is in each case.

This does mean, though, that we need to set up this database separately. Therefore, use the SchemaManager and FixtureManager to create and populate the database (or use the copy in the **chapter18-01** download), and copy the carservDB directory to c:\tmp (Windows) or /tmp (Linux or Mac).

We can run the web app in one of several ways:

- Deploy to an external servlet container.

  For example, in Tomcat this means copying the WAR file to its webapp directory.

- From the command line, get Maven to run using a goal of jetty:run.

  Or, in Eclipse, you can create a run configuration of a Maven build (as we did with Wicket in Chapter 15, *Integrating with Web Frameworks*, on page 269).

- If using the enterprise edition of Eclipse, then you can use its Web Tools Platform (WTP) functionality to run the application as a web application.

  Select the webapp project, then use Run > Run As > Run on Server, and then point to an instance of any JEE container.

- Run the application as a Naked Objects WebServer.

This differs from using the HTML viewer in the commandline project because the WebServer simply runs whatever it finds in the web.xml file. To use this option, temporarily comment back in the webserver module in the webapp project's pom.xml, and then use the launch configurations in the same project's ide/eclipse/launch.

When you deploy for real, you'll want to use the first of these options (copying the WAR file to an external runtime). Any of the other options are useful for checking that the web.xml file is correct, though.

Our next option goes back to using the DnD viewer, but this time client-server.

Client-Server Remoting Over Sockets

Naked Objects comes with the ability to run in client-server mode. The client application runs the DnD viewer and (just as in single-user mode) holds a cache of objects that the user has searched for or navigated to. However, when we invoke an action on these objects, the action is *not* performed locally. Instead, the request is sent to a remote server, which retrieves the (latest version of the) object from the database and invokes the action there. Any changes are then sent back to the client.

Before we deploy the application in this mode, let's just see the application running in client-server mode from within Eclipse (**chapter18-03**):

1. In the commandline project, first start up the server using the server#viewer_encoding-sockets.launch launch configuration.

2. Also, in the commandline project, then start up the client using the client#viewer_dnd#connector_encoding-sockets launch.

As for single-user mode, we'll need to log in first (user *sven*, password *pass*). It probably won't immediately be obvious that we're running in client-server mode, so if you're curious to see the messages being sent between the client and server, add the following to the logging.properties file:

chapter18/sockets/logging.properties

```
log4j.logger.org.nakedobjects.metamodel.commons.encoding.FieldType=DEBUG
```

Restart the application, and in Eclipse's console view (as shown in Figure 18.2, on the next page) you should see the message requests and their responses.

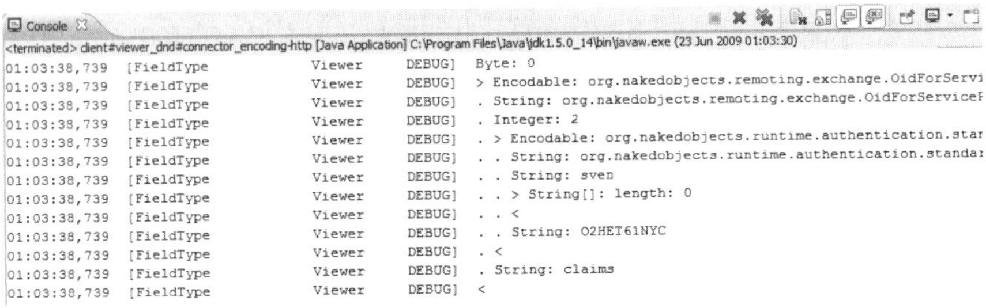

Figure 18.2: MESSAGES FLOW BETWEEN CLIENT AND SERVER.

OK, but what we want to do is to deploy the application as a client or as a server. Since both client and server are run from the command line, all we need is to assemble the application to run with different command options. In the commandline project, you'll see the original naked-objects.bat/sh batch files has been replaced by equivalent client.bat/sh and server.bat/sh files. This is the line that is different for the client:

chapter18/sockets/client.bat

```
set DEPLOYMENT_FLAGS=--type client --viewer dnd \
                     --connector encoding-sockets
```

while for the server the line that is different is as follows:

chapter18/sockets/server.bat

```
set DEPLOYMENT_FLAGS=--type server --viewer encoding-sockets
```

Before we package up the application, also specify the hostname or IP address of the host that will run the server. This is specified in config/transport-sockets.properties; the original version just specifies *local-host*:

chapter18/sockets/transport-sockets.properties

```
nakedobjects.transport.sockets.host = localhost
nakedobjects.transport.sockets.port = 9580
```

The location of the database for this deployment is again absolute (in /tmp/carservDB), so if necessary, set it up in the same way as previously. Then, we just need to assemble the ZIP file, using mvn clean package once more. The ZIP file is in the commandline project's target directory and can then be unzipped on both client and server and run using the appropriate batch file. Obviously, make sure you run the server on the correct host, or the client won't find it!

Let's move onto our most involved deployment, client-server over HTTP.

Client-Server Remoting Over HTTP

Although client-server over sockets works well enough, in production we probably would not want to run a server from the command line. Instead, we'd want it deployed to some managed infrastructure software. We might also want access to the server through firewalls.

So, Naked Objects lets us run the server side of our application within a web app. The client performs an HTTP POST to a single servlet, namely, EncodingOverHttpRemotingServlet, passing the request as a serialized byte stream. The servlet then delegates to the rest of the Naked Objects runtime in the usual manner and returns the result as another bunch of bytes. So, this isn't a servlet that supports HTML, but it does let us do what we want—to deploy the server within a managed environment.

Again, let's start by running client-server within Eclipse (**chapter18-04**). In the commandline project, first start up the server using the server#viewer_encoding-http.launch launch configuration; this bootstraps Naked Objects and its servlet in an embedded web server. Then, start up the client using the client#viewer_dnd#connector_encoding-http launch config. It should then work as before.

To deploy the server side of this application, we use the webapp project that we previously used to package the HTML viewer. The web.xml has been updated with the single entry for EncodingOverHttpRemotingServlet entries, with the HTML viewer's servlets removed:

chapter18/http/web.xml

```
<web-app>
  ...
  <servlet>
    <servlet-name>EncodingOverHttpRemotingServlet</servlet-name>
    <servlet-class>
org.nakedobjects.plugins.remoting.http.EncodingOverHttpRemotingServlet
    </servlet-class>
  </servlet>
  ...
  <servlet-mapping>
    <servlet-name>RemotingServlet</servlet-name>
    <url-pattern>/remoting.svc</url-pattern>
  </servlet-mapping>
  ...
</web-app>
```

Likewise, the commandline project has been updated with the naked-objects.bat/sh batch files renamed to client.bat/sh:

chapter18/http/client.bat

```
set DEPLOYMENT_FLAGS=--type client --connector encoding-http
```

Before we package up the application, we should also change the URL to point to the location where the remoting servlet will be deployed. This lives in the config/transport-http.properties file:

chapter18/http/transport-http.properties

```
nakedobjects.transport.http.url = http://localhost:8080/remoting.svc
```

Packaging the application up is once more just a matter of running mvn clean package. The server WAR will be in the webapp project's target directory, and the client's ZIP will be in the commandline project's target directory. Use them the same as before.

Let's now turn to the topic of securing the application.

18.2 Securing the Application

We're going to focus on the two main aspects of security here: authentication (who are you?) and authorization (what can you do?). Let's look at Naked Objects' (purposefully simple) default implementations for each; then we'll talk about alternatives.

Authentication

As we have seen, the default implementation for authentication just reads logins from the passwords file. This resides in the config directory if running from the command line (stand-alone or server) or in the WEB-INF directory if running within a web app. The format of this file is as follows:

chapter18/authentication/passwords

```
tom:p4ssw0rd:user_role
dick:s3cr3t:oper_role
harry:0bv10us:user_role|supervisor_role
```

This sets up three users, tom, dick, and harry. They have their own respective passwords and are in different roles.

The class that implements this logic is FileAuthenticator, which is created in turn by the FileAuthenticationManagerInstaller. These "installers" act as component factories, with the InstallerLookupDefault class acting as a sort

Other Security Concerns

We've only focused here on authentication and authorization, but of course there's a lot more involved in securing an enterprise application.

You'll probably want to introduce auditing ("what did you do?") somewhere in the mix; the database is an obvious place to implement this.

For client-server deployment, we should also think about network encryption ("no, you can't look"); otherwise, passwords will be sent around in plain text. The easiest way to do this is to use HTTP remoting and then deploy the remoting servlet using SSL (that is, using a URL starting with https://).

For client-side deployments, you'll also want to ensure that the configuration files are read-only for the end user so that they cannot disable security. You might also want to consider packaging up the application as a single signed JAR set up so that the configuration files are read only from the classpath rather than from files in directories.

of factory of factories. If you were to look at the InstallerLookupDefault's authenticationManagerInstaller() method, you'd see this:

`chapter18/InstallerLookupDefault.java`

```
public AuthenticationManagerInstaller
        authenticationManagerInstaller(String requested) {
    return getInstaller(
            AuthenticationManagerInstaller.class, requested,
            SystemConstants.AUTHENTICATION_INSTALLER_KEY,
            SystemConstants.AUTHENTICATION_DEFAULT);
}
```

This attempts to look up the *nakedobjects.authentication* property key from the nakedobjects.properties file and falls back to the default value file otherwise. The value is then used to look up the implementation from the installer-registry.properties file part of the Naked Objects runtime JAR, namely, the FileAuthenticationManagerInstaller mentioned earlier.

That takes care of configuring the default file-based authentication. We will look at alternatives in a minute, but for now let us move onto authorization.

Authorization

Naked Objects supports authorization at two levels—whether a class member (property, collection, or action) is visible and whether it is usable. Out of the box, though, authorization is disabled (even in client or server deployment types); whereas a default authenticator can always be provided, authorization is specific to an application. To enable authorization, we need to uncomment the following in the nakedobjects.properties file:

chapter18/authorization/nakedobjects.properties

```
nakedobjects.reflector.facets.include=\
    org.nakedobjects.runtime.authorization.standard.\
                                        AuthorizationFacetFactoryImpl
nakedobjects.authorization.learn=true
```

The first key enables authorization, while the second puts the authorization manager into a special mode so that it can "learn" about the protected resources and therefore help us create our allow configuration file.

It's probably easiest to see this by doing. Start up CarServ, logging in with a user who has at least one role (look in the passwords file mentioned earlier). You should be able to use the application as normal. Then take a look at the allow configuration file. There will be an entry in the file for the class member accessed, for example:

chapter18/authorization/allow

```
com.pragprog.dhnako.carserv.dom.customer.Customer#notes:role1
com.pragprog.dhnako.carserv.dom.customer.Customer#vehicles:role1
com.pragprog.dhnako.carserv.dom.customer.Customer#since:role1
com.pragprog.dhnako.carserv.dom.customer.Customer#\
    newVehicle(com.pragprog.dhnako.carserv.dom.vehicle.Model):role1
...
com.pragprog.dhnako.carserv.dom.vehicle.Model#name:role1
com.pragprog.dhnako.carserv.dom.vehicle.Model#make:role1
com.pragprog.dhnako.carserv.dom.vehicle.Model#vehicleType:role1
...
```

You can now edit this file by doing the following:

- Using just the class name as a wildcard for all its class members

- Using just the class name and action name as a wildcard for all overloaded versions of the action

- Specifying multiple roles, in a comma-separated list

- Qualifying a permission as visible but not usable using a *-ro* suffix (for example, role1-ro) and removing the original unqualified role name from the list

For example, here's an updated allow file:

chapter18/authorization/allow-updated

```
com.pragprog.dhnako.carserv.dom.customer.Customer#notes:user_role
com.pragprog.dhnako.carserv.dom.customer.Customer#vehicles:user_role
com.pragprog.dhnako.carserv.dom.customer.Customer#since:admin_role
com.pragprog.dhnako.carserv.dom.customer.Customer#newVehicle:user_role
...
com.pragprog.dhnako.carserv.dom.vehicle.Model:user_role-ro,admin_role
...
```

Sometimes, though, it's easier to specify the permissions that users *don't* have rather than the permissions than they *do*. To do this, in the allow file, grant permissions to everything, and then in a new disallow file specify the permissions that users don't have. The format is the same. You also need to tell Naked Objects about this file in the nakedobjects.properties file:

chapter18/authorization/nakedobjects-blacklist.properties

```
nakedobjects.authorization.file.blacklist=disallow
```

The class that implements all the previous is FileAuthorizor, which has its own installer, FileAuthorizationManagerInstaller.

As mentioned, these default implementations for authentication and authorization are purposefully simple. However, it is easy to change the implementation to integrate with whatever security infrastructure your company uses, so let's see how.

Alternative Implementations

Rather than administer security on an application-by-application basis, many organizations prefer to use centralize administration of authentication, certainly, and sometimes authorization too. Typically this is done using a technology such as Active Directory or LDAP.

Because Naked Object's security is pluggable, we can replace both the authenticator and the authorizer with different implementations. For example, Naked Objects does also ship with an implementation of both for LDAP.

> ### Deploying Naked Objects = Choosing the Components
>
> As I'm sure you now appreciate, Naked Objects is a component-based framework, so deployment is really a matter of choosing and configuring the correct set of components.
>
> The minimum components you need to configure are those for persistence (the object store), the presentation layer (viewers), and security. There are a number of other components that we can customize too, though. For space reasons, we won't be covering them here, but if customizing frameworks is your thang, then see Naked Objects' own documentation for further details, or hit the Web.

To specify LDAP authentication, add the following (changing the LDAP server as required):

`chapter18/authentication/nakedobjects-ldap.properties`

```
nakedobjects.authentication=ldap
nakedobjects.authentication.ldap.server=ldap://localhost:10389
nakedobjects.authentication.ldap.dn= dc=nakedobjects, dc=org
```

The Naked Objects documentation has full details.

Similarly, we can use LDAP for authorization:

`chapter18/authorization/nakedobjects-ldap.properties`

```
nakedobjects.authorization=ldap
nakedobjects.authorization.ldap.server=ldap://localhost:10389
nakedobjects.authorization.ldap.dn= dc=nakedobjects, dc=org
nakedobjects.authorization.ldap.application.dn= \
            cn=expenses, dc=apps, dc=nakedobjects, dc=org
```

Again, the Naked Objects documentation has full details.

If you aren't using LDAP, though, it is an easy enough job to implement your own authenticators and authorizers. Since Naked Objects' default implementations are quite simple, they make good starting points on which to base your own implementation that integrates with whatever security infrastructure your company uses. You might also find that existing open source products such as Spring Security or Apache Shiro can do much of the heavy lifting for you.[2]

Suppose you've now written your own SuperDuperAuthenticator and corresponding SuperDuperAuthenticationManagerInstaller. Obviously, you're not expected to crack open and recompile Naked Objects with an updated installer-registry.properties. Instead, you can just specify the authenticator in nakedobjects.properties using the fully qualified class name:

chapter18/authentication/nakedobjects-superduper.properties

```
nakedobjects.authentication=\
    com.mycompany.auth.SuperDuperAuthenticationManagerInstaller
```

The process for replacing this authorization with your own implementation is the same (using the *nakedobjects.authorization* property key).

So, that's our application deployed and secured. We've focused so far on deploying the DnD viewer and the HTML viewer, but as has been mentioned in earlier chapters, several sister projects offer alternative viewers. Let's review those now.

18.3 Deploying the Sister Projects

First, a caveat: at the time of writing, some of the following are still prerelease. Still, open source moves quickly; by the time you read this, they could well be released.

Restful Objects

We met Restful Objects in Chapter 17, *Integrating Within the Enterprise*, on page 311, and saw how it provides an XHTML-based RESTful API so that client programs can use our domain application through web services. Since this is just a web app, it can also be deployed as a WAR file, similar to the HTML viewer and the HTTP remoting servlets discussed in Section 18.1, *Deploying the Application*, on page 333.

One thing that Restful Objects does not provide at the time of writing is any authentication support; there is no built-in way to propagate the identity of the client application to the RESTful server. This will undoubtedly be rectified in time.

---

2. Spring Security (previously called Acegi) is hosted at http://static.springsource.org/spring-security/site/index.html. Apache Shiro (previously called JSecurity) is hosted at http://cwiki.apache.org/confluence/display/SHIRO.

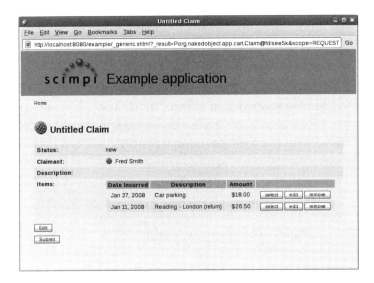

Figure 18.3: SCIMPI PROVIDES CUSTOMIZABLE HTML VIEWS.

Scimpi

Scimpi describes itself as "an ultra-light framework for developing web applications based on strong domain models."[3] Essentially it provides a set of XML tags that you can include within your XHTML; these tags allow domain objects to be easily displayed. It lets the Naked Objects framework take care of the rest.

As you can see in Figure 18.3, out-of-the-box *Scimpi* is similar to the original HTML viewer, providing a generic view for any domain object. This view is specified using a generic template:

`chapter18/scimpi/generic/object.shtml`

```
<swf:page-title><swf:title icon="no" /></swf:page-title>
<swf:template  file="../style/template.shtml" />

<h2><swf:title /></h2>
<swf:long-form link="_generic.shtml" />

<swf:methods />
```

---

3. *Scimpi* is licensed under the Apache License 2.0 and is hosted at SourceForge. Its home page is http://www.scimpi.org.

<swf:long-form> shows properties and collections for the object, while *<swf:methods>* lists the actions available to us.

The clever bit, though, comes through the use of simple naming conventions to identify the HTML page to use to render the object. For example, a Claim object would use Claim.shtml if available, and it would fall back to the standard view otherwise. These custom views can include a variety of more sophisticated tags.

Here's an example:

chapter18/scimpi/Claim/object.shtml

```
<div id="content">
    <h1>Claim</h1>
    <h3><swf:title/></h3>
    <swf:long-form >
        <swf:link name="approver"/>
        <swf:exclude name="claimant"/>
    </swf:long-form>
    <swf:specification always="yes"/>
    <div class="form">
        <div>
            <swf:label field="claimant"/>:
            <swf:field field="claimant" icon="false"/>
        </div>
        <div>
            <swf:label field="description"/>:
            <swf:field field="description" truncate="16"/>
        </div>
        <div>
            <swf:label field="status"/>:
            <swf:field field="status"/>
        </div>
    </div>
    <swf:edit>
        <swf:selector field="approver" object="service:claims"
                      methods="allClaims"/>
    </swf:edit>
    <swf:action-link object="service:claimants" method="allClaimants"/>
    <swf:methods/>
</div>
```

Because *Scimpi* is a web app, deployment is done the same way as the other web apps. Authentication and authorization is done through Naked Objects; *Scimpi* really just replaces the HTML viewer.

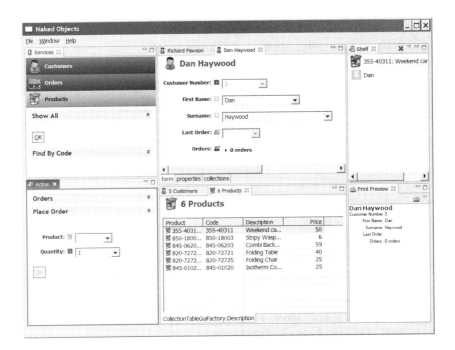

Figure 18.4: THE RICH CLIENT OBJECTS VIEWER USES FAMILIAR IDIOMS.

Rich Client Objects

Like the DnD viewer, the *Rich Client Objects* viewer is a desktop application but uses Eclipse RCP as its base platform.[4] This gives a more familiar UI, as shown in Figure 18.4.

Its user-interaction paradigm is approximately halfway between the DnD viewer and the HTML viewer. Like the DnD viewer, it supports drag and drop, with a *Shelf* view used as a place to hold references temporarily. However, like the HTML viewer, only a single object has focus in the editor, similar to the way that a developer using the Eclipse IDE is only ever working on one Java file at a time. The *Actions* view shows the methods available for the object whose editor has focus.

One of the key objectives for Rich Client Objects is to allow the viewer to be extended, using Eclipse extension points. For example, in

---

4. Rich Client Objects is licensed under Eclipse Public License v1.0 and is hosted on SourceForge. Its home page is accessed from http://starobjects.org.

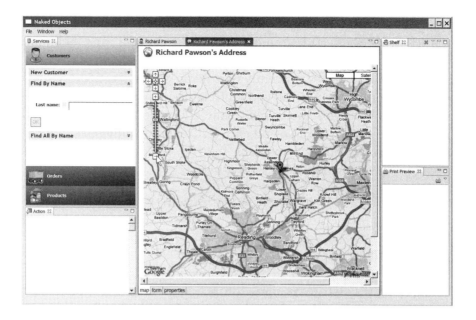

Figure 18.5: RICH CLIENT OBJECTS SUPPORTS CUSTOM VIEWS.

Figure 18.5, we can see an Address object displayed in an embedded Google Maps mashup.

It's still a bit too early in this project's development to talk about deployment. However, I expect at some point that the Naked Objects runtime will also be made available as an OSGi bundle, meaning that it can easily integrate into all the existing mechanisms that the Eclipse platform provides for distributing applications.

Wicket

While not a sister project, we did see in Chapter 15, *Integrating with Web Frameworks*, on page 269 that we can integrate Naked Objects with third-party web frameworks such as Apache Wicket. If you are taking this route, then at some point you'll want to package them up for deployment.

If you go back to that chapter's versions of CarServ (**chapter15-01** and **chapter15-02**), you'll see that the Wicket projects are just regular web app modules, so you'll be to package up the WAR file using mvn clean package.

Of the various ways to deploy Naked Objects, four of them involve web apps (HTML viewer, HTTP remoting, Restful Objects, and Scimpi). I probably don't need to point this out, but there's no intrinsic reason not to run all of these concurrently in a single web app context, thereby supporting multiple different types of clients concurrently. Moreover, doing so will give you the benefit that any second-level caching by object stores will be shared by all clients. The only fiddly part of such a megadeployment would be ensuring that the various servlet and filter mappings are compatible with each other.

And with that, it's about time we started wrapping up this book.

18.4 A CarServ Retrospective

Throughout the book, we've used CarServ to illustrate how to develop domain applications using Naked Objects. Let's just reflect on what we've learned:

- We have seen how to build a *ubiquitous language* consisting of domain objects, where every class (such as Customer and Car) has meaning to both the domain expert and the developer.

- We learned to push complexity out of entities and into value types (such as RegistrationNumber), extending the *ubiquitous language* further.

- By refactoring and decoupling, we've found deeper abstractions that weren't immediately obvious (such as Payable and Vehicle-Owner). We used design patterns to further deepen the design.

- We saw how to test the application from both the domain experts' perspective using scenario tests and from the developers' implementation perspective using developer tests.

- Using injected domain and infrastructure services, we linked our domain objects into the outside world.

- We saw how to integrate our application with other layers of the application putting on custom user interfaces on the one hand and integrating to an RDBMS on the other.

- We learned how to deploy our domain application in multiple ways, allowing its domain logic to be reused in different contexts.

- And throughout we've used standard tools such as Eclipse and Maven within a productive development environment.

Now you've been through the book, I doubt you'll have much need to refer to the earlier versions of CarServ. But as you develop your own domain applications, you might find some of the later versions to be a useful reference: "How do you go about deploying RESTful web services again? What was that thing about a headless viewer?"

18.5 The DSFA Application

Many of the ideas and techniques in this book are borne out of a substantial Naked Objects project that's been running in Ireland for the last five years. So, let me give a flavor of what a Naked Objects real-world application looks like.

The Department of Social and Family Affairs (DSFA) is an Irish government department responsible for administering and paying out benefits such as pensions, child benefits, and about forty other benefits. The online benefits administration system is an application implemented using Naked Objects, rolled out to 600+ users in multiple offices around the country. The system as a whole paying out something like 5bn a year to claimants.

Development started in 2004, and the system went live in 2006. Richard Pawson and I wrote the bulk of the common domain object model (120 classes and about 60,000 lines of code); three others wrote the main pensions domain object model of comparable size. The scope of the system is steadily expanding, with a new release each month; the department intends to eventually migrate all its benefits systems to run on it. Microsoft's Team Foundation Server is used for configuration management; Cruise Control is used for continuous integration, and FitNesse is used for scenario testing. The scenario tests run both against an in-memory object store and also end to end.

The system runs in client-server mode using the DnD viewer as the front end. The server side is deployed on a pair of multicore application servers that act as hot standby to each other; network infrastructure balances the load over the two servers. The customized remoting mechanism invokes SOAP web services.

The application servers in turn talk to two databases. Most of the data lives on a SQL Server database (about 0.5Tb at the time of writing), and there is also a legacy database. Most transactions are local and hit only the SQL Server database, but where necessary distributed transactions are used. Because of the legacy database, a custom object store implementation was used. To date, no second-level caching has been introduced.

Authentication is performed against Active Directory, and authorization uses a custom implementation. According to their roles, different officers have access to different repositories (icons) and actions; some specialize in pensions, others in administering child benefit, and so on. Auditing is performed both in the database level and also at the domain layer using RecordedActions, which are domain objects that represent changes. These can optionally be signed for nonrepudiation, implemented as a secondary password against a certificate server.

In addition to the online system, there is a batch system that performs bulk processing, such as the generation of the payments. Low-volume batch jobs are also performed using logic within the domain model.

The system interacts with a number of other systems both within the department and in other government departments. BizTalk acts as a messaging bus, in effect defining a published language. Other systems publish messages onto the bus, which are received and processed by domain objects. Forms completed on the Web are processed this way, for example. Conversely, the domain objects can also publish messages onto the bus; SMS text is sent out in this fashion.

As you read the previous text, I'm sure you'll have noticed many of the same areas as we've covered in this book. It's my ongoing involvement with the DSFA application that has played a large part in scoping what is in this book: I'd like you to be able to build Naked Objects applications as substantial and successful as the DSFA's.[5]

18.6 Closing Thoughts

Throughout all the preceding chapters we've been assiduously learning the tools, techniques, and practices for developing domain application using Naked Objects. No doubt by now you've started to develop your own ideas as to how you might put Naked Objects to work to develop

---

5. Niall Barry, the DSFA's Directory of Information Systems, stated, "In thirty years of managing IT projects, I have never been more satisfied [than with the Naked Objects application]." See http://www.nakedobjects.org/case-study/dsfa-intro.shtml for more details.

your next masterpiece. But I'd like to conclude the book with a few thoughts of my own. As they say in those legalese disclaimers, all views expressed herein are those of the author!

Naked Objects and DDD

I first learned about Naked Objects at the Object Technology (now SPA) conference at Oxford in 2002. Richard Pawson, the inventor of the pattern, and Robert Matthews, the chief architect of the framework, were demonstrating an early version of the framework. Only really suitable back then for prototyping, it nevertheless caught my imagination. I had just cowritten a book, *Better Software Faster* [CH02] on TogetherJ, and the synergies between the two technologies were immediately obvious; TogetherJ synchronized the code and UML class diagrams at design time, while Naked Objects synchronized the code and the user interface at runtime.

A couple of years on, Eric Evans published his classic book, *Domain Driven Design*, and that gave another set of synergies to explore. Although strictly speaking DDD doesn't require that we use object-oriented models, it does seem that most people, most of the time, are applying DDD with the context of OO-based systems. In the Naked Objects community, we started adopting the DDD terminology and used it to influence the design of newer versions of the framework. For example, in Naked Objects 3.0, we replaced **static** methods on classes with actions on repositories and services, while Naked Objects 4.0 has introduced support for value types using the @Value annotation.

Earlier this year (2009), Evans gave a presentation on what he has learned about DDD since he published his book. One thing he emphasized was how essential exploration and experimentation are—to be prepared to shape and reshape the *ubiquitous language*, while requiring the creative collaboration of domain experts and software experts. So (I hope!) by now you'll agree that with Naked Objects we have a rich tool set to do this. Whether we skin the domain model later with a custom UI, being able to rapidly prototype our application is key to fostering this experimentation.

Strategic Design

Evans also now emphasizes the value of strategic design: recognize that no substantial system will be perfectly well-designed, so put the effort into the *core domain* and not the supporting *subdomains*.

A great example of a supporting domain is the persistence layer; we use ORMs such as Hibernate to do the heavy lifting. Indeed, a quote recently doing the rounds on the blogosphere: "If you're writing [database] code by hand, then you are stealing from your. . . client."[6]

We could say that Naked Objects' philosophy is that the presentation layer is also a supporting domain for many enterprise applications, perhaps especially so for sovereign applications (see Section 13.3, *Which Option to Choose?*, on page 246). All other things being equal, we should spend our efforts improving the design of the *core domain*, not tweaking font sizes on the user interface (see the sidebar on the next page for more of a rant on this subject).

Be a Problem Solver. . .

While the objectives of DDD and Naked Objects overlap substantially, it's not a perfect intersection. Naked Objects doesn't have much to say about non-OO models, for example. Similarly, the DDD ideas of bounded contexts and context maps (as catalogued in Chapter 17, *Integrating Within the Enterprise*, on page 311) are very helpful and are something you can use with or without Naked Objects.

Conversely, Naked Objects isn't only about domain-driven design. One of the metaphors that Richard Pawson developed to explain Naked Objects at the DSFA was in the shape of the game the Incredible Machine.[7]

In this game, the player must use objects in order to meet some goal, which might be something like "help Newton Mouse get to his mouse hole," as shown in Figure 18.6, on page 358. To solve the problem, the game player must move the cheese, connect the pulley, blow up the balloon, or any of a hundred other different activities. These things have state, have behavior, have identity. . . they're objects. But objects are also what underpin enterprise business systems. What Richard asked was, "Why can't business systems be as engaging as the Incredible Machine game?"

---

6. Quotation taken from http://codebetter.com/blogs/jeremy.miller/archive/2008/11/07/how-to-design-your-data-connectivity-strategy.aspx
7. This game is also known as Contraptions. It doesn't appear to be sold anymore, but if you do an Internet search for *Even More Contraptions Demo*, you should be able to download a copy to play with.

The Dangers of Custom UIs

Although the viewers that ship with Naked Objects and its sister projects are steadily becoming more sophisticated, many developers will want to put a custom skin on their domain applications (as we did with Wicket in Chapter 15, *Integrating with Web Frameworks*, on page 269).

There's nothing wrong with that, but—just as we do with the database—we should defer that step as late as possible. Once implemented, database schemas and user interfaces tend to bake in a domain model and make it that much harder to refactor.

Jumping too prematurely to a custom UI also means that insights into the domain can get lost. In the main text, I said not to waste time tweaking font sizes, but we should also ask *why* we would want the font size larger in one place in the UI than another. It presumably isn't arbitrary, which means there's probably some domain knowledge waiting to be discovered.

Another example is in grouping fields together, such as firstName, lastName, and title. That user interface group could well be masking an undiscovered Name domain object.

And the most obvious danger of having a custom-written UI is that we can very easily start writing business logic directly in the presentation layer. What starts out as a quick check for a nonnegative number soon mushrooms into a huge chunk of logic that really should reside on a domain object.

So, this is one of the core Naked Objects philosophies; allow the end user to *be a problem solver, not a mere process follower.* One of the most difficult aspects in building any enterprise application is figuring out where the boundary of the system should lie. Computers are great for highly repetitive, well-defined tasks but pretty poor at anything that requires a bit of discretion or good old common sense. And human beings are just the opposite. Too often, though, enterprise applications encroach on the human being's territory, unsuccessfully automating behavior that should remain in the end users' heads. Naked Objects lets us build applications that give the end user the flexibility to interact with whichever domain objects they need to in order to get the job done.

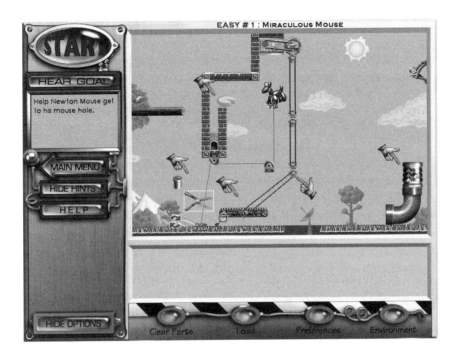

Figure 18.6: THE INCREDIBLE MACHINE WAS AN EARLY METAPHOR FOR NAKED OBJECTS.

It's Not About the Viewers

Naked Objects' unique selling point is its ability to automatically generate the user interface for free, so the title of this section might seem strange. Surely, Naked Objects is *all* about the viewers?

Well, no, not really. If you were to walk around the project room in Ireland where the DSFA application is developed, you won't hear anyone talk about the user interface. Instead, the talk relates to the domain objects for benefits administration: Customers, Schemes, Entitlements, Addresses. Moreover, the business's domain experts use these same terms too. So, what Naked Objects genuinely delivers a *ubiquitous language.*

So, for me at least, what Naked Objects is about is the ability to rapidly develop domain models quickly. Whether they are rendered automatically by Naked Objects or skinned in a custom presentation layer really is secondary. It's the rapid development coupled with a *ubiquitous language* that gives the team more time to uncover the subtleties and nuances in future iterations; moreover, Naked Objects ensures that domain semantics stay put where they should, in the domain layer.

From a technical perspective, Naked Objects is about the metamodel as much as the viewers; all of the clever wizardry that Naked Objects also supports (such as FitNesse and RESTful web services) can only be accomplished because of this metamodel. The way in which the metamodel was built was completely rewritten in Naked Objects 4.0, making it easy to customize the programming conventions. In this book I've hinted about the capabilities of Naked Objects' metamodel, but it's a rich area to explore.

As a developer, not having to explicitly code the user interface means that one tends to start to ignore or forget about it. What I find more unexpected is that in *using* the application one tends to ignore or forget about the user interface too. The connection between presentation layer and domain objects is so immediate that you forget that you are seeing a *representation* of a domain object; instead, it seems that you are dealing with the *actual* domain object.

It's been said (though I can't find out who said it first) that the best user interface is no user interface. A VCR that automatically picks up the time is an improvement on one that requires you to set the time through some fiddly buttons. In building our enterprise applications, we can't get rid of the user interface, but one that becomes invisible over time is the next best thing.

Coming Up Next

In this chapter, we saw how to package up our domain application to run either from the command line or as a web app, and we learned how to configure security and the basis for rolling our own. We also reviewed some of viewers of the Naked Objects' sister projects. Finally, we saw how DDD and Naked Objects intersect—and how they don't.

This is the final chapter, so what's coming up next is, well, whatever you decide. In the five-plus years since Eric Evans wrote his book, domain-driven design continues to garner interest, and that can only be a good thing. There are now dedicated tracks at major conferences, and there has been at least one conference devoted solely to the topic.

Meanwhile, Naked Objects exists on both the Java and .NET platforms, under the stewardship of Richard Pawson and Robert Matthews' company, Naked Objects Group Ltd. In this book we've been using the open source Java version, so you are free to develop and deploy your applications as you will. If you use the .NET platform, then (as mentioned briefly in the preface) there are prototyping and enterprise editions available.

The Java and .NET versions tend to track each other (they both originate from the same codebase), so innovations on one tend to get implemented on the other sooner or later. With respect to the open source version, the following are some of the things on the radar:

- Extending the capabilities of the DnD viewer.

- Ongoing development of Scimpi and Rich Client Objects to provide alternative extensible viewers for both the Web and the desktop.

- Ongoing development of Restful Objects to include support for authentication and the JSON protocol.

- Further new RIA viewers, perhaps using Flex, JavaFX, GWT, and (who knows?) Silverlight. Some of these may exploit the Restful Objects project.

- Restarting development on the Eclipse-bascd IDE (mothballed while I wrote this book!).

- Developing a Maven plug-in to validate domain models at compile time.

- More built-in support for further value types, such as JSR-310, JScience, or JodaTime.[8]

- A user action recorder to allow scenario tests and user guides to be automatically generated just by using the application.

- The ability to provide auditing at the domain layer (rather than in the database), such as using an @Audited annotation.

- Support for authenticated actions requiring the presence of some credentials (for example, using a fingerprint reader) to invoke.

- The ability to contribute properties as well as actions.

---

8. JSR-310 is a proposed replacement for the JDK's date and time classes; see https://jsr-310.dev.java.net. JScience is hosted at http://jscience.org/. JodaTime is hosted at http://joda-time.sourceforge.net/.

As project lead of many of the sister projects and a committer to the core framework, I intend to push forward on as many of the previous as I have capacity to do, but open source projects live or die first from their community and second by their contributors. If you're interested in helping out on any of the previous (or any of your own ideas, of course), then I'd love to hear from you.

But otherwise, that's us just about done. Good luck writing your domain applications. Let me know how you get on!

Exercises

Just because it's the last chapter doesn't mean there aren't any exercises, you know!

First up, try bundling your application as a single-user application. Make sure when you unzip the ZIP file that it runs fine. Then, have a go bundling it up as a WAR file (remember to copy the configuration files from the config directory to the src/main/webapp/WEB-INF directory). Finally, try client-server remoting mode first using sockets and then over HTTP.

Once you're done with that, enable authorization. Try the authorization's "learn" mode, and use the entries to try some whitelisting or blacklisting.

As mentioned in the main text, Naked Objects does actually ship with an LDAP authenticator and authorizer, so if you have an LDAP server, then you could have a go at configuring these. Alternatively, you might want to try implementing your own authenticator and authorizer.

And finally, if you've been doing the exercises at the same time, then by this stage you'll also have your own domain application. Having written one, why don't you go and write another, but this time with the full set of tools, techniques, and practices under your belt?

Part IV

Appendixes

Programming Model Cheat Sheet

The Naked Objects programming model is a set of naming conventions and supporting annotations for writing domain-driven applications. Any application written to these conventions will run on Naked Objects with any of the standard viewers. The programming model can also be extended to support your own conventions (though that isn't something we cover in this book).

Convenience Superclasses

The applib provides a number of convenience superclasses to inherit from. It isn't mandatory to inherit from these, but it does simplify the code. For further discussion, see Section 14.2, *Decoupling from the Framework*, on page 260.

Superclass	Description
AbstractDomainObject	Any domain object, though usually an entity.
AbstractFactoryAndRepository	Factories and in-memory repository implementations.
AbstractFixture	Fixture for use in prototyping or testing using the in-memory object store.
AbstractService	Any service (superclass of AbstractFactoryAndRepository).
AbstractSpecification	As referenced by @MustSatisfy annotation, specifies validation of an object, object member, or action parameter.
AbstractValueSemanticsProvider	As referenced by @Value annotation to provide value semantics to framework.

Annotations Reference

Declarative business rules and other metadata are provided through annotations. Many of these are discussed in Part I of the book.

Annotation	Description
@ActionOrder	Order of actions in the UI, comma-separated. Preferred is @MemberOrder.
@Aggregated	Indicates that object is wholly contained within another. Not currently used in Naked Objects 4.0.
@Bounded	The number of instances of a type is fixed and (relatively) small. Typically shown as drop-down lists.
@Debug	Action intended for diagnostics or debugging, typically for use only by support staff. Use Shift +right-click in DnD viewer; use *debugon.app* and *debugoff.app* in HTML viewer. See also @Exploration.
@Defaulted	Specify a DefaultsProvider to provide a default for a property when an object is first instantiated. @Encodeable and @Parseable are similar; may be implied by @Value.
@DescribedAs	A description of a class, class member, or action parameter. Shown as a tooltip or similar in the UI. See also @Named, @Plural.
@Disabled	Whether class member is usable, based on object's persistence. Grayed out in UI if disabled. See also @Hidden.
@Encodeable	How to serialize type for client-server. @Defaulted and @Parseable are similar; may be implied by @Value.
@EqualByContent	Part of defining value semantics. Not used directly in Naked Objects 4.0. May be implied by @Value.
@Executed	In client-server deployments, whether action should be invoked on the client or server side.
@Exploration	Action not intended for production use. Shown in UI only in exploration mode. See also @Debug.
@Facets	Specify arbitrary facets.
@FieldOrder	Order of properties and collections in the UI, comma-separated. Preferred is @MemberOrder.
@Hidden	Whether class member is visible in UI, based on object's persistence. See also @Disabled.
@Ignore	Instructs framework to ignore this method.

Annotation	Description
@Immutable	Object may not be modified, is read-only in UI. May be implied by @Value.
@Mask	Validation mask for string property. See also @RegEx.
@MaxLength	Maximum length of string property. Dictates size of field in UI. See also @TypicalLength.
@MemberOrder	Order of class members, either fields or menu items. Preferred over @ActionOrder and @FieldOrder.
@MultiLine	Displays string property as text box rather than field.
@MustSatisfy	Validation against a *specification*.
@Named	Override inferred name, used for title or label in UI. See also @Plural, @DescribedAs.
@NotPersistable	Transient instance; no save button in UI.
@NotPersisted	Derived property; read-only in UI.
@Optional	Property is not mandatory, can be saved when null.
@Parseable	Object can be parsed from string, shown as editable field rather than reference. @Encodeable and @Parseable are similar; may be implied by @Value.
@Plural	Plural form of name if irregular; used in UI for title of collections. See also @Named, @DescribedAs.
@RegEx	Regular expression validation for string property. See also @Mask.
@TypeOf	Type of element held in collection. In UI, may display a table where otherwise would have been just a list.
@TypicalLength	Typical length of a string property. Determines length of field. See also @MaxLength.
@Value	Has value semantics. May also imply @Defaulted, @Encodeable, @Parseable, @Immutable, and @EqualBy-Content.

Reserved Methods

A number of method names are effectively reserved but can be used if annotated with @Ignore.

Method Name	Description
title()	Current title of domain object.
iconName()	Current icon for domain object (do not include file extension).
validate()	Validate entire object, vetoing persisting or update if invalid.

Supporting Method Prefixes

Imperative business rules are implemented using supporting methods with well-defined prefixes.

Method Prefix	Property	Collection	Action
modifyXxx()	Yes	No	No
clearXxx()	Yes	No	No
addToXxx()	No	Yes	No
removeFromXxx()	No	Yes	No
validateXxx()	Yes	No	Yes
validateAddToXxx()	No	Yes	No
validateRemoveFromXxx()	No	Yes	No
disableXxx()	Yes	Yes	Yes
hideXxx()	Yes	Yes	Yes
defaultXxx()	Yes	No	Deprecated
defaultNXxx()	No	No	Yes
choicesXxx()	Yes	No	Deprecated
choicesNXxx()	No	No	Yes

Life-Cycle Callback Methods

Life-cycle callbacks are hooks into the object life cycle but will be ignored if annotated with @Ignore.

Method Name	Description
created()	Transient object just instantiated.
persisting()	Transient object just about to be persisted (saved) to object store.
persisted()	Object just persisted (saved) to object store (and is now persistent).
loading()	Persisted object reinstantiated and about to be reloaded from object store.
loaded()	Object just reloaded from object store.
updating()	Persisted object about to be updated in object store.
updated()	Object just updated in object store.
removing()	Persisted object about to be removed (deleted) from object store.
removed()	Object just removed (deleted) from object store (and is now transient).

Eclipse Templates

These templates are provided with the Naked Objects' download. Import them using Window > Preferences > Java > Editor > Templates.

Domain Objects

These templates speed up developing domain objects.

Properties, Collections, and Actions

These templates follow the general pattern of noXYYY, where X is a (action), c (collection), or p (property) and optionally YYY stands for a supporting method: cho (choices), def (defaults), val (validation), dis (disabling) or hid (hiding).

Template	Description
nop	*Get*ter and *set*ter for property, along with outer comment region.
nopmod	modifyXxx() and clearXxx() supporting methods, plus hooks for any other business logic.
nopcho	choicesXxx() supporting method providing choices for property.
nopdef	defaultXxx() supporting method, providing default for property when first created.
nopval	validateXxx() supporting method, validating proposed value for property.
nopdis	disableXxx() supporting method, disabling property based on object's state.
nophid	hideXxx() supporting method, hiding property based on object's state.

Template	Description
nocl	*Getter* and *setter* for collection of type java.util.List, along with outer comment region.
nocs	*Getter* and *setter* for collection of type java.util.Set, along with outer comment region.
nocmod	addToXxx()/removeFromXxx() supporting methods, plus hooks for any other business logic.
nocval	validateAddToXxx() and validateRemoveFromXxx() supporting methods, validating proposed elements to add to or remove from collection.
nocdis	disableXxx() supporting method, disabling collection based on object's state.
nochid	hideXxx() supporting method, hiding collection based on object's state.

Template	Description
noa	Action, plus comment region.
noacho	choicesNXxx() supporting method providing choices for action's Nth argument.
noadef	defaultNXxx() supporting method, providing default for action's Nth argument.
noaval	validateXxx() supporting method, validating all action arguments.
noadis	disableXxx() supporting method, disabling action based on object's state.
noahid	hideXxx() supporting method, hiding action based on object's state.

Common

These are other commonly used templates for domain objects.

Template	Description
noidtitle	title() identification method.
noidicon	iconName() identification method.
noval	validate() object-level validation method.
nod	Comment region for all injected dependencies.
nods	*Setter* for injected service.

Bidirectional Relationships

These templates make it easy to convert unidirectional relationships into bidirectional relationships.

Template	Description
nop-11c	modifyXxx()/clearXxx() supporting methods for 1:1 bidirectional relationship; child side. See also nop-11p.
nop-11p	modifyXxx()/clearXxx() supporting methods for 1:1 bidirectional relationship; parent side. See also nop-11c.
nop-m1	modifyXxx()/clearXxx() supporting methods for m:1 bidirectional relationship; implicitly child side. See also noc-1m.
noc-1m	addToXxx()/removeFromXxx() supporting methods for 1:m bidirectional relationship; implicitly parent side. See also nop-m1.
noc-mmp	addToXxx()/removeFromXxx() supporting methods for m:m bidirectional relationship; parent side. See also noc-mmc.
noc-mmc	addToXxx()/removeFromXxx() supporting methods for m:m bidirectional relationship; child side. See also noc-mmp.

Life-Cycle Methods

These templates create callbacks corresponding to the object's life cycle.

Template	Description
nol	Comment region for all life-cycle methods.
nolc	created() life-cycle method (called immediately post-creation).
nols	saving() and saved() life-cycle methods (called before/after initially persisting object).
nolu	updating() and updated() life-cycle methods (called before/after updating persisted object).
nold	deleting() and deleted() life-cycle methods (called before/after deleting persisted object).

In-Memory Repository (Also Fixtures)

These templates are useful for in-memory repository implementations and will also work within fixtures.

Template	Description
nosa	Search for all instances.
nosafil	Search for all instances matching the provided filter.
nosffil	Search for first instance matching the provided filter.
nosufil	Search for a unique instance matching the provided filter.

Factory (Also Fixtures)

These factory methods are typically combined with repository implementations.

Template	Description
noft	Factory method to create new still-transient instance.
nofp	Factory method to create new already-persisted instance.

Bibliography

[Adz09]   Gojko Adzic. *Bridging the Communication Gap.* Neuri, Ltd., London, 2009.

[Amb02]   Scott Ambler. *Agile Modeling: Effective Practices for Extreme Programming and the Unified Process.* John Wiley & Sons, New York, 2002.

[BK06]   Christian Bauer and Gavin King. *Java Persistence with Hibernate.* Manning Publications Co., Greenwich, CT, 2006.

[Blo08]   Joshua Bloch. *Effective Java.* Addison Wesley Longman, Reading, MA, second edition, 2008.

[CH02]   Andy Carmichael and Dan Haywood. *Better Software Faster.* Prentice Hall PTR, Englewood Cliffs, NJ, 2002.

[CLL99]   Peter Coad, Eric Lefebvre, and Jeff De Luca. *Java Modeling In Color With UML: Enterprise Components and Process.* Prentice Hall, Englewood Cliffs, NJ, 1999.

[Com08]   Sonatype Company. *Maven: The Definitive Guide.* O'Reilly & Associates, Inc, Sebastopol, CA, 2008.

[DH08]   Martijn Dashorst and Eelco Hillenius. *Wicket In Action.* Manning Publications Co., Greenwich, CT, 2008.

[Eva03]   Eric Evans. *Domain-Driven Design: Tackling Complexity in the Heart of Software.* Addison-Wesley Professional, Reading, MA, first edition, 2003.

[Fea04]   Michael Feathers. *Working Effectively with Legacy Code.* Prentice Hall, Englewood Cliffs, NJ, 2004.

[Fow96]   Martin Fowler. *Analysis Patterns: Reusable Object Models.* Addison Wesley Longman, Reading, MA, 1996.

[Fow03]   Martin Fowler. *Patterns of Enterprise Application Architecture.* Addison Wesley Longman, Reading, MA, 2003.

[GHJV95]   Erich Gamma, Richard Helm, Ralph Johnson, and John Vlissides. *Design Patterns: Elements of Reusable Object-Oriented Software.* Addison-Wesley, Reading, MA, 1995.

[Hay96]   David C. Hay. *Data Model Patterns: Conventions of Thought.* Dorset House Publishing, New York, 1996.

[HFR00]   Neil Harrison, Brian Foote, and Hans Rohnert. *Pattern Languages of Program Design 4.* Addison-Wesley, Reading, MA, 2000.

[HT00]   Andrew Hunt and David Thomas. *The Pragmatic Programmer: From Journeyman to Master.* Addison-Wesley, Reading, MA, 2000.

[Hun08]   Andy Hunt. *Pragmatic Thinking & Learning: Refactor Your Wetware.* The Pragmatic Programmers, LLC, Raleigh, NC, and Dallas, TX, 2008.

[HW04]   Gregor Hohpe and Bobby Woolf. *Enterprise Integration Patterns: Designing, Building, and Deploying Messaging Solutions.* Addison Wesley Longman, Reading, MA, 2004.

[Mar02]   Robert C. Martin. *Agile Software Development, Principles, Patterns, and Practices.* Prentice Hall, Englewood Cliffs, NJ, 2002.

[MC05]   Rick Mugridge and Ward Cunningham. *Fit for Developing Software: Framework for Integrated Tests.* Prentice Hall PTR, Englewood Cliffs, NJ, 2005.

[MRB97]   Robert C. Martin, Dirk Riehle, and Frank Buschmann. *Pattern Languages of Program Design 3.* Addison-Wesley Professional, Boston, MA, 1997.

[Ode98]   James J. Odell. *Advanced Object-Oriented Analysis & Design using UML.* Cambridge University Press, Cambridge, 1998.

[PM02]   Richard Pawson and Robert Matthews. *Naked Objects*. John
            Wiley & Sons, New York, 2002.

[RR07]   Leonard Richardson and Sam Ruby. *RESTful Web Services*.
            O'Reilly & Associates, Inc, Sebastopol, CA, 2007.

Index

X

The Pragmatic Bookshelf

Available in paperback and DRM-free PDF, our titles are here to help you stay on top of your game. The following are in print as of November 2009; be sure to check our website at pragprog.com for newer titles.

Title	Year	ISBN	Pages
Advanced Rails Recipes: 84 New Ways to Build Stunning Rails Apps	2008	9780978739225	464
Agile Coaching	2009	9781934356432	250
Agile Retrospectives: Making Good Teams Great	2006	9780977616640	200
Agile Web Development with Rails, Third Edition	2009	9781934356166	784
Augmented Reality: A Practical Guide	2008	9781934356036	328
Behind Closed Doors: Secrets of Great Management	2005	9780976694021	192
Best of Ruby Quiz	2006	9780976694076	304
Core Animation for Mac OS X and the iPhone: Creating Compelling Dynamic User Interfaces	2008	9781934356104	200
Core Data: Apple's API for Persisting Data on Mac OS X	2009	9781934356326	256
Data Crunching: Solve Everyday Problems using Java, Python, and More	2005	9780974514079	208
Debug It! Find, Repair, and Prevent Bugs in Your Code	2009	9781934356289	232
Deploying Rails Applications: A Step-by-Step Guide	2008	9780978739201	280
Design Accessible Web Sites: 36 Keys to Creating Content for All Audiences and Platforms	2007	9781934356029	336
Desktop GIS: Mapping the Planet with Open Source Tools	2008	9781934356067	368
Developing Facebook Platform Applications with Rails	2008	9781934356128	200
Enterprise Integration with Ruby	2006	9780976694069	360
Enterprise Recipes with Ruby and Rails	2008	9781934356234	416
Everyday Scripting with Ruby: for Teams, Testers, and You	2007	9780977616619	320
FXRuby: Create Lean and Mean GUIs with Ruby	2008	9781934356074	240
From Java To Ruby: Things Every Manager Should Know	2006	9780976694090	160
GIS for Web Developers: Adding Where to Your Web Applications	2007	9780974514093	275
Google Maps API, V2: Adding Where to Your Applications	2006	PDF-Only	83
Grails: A Quick-Start Guide	2009	9781934356463	200

Continued on next page

Title	Year	ISBN	Pages
Groovy Recipes: Greasing the Wheels of Java	2008	9780978739294	264
Hello, Android: Introducing Google's Mobile Development Platform	2009	9781934356494	272
Interface Oriented Design	2006	9780976694052	240
Land the Tech Job You Love	2009	9781934356265	280
Learn to Program, 2nd Edition	2009	9781934356364	230
Manage It! Your Guide to Modern Pragmatic Project Management	2007	9780978739249	360
Manage Your Project Portfolio: Increase Your Capacity and Finish More Projects	2009	9781934356296	200
Mastering Dojo: JavaScript and Ajax Tools for Great Web Experiences	2008	9781934356111	568
Modular Java: Creating Flexible Applications with OSGi and Spring	2009	9781934356401	260
No Fluff Just Stuff 2006 Anthology	2006	9780977616664	240
No Fluff Just Stuff 2007 Anthology	2007	9780978739287	320
Practical Programming: An Introduction to Computer Science Using Python	2009	9781934356272	350
Practices of an Agile Developer	2006	9780974514086	208
Pragmatic Project Automation: How to Build, Deploy, and Monitor Java Applications	2004	9780974514031	176
Pragmatic Thinking and Learning: Refactor Your Wetware	2008	9781934356050	288
Pragmatic Unit Testing in C# with NUnit	2007	9780977616671	176
Pragmatic Unit Testing in Java with JUnit	2003	9780974514017	160
Pragmatic Version Control Using Git	2008	9781934356159	200
Pragmatic Version Control using CVS	2003	9780974514000	176
Pragmatic Version Control using Subversion	2006	9780977616657	248
Programming Clojure	2009	9781934356333	304
Programming Cocoa with Ruby: Create Compelling Mac Apps Using RubyCocoa	2009	9781934356197	300
Programming Erlang: Software for a Concurrent World	2007	9781934356005	536
Programming Groovy: Dynamic Productivity for the Java Developer	2008	9781934356098	320
Programming Ruby: The Pragmatic Programmers' Guide, Second Edition	2004	9780974514055	864
Programming Ruby 1.9: The Pragmatic Programmers' Guide	2009	9781934356081	960
Programming Scala: Tackle Multi-Core Complexity on the Java Virtual Machine	2009	9781934356319	250
Prototype and script.aculo.us: You Never Knew JavaScript Could Do This!	2007	9781934356012	448
Rails Recipes	2006	9780977616602	350

Continued on next page

Title	Year	ISBN	Pages
Rails for .NET Developers	2008	9781934356203	300
Rails for Java Developers	2007	9780977616695	336
Rails for PHP Developers	2008	9781934356043	432
Rapid GUI Development with QtRuby	2005	PDF-Only	83
Release It! Design and Deploy Production-Ready Software	2007	9780978739218	368
Scripted GUI Testing with Ruby	2008	9781934356180	192
Ship it! A Practical Guide to Successful Software Projects	2005	9780974514048	224
Stripes ...and Java Web Development Is Fun Again	2008	9781934356210	375
TextMate: Power Editing for the Mac	2007	9780978739232	208
The Definitive ANTLR Reference: Building Domain-Specific Languages	2007	9780978739256	384
The Passionate Programmer: Creating a Remarkable Career in Software Development	2009	9781934356340	200
ThoughtWorks Anthology	2008	9781934356142	240
Ubuntu Kung Fu: Tips, Tricks, Hints, and Hacks	2008	9781934356227	400
iPhone SDK Development	2009	9781934356258	576

Fun with Java and the Web

Stripes

Tired of complicated Java web frameworks that just get in your way? Stripes is a lightweight, practical framework that lets you write lean and mean code without a bunch of XML configuration files. Stripes is designed to do a lot of the common work for you, while being flexible enough to adapt to your requirements. This book will show you how to use Stripes to its full potential, so that you can easily develop professional, full-featured web applications. As a bonus, you'll also get expert advice from the creator of Stripes, Tim Fennell.

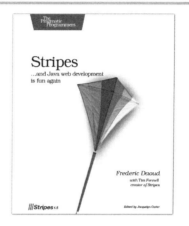

Stripes: ...And Java Web Development Is Fun Again
Frederic Daoud
(375 pages) ISBN: 978-1934356-21-0. $36.95
http://pragprog.com/titles/fdstr

Prototype and script.aculo.us

Tired of getting swamped in the nitty-gritty of cross-browser, Web 2.0–grade JavaScript? Get back in the game with Prototype and script.aculo.us, two extremely popular JavaScript libraries that make it a walk in the park. Be it Ajax, drag and drop, autocompletion, advanced visual effects, or many other great features, all you need is to write one or two lines of script that look so good they could almost pass for Ruby code!

Prototype and script.aculo.us: You Never Knew JavaScript Could Do This!
Christophe Porteneuve
(330 pages) ISBN: 1-934356-01-8. $34.95
http://pragprog.com/titles/cppsu

Boost your Career

Pragmatic Thinking and Learning

Software development happens in your head. Not in an editor, IDE, or design tool. In this book by Pragmatic Programmer Andy Hunt, you'll learn how our brains are wired, and how to take advantage of your brain's architecture. You'll master new tricks and tips to learn more, faster, and retain more of what you learn.

• Use the Dreyfus Model of Skill Acquisition to become more expert • Leverage the architecture of the brain to strengthen different thinking modes
• Avoid common "known bugs" in your mind
• Learn more deliberately and more effectively
• Manage knowledge more efficiently

Pragmatic Thinking and Learning:
Refactor your Wetware
Andy Hunt
(288 pages) ISBN: 978-1-9343560-5-0. $34.95
http://pragprog.com/titles/ahptl

The Passionate Programmer

This book is about creating a remarkable career in software development. Remarkable careers don't come by chance. They require thought, intention, action, and a willingness to change course when you've made mistakes. Most of us have been stumbling around letting our careers take us where they may. It's time to take control.

This revised and updated second edition lays out a strategy for planning and creating a radically successful life in software development *(the first edition was released as My Job Went to India: 52 Ways To Save Your Job)*.

The Passionate Programmer: Creating a
Remarkable Career in Software Development
Chad Fowler
(200 pages) ISBN: 978-1934356-34-0. $23.95
http://pragprog.com/titles/cfcar2